James Luther Adams

Prophet to the Powerful

James Luther Adams
Prophet to the Powerful

Edited by Herbert F. Vetter

Harvard Square Library, Cambridge

James Luther Adams: Prophet to the Powerful

Published by Harvard Square Library
www.harvardsquarelibrary.org

ISBN: 978-0-615-25994-9

Contents

For a bibliography of the writings of James Luther Adams, see *Not Without Dust and Heat: A Memoir* by James Luther Adams, published by Exploration Press, Chicago Theological Seminary, Chicago, Illinois, 1995.

*This section is published courtesy of *The Unitarian Universalist Christian*, Spring/Summer, 1977, Vol. 32, Nos. 1-2

** This section is published courtesy of *The Unitarian Universalist Christian*, Fall 1993/Winter 1994, Vol. 48, Nos. 3-4

James Luther Adams Foundation
Promoting the thought and work of James Luther Adams

The James Luther Adams Foundation is pleased to be a sponsor and a supporter of James Luther Adams. Prophet to the Powerful. The Foundation was formed in 1977 to help Adams continue his scholarly work during his retirement. It provided him with secretarial help and produced on videotape and DVD Adams and the church historian, George H. Williams, discussing the films Adams had taken in Germany during the rise of Nazi power in 1936. It also arranged the disposition of Adams' papers at the University of Syracuse research library.

Since the death of James Luther Adams in 1994, the JLA Foundation has concentrated on maintaining Adams' intellectual history. It does this by continuing the preservation of his tapes and papers and sponsoring the annual James Luther Adams Forum on Religion and Society. Here lectures are given on topics associated with Adams' particular concerns for relating Christian faith to society. For maximum exposure, they are moved around the country.

More information about the Foundation can be found on its web site, www.jameslutheradams.org, or by contacting it at 11 Miller Road, Beverly MA 01915-1315 or scmott@comcast.net (telephone and fax: 978-927-0216).

There are eight other anthologies of Adams' essays (cf. the web site for more information on these). James Luther Adams. Prophet to the Powerful stands out, however, in several ways. Starting with four essays on his life, the papers progress in a manner that indicates his evolving social concerns over the several decades of his writing. Most of the essays were previously published in a journal, The Unitarian Universalist Christian, which unfortunately is not widely distributed. Now these essays are in a book and so available for purchase, easily located, and entering libraries that do not carry the journal. Finally, the entire book is also online, making it accessible at all times in many parts of the world. This book is a distinct contribution to the maintenance of the diverse and penetrating intellectual heritage of James Luther Adams. For this the Foundation is deeply grateful to Herbert F. Vetter and the Harvard Square Library.

Stephen Charles Mott, President
The James Luther Adams Foundation

I.
The Life of
James Luther Adams

Taking Time Seriously

By James Luther Adams

I

My earliest recollection goes back to the year 1906 when I was four years old. Our family was kneeling in prayer, all of us burying our heads in pillows. We could scarcely breathe, for our farmhouse was in the path of one of the worst dust storms of a decade in the Pacific Northwest, and we were praying for relief. A few minutes before, blinded by the dust, I had lost my way in the farmyard, and on rejoining the family circle my prayer may well have been one of thanksgiving for having found the path to the house as well as of petition for the quieting of the wind. I was told much later that my father, a Baptist country preacher of premillenarian persuasion, prayed then and there for the Second Coming.

At one time my father was what might be called a circuit rider and I can remember riding behind him on horseback on some of his trips. Later on, I used to take my violin along to accompany the hymn singing.

My father was as otherworldly as the head of a family could possibly be. Very often he would tell us after family prayers before retiring at night that we might not see each other again on this earth. Christ might come before the morning and we should all meet him in the air. He interpreted the World War as evidence of the approaching end of the present "dispensation." Later on, after he had joined the Plymouth Brethren, he refused on religious principle, to vote. He gave up his life insurance policy because he felt it betrayed a lack of faith in God. When he was employed by the American Railway Express Company he refused to join the union on the grounds that it was a worldly organization with worldly aims. Indeed, he had taken up railway work because of his decision to follow St. Paul's example and refuse to accept wages for preaching the gospel. In short, my father was a man of principle.

By the age of eleven I knew the whole plan of salvation according to the Scofield Reference Bible, and I testified for it in season and out. I even preached on the street and at the Salvation Army during my earlier years in college. The break came before I left college, but I did not give up religion. I simply changed my attitude: I decided that it was my mission to attack religion in season and out. I became a "campus radical" and joined with some other quondam fundamentalists to publish an undergraduate freelance sheet which we smugly called the Angel's Revolt. My new law was in the scientific humanism of John Dietrich and my new prophecy was in the anti-Rotarianism of H. L. Mencken.

One of the great surprises of my life came at the end of my senior year in college. I had been taking a course in public speaking and all my speeches had been vicious attacks on religion as I knew it—at least, they had been as vicious as I could make them. Then the shock came one day when on leaving the classroom I happened to say quite casually to the professor that I did not know what I was going to do after graduation. I was already profitably engaged in business, but I was thoroughly discontented. The professor replied in a flash, "You don't know what you are going to do? Why I have known for months. Come around and talk to me some day." And then, right there in the presence of my enemies, the fundamentalists, he smote me. "There is no possible doubt about it," he said. "You are going to be a preacher!" Later, I went by night, like Nicodemus, to question this strange counselor, Professor Frank Rarig. Within six weeks the arrangements were complete. I was to attend Harvard Divinity School.

II

The changes that have taken place in me since then have been changes largely characterized by a slow process of deprovincialization, and yet by a process that has found its frame of reference for the most part in the catholic tradition of Christianity. The thread of continuity running through these changes has been an interest in history. Hence the French proverb that the more human nature changes the more it remains the same, may find some illustration in my own thinking. After all, the expectation of the Second Coming "when time shall be no more" involved at least an otherworldly, negative interest in history. The major change (aside from a difference in attitude toward science and toward the kind of authority the Bible possesses) centers around a change of attitude toward, rather than a diminution of interest in, time. Whereas in my youth I felt myself to be a stranger in time, a pilgrim on a foreign strand, now (largely under the influence of Dewey, Whitehead, Tillich, and the Bible) I believe time itself to be of the essence of both God and human being. Whereas formerly I thought of salvation as an escape of the elect from time, I now envisage it as taking place in community and in time, whether here, or hereafter.

III

At the beginning of this decade, I was a disciple of Irving Babbitt, the leader of the movement known as literary humanism. As I look back on this phase of development, it seems to me that there was little at variance between what I took from Babbitt and what I had gained from the theological and historical disciples of the divinity school. Babbitt (along with Paul Elmer More) did for me what he did for hundreds of others. He made the religious ideas of Plato, the Buddha, and Jesus, as well as Christian theology, come alive. He led us back to fundamental ideas, but by a path that seemed new.

Scientific humanism had stressed a faith in education and in progress through science. At the same time it was, when consistent, purely relativistic in its ethics. Literary humanism, to my mind, had a more realistic conception of human nature: It envisaged the central problem of civilization as that of ethical standards and, without being obscurantist, it stressed the necessity of something like conversion, of a change in the will whereby a person would develop an inner ethical control and work toward a richly human, universal norm. Through Babbitt's stress on these ideas I came to understand and value Greek and Chinese humanism, the Christian doctrine of sin and grace, and the Christian emphasis on conversion and humility. I also thus acquired a skepticism of the romantic liberal conception of human nature which was later to be so severely scrutinized by "realistic theology."

Yet literary humanism, despite its challenging sense of the past, did not possess a dynamic conception of history. The meaning of history tended to be localized more in the individual than in society. This was, to be sure, a needed emphasis at a time when humanitarianism was equated with Christianity by many of the "social gospelers," and with religion by scientific humanists. But, with the reading of Karl Marx and a study of the Anglo-Catholic view of the church and its role in society, I began to look upon literary humanism as more satisfactory as an individual psychology of self-culture than as a social and institutional psychology. Literary humanism did not, except in the schools, elicit participation in the process by which a more just social order and even a humanistic education are to be achieved.

Moreover, the humanistic interpretations of sin and grace and humility were truncated. As I indicated in my long critique of literary humanism, which appeared in *Hound and Horn* in 1932, these interpretations seemed to me to be only humanistic parodies of Christian theology. Humanism envisaged them in too narrow a frame of reference. It reckoned without its host "our neighbor the universe." Both scientific and literary humanism had done what Millet did when he first painted the *Sower*. They and he alike left no room on the canvas for the field into which the sower was casting his seed. Like the Millet of the second (and better known) painting, I felt that the man should be placed in a larger setting, so that there might be two principles rather than one: the man *and* the earth upon which he is dependent for the growth of the seed.

It was only later that the New Testament idea concerning the seed growing of itself was to be impressed upon me by Rudolf Otto. At that time, Henry Nelson Wieman's definition of God provided a great stimulus. Religion, I came to believe, requires the declarative as well as the imperative mood. It has to do with facts as well as with hopes and demands, facts about human beings, especially about the resources upon which we are dependent for growth and re-creation. I began to appreciate again certain aspects of the Christian doctrines of creation and redemption. Humanism, in eschewing metaphysics, presupposed an unexamined metaphysics, and I decided that an unexamined metaphysics was not worth having.

My gratitude to Irving Babbit has increased with the years and will probably continue to increase; indeed I have tried to give expression to it in my contribution to the volume in honor of Babbitt published by some of his students. Nevertheless, I was constrained to go beyond humanism, both scientific and literary. My desire was to find a metaphysics in addition to ethical standards and a meaning in history which would involve them both.

IV

At this time two significant changes took place. One of those changes was brought about through my work as a minister in the liberal church. The other was introduced through my reading of Baron Friedrich von Huegel. But before speaking of these developments, I should like to repeal reticence still further by referring to a personal experience.

At the beginning of this decade I was a graduate student of philosophy and comparative literature at Harvard. During this period I became a member of the Harvard Glee Club. Nathan Soderblom has remarked that Bach's *St. Matthew Passion* music should be called the fifth evangelist. So was Bach for me. One night after singing with the club in the *Mass in B Minor* under Serge Koussevitzky at Symphony Hall in Boston, a renewed conviction came over me that here in the mass, beginning with the *Kyrie* and proceeding through the *Crucifixus* to the *Agnus Dei* and *Dona nobis pacem*, all that was essential in the human and the divine was expressed. My love of the music awakened in me a profound sense of gratitude to Bach for having displayed as through a prism and in a way that was irresistible for me, the essence of Christianity.

I realize now that this was only the culmination of my *preparatio evangelica*. For suddenly I wondered if I had a right even to enjoy what Bach had given me. I wondered if I was not a spiritual parasite, one who was willing to trade on the costly spiritual heritage of Christianity, but who was perhaps doing very little to keep that spirit alive. In the language of Kierkegaard, I was forced out of the spectator into the "existential" attitude. This experience as such was, to be sure, not a new one: It was simply a more decisive one. I could now see what Nietzsche meant when, in speaking of the *Passion* music, he said, "Whoever has wholly forgotten Christianity will hear it there again."

V

As an active minister (which I had been from the time of my graduation from Harvard Divinity School in 1927), I began to feel an increasing uneasiness about religious liberalism. It appeared to me to represent a cultural lag, the tail end of the laissez-faire philosophy of the nineteenth century. Its competitive character and its atomistic individualism forced upon me the question of what the theological method of liberalism is and should be, and also of what its religious content actually is. Reinhold Niebuhr, Walter Marshall Horton, and John Bennett had their share in pointing up these questions, if not in raising them. Especially influential at that time was T. S. Eliot's criticism of Babbitt's cosmopolitanism and the strictures of Hermelink and Otto upon so-called universal religion.

Through these writers as well as through personal experience I came to see that religion lives not only by means of universally valid *ideas*, but also through the warmer, more concrete, historical tradition that possesses its sense of community, it prophets and its "acts" of the apostles, its liturgy and literature, its peculiar language and disciplines. "The spirit killeth, the letter giveth life." Not that I doubted the validity of the principle of disciplined freedom. Rather the question was: Is there a liberal church, or are there only aggregates of individuals, each claiming to search the truth—as though none had yet been found? Despite my (still existing) conviction that the empirical method is the proper one for theology, Anglo-Catholicism and Barthianism with their respective emphases on common faith and "church theology" served as a challenge.

These questions were the source of great distress to me. I even contemplated giving up the ministry and going into teaching. Indeed, I did later become a full-time instructor in English at Boston University, continuing the while my work as a minister.

Some of the younger Unitarian ministers in New England had organized themselves into a study group for the purpose of working out together a critique of liberalism and also of searching for a remedy. Over a period of years this group (later to be known as the Greenfield Group) read, discussed, and wrote papers on the outstanding theologians of the twentieth century as well as on some of the earlier ones, both Roman Catholic and Protestant. They hammered out together a "church theology" that would enable them as liberals to restate in modern terms the Christian doctrines of God and the human being, of sin and grace, and of the church. Pursuing the implications of their group method, they attempted to set forward the principle disciplines that these doctrines seemed to demand. Nor did they confine their attention to the harmless concerns of academic theology. The necessity of carrying their conclusions over into the work of the church and a year spent studying books like Troeltsch's *Social Teachings of the Christian Churches* helped us, as F. R. Barry would say, to make our Christianity relevant. But many of us felt that we had much to do yet before we learned to take contemporary history seriously.

Although von Huegel did not meet this need for orientation in time, his influence upon me and certain other Unitarian ministers in the Greenfield Group was profound. My own interest in von Huegel I owe, like many another fruit-bearing seed, to Dean Willard Sperry of Harvard Divinity School. Von Huegel's philosophy of critical realism, his emphasis on the role of the body, history, and institutions in religion, his attack (along with Maritain's) on the "pure spirituality" of unhistorical, noninstitutional, nonincarnational religion became determinative for my conception of religion. Much of this side of von Huegel was the more impressive because of the way in which he showed how James Martineau, a Unitarian theologian, had espoused similar views. Through reading von Huegel's *Letters to a Niece* I found a new reality in the devotional life, especially because of his insistence that there should remain a tension between the sacred and the secular, and between Hebraism, Hellenism, and science.

I went on from von Huegel to the reading of certain other spiritual directors of history, and especially of St. Francis of Sales. Several groups of Unitarian ministers at about this time were developing cooperatively certain disciplines for the devotional life. One of our groups (the Brothers of the Way), suspicious of the sort of devotions that aim at a cloistered virtue, included within its disciplines weekly visits of mercy to the needy, a "general" discipline of active participation in some secular organization of socially prophetic significance, and an annual retreat where we participated in discussions of social issues and in the sacraments of silence and of the Lord's Supper.

A sense for the ontological, the historical, and the institutional elements in Christianity was by now deeply formed. Still I only vaguely apprehended the relation of all these things to the history that was in the making. This statement seems to me accurate despite the fact that I had been actively involved in strikes (a minister could not live in Salem, Massachusetts, without having something to do with strikes), despite the fact that I knew something about the lot of the laborer by having worked for six years on the railroad, and despite the fact that one of our groups of Unitarian ministers had for a period used St. Francis of Sales and Karl Marx for daily devotional reading. I was not yet taking time seriously. Von Huegel, like Babbitt, had increased in me a sense of the past which gave perspective to immediate interests, but he had no theology for social salvation.

VI

In 1935 and 1936 I spent almost a year abroad in preparation for coming to teach at the Meadville Theological School in Chicago. Because of my interest in the liturgical movement, I devoted a portion of my time to visiting Benedictine monasteries. But I spent the greater part of the year attending lectures in philosophy and theology in French and Swiss universities. I also became familiar with the writings of a French Protestant religious socialist, Andre Philip, a professor of law in Lyons and a member of the Chamber of Deputies.

11

Pursuing still further my interest in the devotional life, I secured through the good offices of Catholic friends in America a spiritual director at the famous seminary of Saint Sulpice in Paris. Two hours a week for a period of three months with one of the finest spirits I have known will not be forgotten. Here I came to know a man for whom the devotional life was far more than discipline. It was a growing in the grace and knowledge of Christ. He did for me what I should have expected from a Protestant: he acquainted me with a living Christ. Yet the Christ he made vivid for me was not the harbinger of the Kingdom, but rather the obedient servant of God in the inner life and in the personal virtues.

On leaving France I went to live with an old Harvard friend, Peter Brunner, who was a professor of theology in a Confessional Front theological school and who had just been released from a concentration camp. Through his aid I became acquainted with Confessional Church leaders in the various sections of Germany. I saw with my own eyes what I had previously not seen even in print. I accompanied one young minister just out of concentration camp on a preaching tour, and I heard him speak out against the government, mincing no words, knowing that very often, the secret police were in his audience.

I soon learned, of course, that these Confessional people had little interest in strictly social and political questions, that they were scarcely aware of the fact that their present plight was tied in with the breakdown of capitalism. But I learned at first hand what it means when we say that the struggle in our world is between paganism and Christianity, between nationalism and Christianity. I talked not only with Martin Niemoller, but also with his enemies and with leaders in the German Christian and pagan movements. I learned what the existential attitude is in a situation where the options are living options. By hearing it read in the homes of the persecuted, I learned again how the Bible may be more than something to be read as great literature. I learned the meaning of decision and commitment.

Then I went to visit Rudolf Otto, who was in retirement and whom I had the good fortune to see for an hour or two a day throughout the summer. The struggle of the church was never for long out of our conversation. But more important for me were the discussions of his last, and greatest, book, *The Kingdom of God and the Son of Man*. In his interpretation of Jesus I saw again the man who took time seriously: "The kingdom of heaven is at hand." Already it has partially entered into time, it grows of itself by the power of God (here again was the seed growing of itself), it demands repentance, it is an earnest of the sovereignty of God. It is a mystery. Yet the struggle between the divine and the demonic is evident to all who can read the signs of the times.

VII

Scarcely a better preparation than the reading of Andre Phillip and the time spent with Otto and among the Confessional Church leaders could have been given me for becoming acquainted subsequently in 1936 and again in 1938 with another group, certain students and admirers of Paul Tillich. I had first become familiar with Tillich's point of view when I was in Germany in 1927. For his appreciation of his use of the voluntarist tradition beginning with Duns Scotus and down through Jakob Bohme and later Friedrich Schelling, I had been prepared also by previous acquaintance with the writings of Kurt Leese of Hamburg.

In Tillich's writings I now found a binding together of many of the more significant things that had attracted me in the preceding decade. In his theology I was confronted by a prophetic restatement of the Kingdom, of the divine and the demonic, of time being fulfilled, of sin and grace, all interpreted in the light of the voluntaristic tradition that I had earlier approached through pragmatism as well as through literary humanism. And, what is more important for me, they were interpreted also in relation to the social (and antisocial) realities that constitute present-day history: self-sufficient nationalism, fascism, communism, capitalism, Bible Protestantism, Roman Catholicism, estheticism, intellectualism on the side of virtual resistance to the grace of God acting in history, and a religious socialism theonomously aware of the dialectical nature of God, human being, and history on the other side.

There is much in Tillich that still remains for me obscure and, where understood, unacceptable. His view of Christ as the center of history and his reading of his own philosophy of religion into Reformation theology are to me unconvincing. Yet, it seems to me that American theologians have much to gain from acquiring a greater familiarity with his work, much of which remains untranslated. In Tillich's view of the dialectical nature of reality, of revelation, of God, of the Kingdom, of human nature and history, I find an interpretation and an application of Christian doctrine which are far more relevant to the social and divine forces that determine the destiny of humanity than in any other theologian I happen to know about. Here, if ever, is a theologian who takes time seriously. This aspect of his thought comes best into relief when he is contrasted with Barth. Indeed, Tillich has made the most penetrating criticism of so-called dialectical theology that has yet appeared, namely, that it is not in truth dialectical.

One who takes time seriously, however, must do more than talk about it. He must learn somehow to take time by the forelock. He must learn to act as a Christian and as a citizen through socially effective institution, to do what E. C. Lindeman has called the humdrum work of democracy. I, for one, now believe that every Christian should be actively and persistently engaged in the work of at least one secular organization that is exercising a positive influence for the sake of peace and justice against the forces of hate and greed. But this is, of course, not enough.

The question is whether the churches as corporate bodies can learn to take contemporary history seriously, whether Christianity will act in time, whether it will not, as at the beginning, be betrayed in its critical moment by those who sit at its table. The danger is, as Stanley Jones has recently warned us, that the church will be more interested in itself than in the Kingdom. Otto Dibelius once inadvertently wrote of the twentieth century as the "century of the church." What has happened since that phrase was coined lends to it an ironic and ominous overtone. This is indeed the century of the church. It is the century in which the church will have to decide unequivocally whether it means business, whether it will play a constructive role in the dynamic process that makes history meaningful. It will have to come to grips with pacifism, nationalism, and capitalism.

This then, is the change that the decade has wrought in me. Christianity is no longer an optional luxury for me. Salvation does not come through worship and prayer alone, nor through private virtues that camouflage public indolence. Time and history are fraught with judgment and fulfillment. We are in the valley of decision. But there is reason for hope, for God will make all his mountains a way.

A Biographical and Intellectual Sketch

By Max L. Stackhouse

In James Luther Adams one finds the curious, and sometimes contradictory, combination of medieval saint, Renaissance humanist, Marxist critic, Enlightenment encyclopedist, sectarian enthusiast, and bourgeois compulsive. Yet he is, in many ways, a prototypical modern man, attempting to find, confess, and, where necessary, carve out a sense of meaning large enough to preserve us from the perennial idolatries and aimlessness that flesh is heir to.

It should be clear that any attempt to delineate the many aspects of his character is no simple task, for he is so multifaceted in his interests and abilities that one cannot be sure where the center is. He sometimes appears, like a model of a complex atom in modern physics, to be primarily a constellation of energy in motion only momentarily and artificially fixed into a given form for pedagogical purposes. Yet it is this dynamic quality that allows such explosive insights and disallows any description that attempts to trace the relationships of all the orbits through which the constituent particulars of his personality move.

In spite of the difficulties, the purpose of this effort is to attempt the construction of such a model, one that remains necessarily a rough sketch by virtue of the subject. The central lines of this sketch will trace the form and development of his thought by means of interlocking analytical and chronological accounts. It will be adorned, as is every conversation with JLA, with anecdotes and impressions.

We begin by characterizing his mode of thinking, for not only must we have some sense of the whole to understand the parts, but it is the quality of his mind and his particular way of approaching problems that is most striking to those who come in contact with him—most striking, that is, besides his sensitivity and personal warmth.

James Luther Adams is a critical and comparative, not a reflective or systematic thinker. He thinks vis-à-vis other minds, external evidence, or objective events. He seldom sets forth a point of view and works through the logical implications thereof, but continually engages one point of view

Max L. Stackhouse, the Rimmer and Ruth Professor of Reformed Theology and Public Life, *Emeritus*, Princeton Theological Seminary, is editor of *On Being Human Religiously* by James Luther Adams (Beacon Press, Boston, 1976).

with the historical alternatives. He plays off, so to speak, one set of cultural repositories against another or others. The variety of approaches, the conflicting ways of looking at a problem, the historical settings of various alternatives, and the consequences of dealing with perennial human problems in one way rather than another—these are the issues that are crucial to him.

A paragraph that over-dramatizes this point but that is thus representative in an "ideal-typical" way appears in his essay "Basic Causes of Progress and Decay in Civilization," wherein he discusses the relationship of religion to civilization.

> Some people view religion as the enemy of civilization; others think of it as the mother of civilization and culture, still others think of civilization and especially of civility as the enemy of true religion. Because of its tendency to preen itself on man's sophistication and on his cultural achievements, urbanity, Spengler asserted, long ago "killed Christianity." In contrast, Gibbon attributed the fall of Rome to the rise of barbarism and religion. Kierkegaard, on quite different presuppositions from Spengler's, insisted that there is a world of difference between the roots and fruits of Christianity and the roots and fruits of urbanity. For Kierkegaard urbane poise freezes the knees of the "man of the world": being completely self-sufficient, he is not capable of genuine religious humility—he aims to be his own redeemer. With still different presuppositions John Henry Newman contrasted the ideal of the gentleman with the ideal of the Christian, sardonically defining the gentleman as one who refuses to cause pain. Harold Laski believes that progress in civilization is possible only with the elimination of religion. In contrast to certain of these views we find Hegel asserting that religion is the womb of culture; Arnold Toynbee believes civilization is the womb of religion, and indeed religion is the only enduring product of civilizations in their rise and fall; and Edmund Burke held that civilization is the result of two things—the spirit of the gentleman and the spirit of religion.

How does it occur that Adams should come to such a way of thinking, writing, and teaching? Suggestions for an answer are found in his life's history.

Of his background we know relatively little in a direct way. James

Luther Adams was born in Ritzville, Washington, in 1901. His father, James Carey Adams, was a Baptist premillenarian country preacher, later to become a Plymouth Brother. His mother, Lella Barnett Adams, was also a "true believer." The details of the name-giving are not known, except that his given names were of earlier use in the family; but the anomaly of James Luther, in view of Luther's opinion of James and Adams' opinion of Luther, not only is now the source of comment in introductions at various functions, but is somehow prophetic of the creative contradictions inherent in the bearer.

The most significant anecdotes of JLA's early history, the ones that he remembers as being most significant, are spelled out in the autobiographical chapter in *Taking Time Seriously* and partially recapitulated in D. W. Soper's *Men Who Shape Belief.* But only the barest outlines are found there, and perhaps the genuine flavor can best be tasted by reading Sir Edmund Gosse's *Father and Son,* an autobiographical study of a Plymouth Brethren lay preacher (a zoologist professionally) and his son whose interest in literature led him into a larger fold, or, as his father thought, out of the fold altogether.

One finds in Gosse's now almost classic account several themes that are indeed applicable to James Luther Adams. Gosse characterizes the type of thinking operant in his household as more that of an attorney than of a philosopher. Positively, the marshaling of historical witnesses as well as the importance of obtaining explicit consensus among the peers and following the rules of justice are precisely the way in which Adams treats a subject in his writing and lecturing. The fact is supplemented by the interest that Adams has in jurisprudence and the precision he demands in ethical casuistry. His interest in the history and philosophy of law appeared early in seminars under Roscoe Pound, William E. Hocking, and Helmut Coing. In his own seminars he has for years promoted the study of Natural Law. His concern for Althusius as a pivotal thinker in the history of Protestant political theory appears full-blown in the work of his former student Frederick Carney. Much of what JLA has presented in the history of Protestant social ethics he has viewed in connection with the work of the jurists, from Althusius through Friedrich Julius Stahl and Otto von Gierke to Rudolf Sohm. Otto von Gierke's *Genossenschaftsrecht* has served as a basis for his own associational philosophy and periodization of Western history. JLA often voices lament for the lack of interest in legal literature and problems among contemporary Protestant theologians. He is fond of speaking of the Three R's—Reformation, Renaissance, and Reception—as the foundation of modern civilization. But his participation in the Civil Liberties Union is perhaps an equally good illustration, for every intellectual concern that is to have reality for Adams must take form in institutional participation. His participation in the Civil Liberties Union has given him occasion repeatedly to become personally involved in the defense of individuals harassed by superpatriots or unjustly snared by the Walters-McCarran Act. Some of his files on these individual cases cover as much as a decade and have entailed an enormous amount of effort. Very often the injustice to be corrected has been the fault of lawmaking or law-enforcement agencies.

But negatively the concern for legal modes of thinking also plays a role in JLA's thinking. The "legalistic" approach to human problems by Gosse's father (and by Adams's) leads one continually to have to establish innocence. This need, so dramatically set forth in the modern mode in the writings of Kafka, leads to such a radical demand for proving innocence that inhumanity is the result. Against this JLA rebelled and continues to protest. One must be willing to get one's hands dirty at the expense of a manicured soul. This rebellion away from withdrawal and toward participation is one of the chief sources of his concern for voluntary associations.

Another significant factor mentioned by Gosse is the fact that professional interests are spoken of as avocations. Again we see a factor that appears in JLA's life and thought. His service to God, to the church, and to other human beings is his real vocation, and the various professional abilities that he has developed are means to that end. Since his early days when, carrying his violin to accompany singing, he went from village to country crossroad on horseback with his father, he has traveled and preached, using his secular excursions as a means for "evangelism." The full vocation of the ministry combines scholarly research, administration, cure of souls, social criticism, and citizenship responsibilities as well as preaching the Word and performing the sacraments. Although other institutions must differentiate in our society, the church must maintain an integrative center, and pastors must be capable of leading the flock in many and varied ways. JLA believes in the prophethood as well as in the priesthood of all believers.

The premillenarian expectation of "meeting Jesus," with all the attendant implications, are an aspect of Gosse's account which also shows up in Adams's own memory.

> My earliest recollection goes back to the year 1906 when I was four years old. Our family was kneeling in prayer, each of us burying his head in a pillow. We could scarcely breathe, for our farmhouse was in the path of one of the worst dust storms of a decade in the Pacific Northwest, and we were praying for relief.... I was told much later that my father... prayed then and there for the Second Coming.... My father was as other-worldly as the head of a family could possibly be. Very often he would tell us after family prayers before retiring at night that we might not see each other again on this earth.

Several themes appear in this passage that are of considerable significance for the understanding of Professor Adams. One is the tension between the necessities of this worldly living and the professing of other-worldly interests. This theme, treated systematically by Troeltsch and Weber in regard to Calvinistic Puritanism, not only describes a major tension in JLA's life and thought, but also accounts for his fascination with the problem of alienation, which, according to the Marxian definition, means having an ideological theory that obscures rather than reveals the true state of affairs.

On the positive side, however, the tension of eschatology with history, and the continual searching in the events of history for signs of the times, is an unceasing endeavor of his life which perhaps derives from this eschatological watching of his youth. Although he recognizes the mechanical way in which this was done by his father and other adherents of "the whole plan of salvation according to the Scofield Reference Bible," the crucial significance of repeatedly asking the whence and whither of human events remained, and indeed has become a dominant theme of his thinking.

One result of the mentality imbued accidentally in his earlier days, but later accepted in a series of self-critical decisions, is the radical "work ethic" that JLA exemplifies.

An account of his working and moneymaking (he has never had difficulty making money, although he has carried heavy responsibilities in view of his father's fiscal incapacity and although he is radically critical of people who make decisions on a financial basis alone) has been sent to me by J. Bryan Allin, his friend since 1920.

At ten years of age JLA (his family called him Luther) was the janitor of the little country schoolhouse for the pay of one dollar a month. During the summer months, he shocked oats and did other farm chores, and for a while he drove a derrick for two dollars a day. He had the constant care of two horses. He was also, part time, a night clerk at a University Club, and sold brushes house to house.

By twelve years of age he was the office boy of Dunham Engineering Company, and sold newspapers on the street during the noon hour. He raised rabbits, besides selling some aluminum goods, knickknacks, and home furnishings made by other boys. A newspaper article in his home town appeared at this time with his picture, saying, "Luther Adams has banked $100."

At fourteen he worked in a carriage shop and carried two paper routes, netting about $15 a week. On the side, he ran errands for a combination collection agency and matrimonial bureau.

At age fifteen, family finances forced him to leave high school. He learned stenography in night school in order to get a job with the prosecuting attorney, at $75 a month. While employed there, he developed his shorthand to the point that his secretaries could still read his script before he switched to tape-recorded dictation. By 1918, when he was seventeen years old, he was the private secretary to the superintendent of the Northern Pacific Railroad and was earning $113 a month. He next became Chief Clerk of the Operating Division.

During these several years it appeared that he might succumb to sheer exhaustion and fatigue. Doubtless the question of the meaning of what he was doing crossed his mind several times, but he persisted, returned to high school, and graduated at the top of his class.

He went to college, where his busy schedule continued, as, indeed, it has until today, although intellectual, cultural, and human interests began to displace commercial ones. Some of the jobs that he held from 1920 to 1924 while he was attending college full time are:

Dispatcher's clerk for the Northern Pacific on the midnight eight-hour shift. Worked at the Minnesota Union (where the men ate). Ran a collection agency. Read to a millionaire, Mr. Bean, at night. Organized a printing company. Worked in a cigar store. Was secretary to Rev. Mr.

Henderson, a Baptist minister, and Professor van Roosbroeck (professor of French). Sold advertising, automatic typewriters, and mailing lists. Organized a radio sales organization. Typed for Professor Swift. Taught salesmanship and Business English. Invested in a book store.

The significance of this energetic involvement is that a pattern was set, a style of life developed, that demanded the utilization of every available moment. He not only takes time seriously in its theological and philosophical senses, but tries also to fill each moment with some useful effort. One manifestation of this is found in his regular attendance at gatherings where decisions are being made. He once said that history in a democracy is made by those who take the time to go to important committee meetings and to stay to the end. By participating in those political, ecclesiastical, and associational organizations that make decisions, JLA is ever engaged in the business of defining and redefining the changing cultural needs, sensitivities, and perceptions of modern social existence.

However remarkable, it is not this aspect of his life in college that was most notable at the time. Rather it was the germinal process of deprovincialization (as he calls it), accompanied by a rather agonizing shaking of the foundations (as Tillich calls it), that really allowed James Luther Adams to become what he is instead of a tycoon, an organization man, or a religious fanatic (although, as he reports, "I preached on the street and at the Salvation Army during my earlier years in college"). Deprovincialization is a painful exorcism for anyone, the more so for one strongly conditioned to an absolute and explicit faith and by continual success in business. The more one was rooted in faith before, the more he must rebel. As JLA himself puts it:

> I decided that it was my mission to attack religion in season and out. I became a "campus radical" and I joined with some other quondam Fundamentalists to publish an undergraduate free-lance sheet which we smugly called the *Angels' Revolt*. My new law was in the scientific humanism of John Dietrich and my new prophecy was in the anti-Rotarianism of H. L. Mencken.
>
> One of the great surprises of my life came at the end of my senior year in college. I had been taking a course in public speaking, and all my speeches had been vicious attacks on religion as I knew it—at least, they had been as vicious as I could make them. The shock came one day when on leaving the classroom, I happened to say quite casually to the

professor that I did not know what I was going to do after graduation. I was already profitably engaged in business, but I was thoroughly discontented. The professor replied in a flash, "You don't know what you are going to do? Why, I have known for months. Come around and talk to me some day." And then, right there in the presence of my enemies, the Fundamentalists, he smote me. "There is no possible doubt about it," he said. "You are going to be a preacher!" Later, I went by night, like Nicodemus, to question this strange counselor. Within six weeks the arrangements were complete. I was to attend Harvard Divinity School.

This Nicodemus indeed arrived at Harvard Divinity School at the start of the following semester. He came as a flaming... but he didn't know what noun was to follow. People who knew him during this period remember him as one passionate for learning, drinking in more than several average students, and moving into conversation with professor, janitor, and cook alike, receiving-antennae constantly sensitized. He was assigned field work at All-Souls Church in Lowell, where his own enthusiasm for scholarship and literature, even if unfocused, was transmitted to people previously untouched or unmoved by the world of letters. The picture of a young theolog, sitting on the woodpile reading to and discussing with workers who swore and smoked as well as ate during the noon hour, made several respectable eyebrows rise.

Indicative of the kind of man that JLA is, are reports of his constant efforts to provide acquaintances with something to "stretch their minds." He bought records, books of poetry, or reprints of paintings to give to landladies, bakers, or other friends. He conducted three-hour sessions of listening to symphonic recordings, relating the music to the other arts, the religious movements, and the events of the period. That this love for music did not express a narrowly artistic interest is shown by JLA's interpretation of the role of Johann Sebastian Bach in his own spiritual development.

> Nathan Soderblom has remarked that Bach's St. Matthew's Passion music should be called the Fifth Evangelist. So was Bach for me. One night as I sang, with the Harvard Glee Club, the Mass in B Minor under Koussevitzky at Symphony Hall, Boston, a renewed conviction came over me that here in the Bach Mass, beginning with the *Kyrie* and proceeding through the *Crucifixus* to the *Agnus Dei* and *Dona nobis pacem,* all that was essential in the human and the divine was expressed. My love of the music awakened in me a profound sense of gratitude to

Bach for having displayed as through a prism and in a way that was i
irresistible for me, the essence of Christianity.

From his training at Harvard Divinity School three influences are
recorded as being most significant, although the fruit was slow in coming
and he was still to pass through the stage of classical humanism. One was
the tradition of social responsibility in Unitarianism and of pluralism
("the uses of diversity") coupled with the historical, critical method
promoted at Harvard. JLA was inducted into this tradition through
his acquaintance with some of the leading young Unitarian ministers
of the New England area. It might be said, for those not familiar with
old Yankee Unitarianism, that it is much less subject to the charge of
theological poverty or to the epithet "non-Christian" than are some of the
syncretistic and scientistic strains of Unitarianism. (JLA, his friends, and
former students are responsible for the journal, *The Unitarian Christian*,
an inherent contradiction only for those not familiar with Unitarian
history.) The issue of these acquaintanceships has been "The Greenfield
Group" and subsequently in the Middle West "The Prairie Group." These
groups with their somewhat rigorous disciplines of study have been a
main bulwark against atomic individualism in Unitarianism. Similar
organizations have formed more recently in New York, Washington, and
California. JLA sometimes explicates one aspect of his doctrine of God
as "a community-forming power," and further explicates the community
as necessarily having some form of explicit faith and discipline. If this
definition is correct, the Greenfield and Prairie Groups are evidence
of God's working. The participants formed a fellowship, or *koinonia,*
and self-consciously assumed a discipline to attempt hammering out a
theology of the church, a more adequate hymnology, liturgy, biblical
criticism, and conception of history, by intensive engagement with the
outstanding theologians of mainline Protestant and Catholic orientations.
Following a pattern adopted by von Huegel, they pursued an elaborate
program that combined the study of theology (or the Bible) and the
study of some other discipline (economics, art, political science)— the
dialectic between grace and its medium. Another group of which JLA
was a charter member, while related to Harvard, was the "Brothers of
the Way." They, too, maintained a discipline, this one requiring every
member to adopt devotional disciplines and also to be a participant in
a controversial "secular" organization, feeling that only by means of the

abrasive clash of important disputes are deep-seated values exposed. These groups and other relationships that JLA has maintained in Unitarian circles have been a theological, intellectual, and social leaven for many in the denomination for over three decades. One long-time associate, Professor John F. Hayward, wrote in his preface to *Existentialism and Religious Liberalism,*

> In the background of all my thinking and in the foreground of my affections, stands my former minister, teacher, one-time colleague at the University of Chicago, and continuing compatriot in the liberal ministry, Professor James Luther Adams. He is foremost among those cherished persons who have led me 'to behold the beauty of the Lord and to enquire in his temple.'

JLA was also influenced by Harvard Divinity School's Dean Willard L. Sperry, especially as he directed Adams's attention to literary studies, to devotional literature, and to the writings of Baron von Huegel. Adams writes:

> Von Huegel's philosophy of critical realism, his emphasis on the role of the body, history and institutions in religion, his attack (along with Maritain's) on the pure spirituality of unhistorical, non-institutional, non-incarnational religion became determinative for my conception of religion.

Much of this side of von Huegel was the more impressive because of the way in which he showed how James Martineau, a Unitarian theologian, espoused similar views. The issue of these themes was not to come to the fore until several years later.

The third influence, although much less direct since he was no longer at Harvard when JLA arrived, was Francis Greenwood Peabody. "Peabody was not only one of the early proponents of the 'social gospel' but also the first teacher in the United States to demand and create a permanent place for systematic Christian social ethics as a University discipline in a liberal education as well as in professional theological education." Further, Peabody "took into account German theological scholarship; he also attempted to come to terms with Marxist literature and with the thought of the European Christian socialists." JLA, as Peabody's spiritual descendant, occupied the Mallinckrodt Chair at Harvard.

He graduated from Harvard Divinity School, was ordained a

Unitarian minister, assumed the pastorate at Second Church, Salem, Massachusetts, spent the summer in Europe, and returned to marry a student of music and a Unitarian, Margaret Ann Young, all in 1927.

The trip to Europe in 1927, just as Hitler and the Nazis were beginning to flex their political muscles, was highly significant, for during that stay JLA first became acquainted with the philosophy and social criticism of Paul Tillich, an acquaintance and an influence that was to stay with him for some time.

Margaret Young was a member of the First Church (Unitarian) in Salem. JLA's business sensitivities of long standing were undoubtedly touched when he took her on an early, if not first, "date" to hear a Bach *Passion* and she requested that he get inexpensive tickets. Puritan frugality, cultural sensitivity, a liberal outlook in politics, and personal charm claimed his heart.

During his pastorate in Salem, where Mrs. Adams's father was a banker, a major strike occurred. It was one of the bitter, townsplitting affairs that occur when workers become articulate and organized, when management feels its prerogatives threatened, when a small number of industries dominate the economy, and when the first signs of structural instability are blinked away. The issues were muddied by Communist agitation. Resolving that something had to be done, the Reverend Mr. Adams proposed to a group of ministers that they take collective action and look into the matter. Several of the clergymen called members of their churches who were managers of the factories, and were assured that the situation was well in hand and that nothing needed to be done. So they did precisely that. But JLA was not to be so easily dissuaded even though his church, too, had its strong share of managers and of managerial sympathizers. He singlehandedly tried to find the facts of the matter. It turned out that the workers (mostly Roman Catholics) had a just grievance, that the managers were distorting the facts in paid advertisements in the newspapers, and that other reporters had not gone beyond the surface. From mill managers in neighboring towns he uncovered the real scandal of the situation, how dishonest the Salem owners were, and decided in the eleventh week of the strike to deliver a sermon on the dispute. The situation became more serious, bitterness increased, and talks between management and labor were on the verge of breakdown. Adams not only preached his sermon at a joint summer service, but went to the newspaper editors and asked them to print his analysis of the situation, at least to let the public look at the other side of the disagreement. When they hesitated, he told them that he had a pulpit and would preach on their reluctance if they would not cooperate. The newspaper hit the streets at 11 a.m., Monday, with the sermon starting on page one and continuing inside. The bargainers were recalled by late afternoon. By 8 p.m. agreement was reached, the strike was over.

The negative reaction was strong on some sides, but JLA maintained that he had not "taken sides" and had only made demand for informed public opinion and open discussion.

No one knows, of course, what the many factors playing into this resolution were, but about three thousand workers, wives, and families thought they knew. They started a victory procession that ended on the front lawn of the Reverend and Mrs. J. L. Adams. Further, when he started to speak at their request and was interrupted and almost attacked by one Communist agitator, the latter was physically (and somewhat indelicately) removed from the area by the workers.

The significance of this painful siege in the life of James Luther Adams is twofold: (1) Like his earlier reaction to Nazism, it is empirical evidence that his thought would be shaped by participation in political and economic struggles, and (2) it appears to have been for him an existential confirmation of *Millhands and Preachers* that those churches claiming to have eternal foundations for their faith are also subject to the dangers of culture-religion, justifying the ways of their contributors.

JLA had previously embarked upon a master's program in English and Greek at Harvard, in part to find another vocation since he saw little of significance in the church, in part to pursue his literary concerns, and in part to study under George Lyman Kittredge, John Livingston Lowes, and Irving Babbitt. Much of his time was devoted to philology, but he became, as his friends report, a raving humanist, almost unbearably so. The influence of Irving Babbitt—whose conservative, classical humanism, with accents on the importance of identification and involvement, shaped several generations of Harvard students—appears to have been internalized and radicalized by JLA. The very intensity of his involvement in this literary humanism was highly significant for Adams in the early 1930's; for while many of the young intellectuals, disillusioned with the Social Gospel in its superficial post-World War I form, and disenchanted with the "American Way of Life" after 1929, turned to scientific humanism, or to various types of relativism, the young Adams was able to maintain a critical attitude against these even while having them broaden and deepen his concerns. While he was indeed to become associated with liberal causes in the 1930's, it is only the undiscerning who could not see the radical differences between his position and dogmatic Marxism. Further, with the realistic view of man involved in the literary humanism of Babbitt, he asserted that "the central problem of civilization [is]... ethical standards and, without being obscurantist,.. stressed the necessity of something like conversion, of a change in the will whereby a man would develop inner ethical control and work toward a richly human, universal norm." As he continues, "Through Babbitt's stress on these ideas I came to understand and value Greek and Chinese humanism, the Christian doctrines of sin and grace, and the Christian emphasis on conversion and humility. I also thus acquired a skepticism of the romantic liberal conception of human nature which was later to be so severely scrutinized by "realistic theology." And by the end of the '20's and into the early '30's, JLA was devouring these "realists." Reinhold Niebuhr, Walter Marshall Horton, Alfred North Whitehead, John Bennett, and von Huegel became crucial figures in opening the doors of criticism, even against the humanism that he endorsed.

The question was asked by this generation: In what kind of context is man to be seen? Surely he does not stand alone, divorced from nature and history, and just decide, *metanoia* without trying to discern where the kingdom is. He is supported, sustained, altered, and influenced by environmental factors of all kinds. The ideational, natural, and temporal settings of man and the influence of these on his decisions became increasingly clear to JLA as he became self-conscious of the provincialized decisions that he himself had made in the past. In short, he began to ask what historical and natural conditions were necessary for mature, self-critical decision-making and for the preservation of a civilization that attempted to have a wide dispersion of decision-making and power.

Suggestions for provisional answers came from several sources, and the style of thinking that we have called comparative-critical began to appear in his scattered essays. Although he was still a pastor (not only in Salem, 1927-33, but later also in the Wellesley Hills First Unitarian Society, 1933-35), his interest in literature found expression in the teaching of English (he still abhors nothing so much as a dangling modifier) at Boston University (1929-32), and in journals such as *Hound and Horn,* whose list of contributors, including T. S. Eliot Archibald MacLeish, Conrad Aiken, Robert Oppenheimer, Francis Fergusson, and Austen Warren, to name a few, reads like a *Who's Who* of that period. His personal acquaintance with T. S. Eliot is particularly treasured. JLA saw Eliot once a week at tea for graduate students in English when Eliot was the Charles Eliot Norton Lecturer at Harvard. They had a chance to renew their acquaintance in London in 1935, when Adams went to Europe to do some research on the literary sources of Bishop Hurd's literary criticism and to devote a year in preparation for his new teaching assignment in Chicago. Through Eliot (also a pupil of Babbitt) he became personally acquainted with certain literary and philosophical figures in England and later in France

To this observer, one *Hound and Horn* article, perhaps only of secondary importance when written, appears to be particularly significant. In the review of *Vigile,* a Paris journal, we see several themes that suggest those percolating concerns that appear repeatedly and increasingly in his writing and lecturing.

One theme is his dialogue with other-worldliness in its more sophisticated expression. Mysticism, in the classical sense and as represented to the modern world in the works of Baron von Huegel and Rudolf Otto, is ever a concern of Adams, for it raises the question of the mediacy or immediacy of revelation and knowledge. He wrote in a commentary on Jacques Maritain's article on St. John of the Cross, "Mysticism, Protestant or Catholic, is always in danger of regarding the means which the church furnishes for uniting God and man as 'intermediary,' as separating God from man. Common sense, as well as tradition, demands that mysticism be always aware of the need for mediators, Christ and the Church." The notion that "nothing but the infinite can save us" just does not fit with *"salus extra ecclesia non est."* The questions became, therefore, (a) since Christ and his church must mediate, how may these best be understood and structured? Or to put it in quite another way, the movement from spiritual bondage to spiritual freedom demands changing the types of social organization. Freedom, to stay free, must organize. And (b) how can an adequate hermeneutical principle be devised to discern where in the plethora of God's creation, human action, and man's thought, God's will is to be known?

While protesting repeatedly against the "un-Catholic desire for pure spirituality" which he sees variously formulated in St. John of the Cross, Rousseau, and Descartes (and others), he appears nevertheless to be continually troubled by and attracted to the self-validating reality of immediate experience. Rudolf Otto, not only because of his sense of the encounter with the Holy, but also because of his historical and eschatological sensitivities as seen in *Kingdom of God and Son of Man*, was influential.

These themes had been present earlier. After assuming the pastorate in Wellesley, JLA turned to a more systematic reading of theology and began to see a significance, not previously clear to him, in the religious life. Indeed, while studying in Europe several years later (1935-1936), he followed the example of von Huegel and secured a spiritual director for a while at the Seminary of St. Sulpice in Paris. He reports of that experience:

> Two hours a week for a period of three months with one of the finest spirits I have known will not be forgotten. Here I came to know a man for whom the devotional life was far more than a discipline. It was a growing in the grace and knowledge of Christ. He did for me what I should have expected from a Protestant: he acquainted me with a living Christ. Yet the Christ he made vivid for me was not the harbinger of the Kingdom, but rather the obedient servant of God in the inner life and in the personal virtues.

This concern with spiritual direction was an analogue to his interest in public worship. The Greenfield Group had given much attention to problems of public worship. They had produced a revision of liturgy which had been adopted in a number of churches; in this connection they had also promoted the adoption of the German chorale in substantial measure in the Unitarian hymnal. During this period (1935-36) in Europe JLA studied liturgies for a semester with Robert Will of the Strasbourg Theological Faculty. He then proceeded to study the Liturgical Movement of the Benedictines, especially at the famous monastery of Maria Laach in Germany. (Later on, Ernst Koenker under Adams's stimulus would write the major Protestant work on the Roman Catholic Liturgical Movement.) In this period he also spent much time with Rudolf Otto in Marburg, considering "the renewal of liturgy" in

Protestantism in its relation to New Testament studies. Liturgy, in Adams's view, is always in danger of becoming a static rite and of inhibiting the prophetic element of Christian faith. Rudolf Otto with his paradoxical "realized eschatology" injected the *dynamis* of directed time into the space of the sacrament.

The problem of history, of time, plagued him. The content of supposedly pure spirituality was subject to temporal influence. That was empirically and existentially so. One must see the mediate character of the spirit. What are the factors that mediate the spiritual reality? Increasingly he came to the conclusion that language is insufficient. Writing, confessing, speaking, and preaching, even the whole literary heritage he loved, as important as they were, did not finally determine the spiritual destiny of nations. It is concrete historical institutions that shape life most massively. Institutions, indeed, provide the nexus for preservation, transmission, and alteration of language and cultural memory, as well as the conditions for receptivity to alternative choices in conversion. Selection and definition of terms and remembered events are primarily, although not exhaustively, social processes. It thus was not accidental that Adams, during this period, became acquainted personally with the French Protestant religious socialist, André Philip, a professor of law in Lyons and a member of the Chamber of Deputies. In the efforts of the religious socialists Adams found an attempt to link theology and the world in a way that took history and institutions seriously, even if they, like the members of the *Kairos* circle in Germany, were sometimes more theoretical than participating.

The problem of history also began to become clear to him in other ways, for even as he had been aware of the importance of the Radical Reformation through his involvement with the Unitarians and through his reading of Troeltsch, it was during the next decade that he became more systematically concerned with a "third history" of the Reformation. As the Catholics could not be counted on for a full account of the Reformation movement and the Lutheran and Calvinist historians tended to read the data of the Reformation in a way not to the liking of Catholic historians, so neither could be counted on to portray accurately the "Left Wing." The Anabaptists, the Mennonites, the Münsterites, and all the other varieties of wilding growth are not to be dismissed out of hand just because they were successfully suppressed during the sixteenth century. This concern flowered, as did many of his interests, in Adams's students—in this case most notably in George H. Williams. Even more important to American history are the proto-democratic and quasi-equalitarian sectarian movements in and around the Cromwellian Revolution. The Diggers, the Levellers, the Seekers, the Separatists, and the whole range of such groups represent a variety of social creativity that has shaped the modern world more than it acknowledges. (It was the study of these movements that initially brought Adams and D. B. Robertson into association; Adams read D. B. Robertson's doctoral dissertation, *The Religious Foundations of Leveller Democracy*, before it went to press in 1951.)

Adams came to see that the Marxists and the sectarians themselves, while treating the material in a highly ideological way, had done a service in turning attention to these movements and figures once again. Even more important became the theorists of voluntary associations who recognized the crucial importance, limitations, and perversions of these groups—Figgis, Maitland, Barker, and Channing.

Further, the problem of the relation of nature to immediate history struck James Luther Adams at this time in full vigor. It appeared in two ways: politically and theoretically. Both during the 1935-1936 trip to Germany and later in 1935, JLA was inevitably concerned about the emerging power of Hitler and the inability of the church, even where willing and sensitive to the need, to head off the demonic appeal to "the German nature."

The fact that so few effective, free-wheeling, voluntary associations had ever developed in Germany since the assassinations of the leaders of the Left Wing in the Reformation was, according to JLA's perspective, a contributing factor. The limited historical possibilities of human action and association had not been able to contain the laws of tooth and claw inherent in nature in the time of crisis. Indeed, the historical church and the theological tradition in many cases contributed to their own dissolution.

More personally, he began to ask what he was doing to prevent something like that from happening in America. (He had once resisted the organization of an anti-Nazi demonstration on Boston Common.) This reflection and self-examination resulted ultimately in many efforts and actions. Among these are some of the earlier protests against racial segregation.

JLA happened to be chairman of the library committee of the Federated Theological Faculty of the University of Chicago during a WPA project to catalogue a huge stack of some 70,000 pamphlets dating before the Civil War. Adams noticed that no Negroes were among the employed, brought the matter before the committee, and got unanimous agreement that the personnel should be integrated. After carrying on correspondence about the matter for some time, with no results, he went in person to see the director of the projects in that area. He confronted the executive, a prominent businessman weighing some 250 pounds who enjoyed, as Adams tells it, "physically and spiritually throwing his weight around." The executive resisted any recommendations concerning his authority, his policy, or the program in the libraries. Finally the time came for a showdown session.

The administrator invited Adams to his office (in the midst of an enormous outlay of glass-partitioned bureaus) at 5:15 after all other employees had left. For about an hour and a half, the conversation became more and more heated until finally something like the following climax was reached:

"Obviously, you are just a professor; you have never had to meet a payroll, and haven't the slightest notion of the problems of an executive. We're going to have great trouble if we introduce Negroes into the project. The workers won't stand for it!"

"Well, I'm not convinced that they won't stand for it. I am convinced, and I have talked with some of them, that some of them are also displeased. There are others, of course, that won't like it, but after all, the Negroes are American citizens, they pay taxes, WPA is a federal project, and the WPA ought to join the United States. I am speaking to you in the name of a committee that agrees unanimously on this policy. And if you don't want to follow the policy, which is, really, in accord with the United States Constitution, you can just take the project out."

The executive was shocked. He could scarcely believe this, but Adams continued:

"And I think that we ought to take it out right now. We want nothing to do with it."

"You mean you don't want those books, you don't want those thousands of pamphlets catalogued?"

"No! They have not been catalogued for over a century, and they can wait until this becomes a possibility within the framework of the American Constitution."

"But you don't realize the complexity of executive decision-making. There would be pandemonium if I tried to introduce such a policy overnight. You have to realize the problems of being an administrator and an executive."

"I don't have to discuss with you *my* executive abilities. You are the executive, and you are the one who has the executive ability, as I understand it. But I have to tell you that in this instance I have the authority and the power to tell you what to execute. Perhaps you do not often find yourself in a position when others have power over you, but you are in one now. So, if you have such great executive ability, will you show me how? Do your stuff. Now, what are you going to do with me, and what are you going to do with the library committee? I am your 'problem.' They are your 'problem.' Do your stuff."

The executive had to surrender.

"Well, there will be a lot of trouble!"

"I don't think there will be trouble. But if anybody doesn't want to work for the WPA, and if he would rather be unemployed, he is free to leave the job. But, despite my alleged lack of executive ability, I venture to predict that no one will leave just because Negroes are brought in."

So the project was integrated. No one left the project.

But not all efforts were so successful. In one lecture that he gave recurrently to American servicemen (in officers' training) to teach them about the Nazi enemy, he outlined the Nazi racist philosophy in such a way that the audience became thoroughly incensed. Many of them would not recognize, however, that their attitudes about the Negroes were closely allied with the dominant racist motifs of the Axis, nor would they admit that "America First" and "Deutschland über Alles" were close cousins. He was quietly relieved of his duties.

But even while he was still in Germany, his interest turned to those groups actually involved in resistance. By 1938 this interest was more intense, and Adams in the company of Peter Brunner (now on the Heidelberg faculty) spent several months observing underground movements and the behavior of the churches in the face of this "natural nationalism." He interviewed numerous Nazi and anti-Nazi leaders, taking some home movies that would make several leading German theologians, some of whom are still living, quiver in their boots with many a *mea culpa*. "The Cult of Authority," to quote Georg Iggers's book title out of context, was in full reign and was not to be vanquished, as Bonhoeffer (if not many Bonhoefferians of today) learned, by confessional statements alone.

Never one to stand in the wings of a dispute, JLA became so involved that he was apprehended by the Nazis and had his passport withheld for a while. Ostensibly, he was questioned for having been seen on the streets with a Jew, but he has always felt that his involvement with resistance groups was known to them.

Several important events occurred between his visits to Europe. Upon his return from the 1935-36 visit, the Reverend James Luther Adams became Professor James Luther Adams, teaching Psychology and Philosophy of Religion at The Meadville Theological School in Chicago. The impact of this young teacher on the students at Meadville, according to their reports, cannot be overestimated. The excitement of the intellectual enterprise, the expanding of horizons historically, internationally, and socially, and the direct importance of commitment and involvement left its mark on a whole generation of Unitarian pastors and scholars. For Adams himself, it was in this position that he began to deal with the theoretical aspects of the relationship of nature and history.

Since 1927, JLA had been intrigued by the thought of Paul Tillich, eventually writing his doctoral dissertation on "Paul Tillich's Philosophy of Culture, Science, and Religion" (published in 1965 by Harper and Row). Tillich, along with Troeltsch, has been a crucial influence on Adams's thought. And in Chicago, he encountered again "process philosophy," confirming a philosophical interest initially stimulated by courses taken under Whitehead at Harvard. Both Tillich and the "process philosophers" had a sense of the ontological rootage of man in the nature of being and the pertinence of that problem to the human situation in history. Sensitivity to Being, Becoming, and Time were necessarily bound up with discerning "the times." The attempt to relate ontological, historical, and institutional matters, a concern of long standing, was a crucial part of Adams's critical reading of the conflict between Tillich and the process thinkers. While he always pressed the question of what the more theoretical formulations mean in terms of social organizational structure and the distribution of authority, the continuing dialogue on the relationship of history, metaphysics, and politics in which Tillich tends to ontologize history and the process philosophers tend to historicize ontology fed and nurtured Adams's ever-questioning drive. Even while he can say, "There is much in Tillich which still remains for me obscure and where understood unacceptable," and while he can call some process philosophy an ontological evasion of the institutional dimension of existence, the fact remains that this debate strongly influenced his view of the relationship of nature and history, and the theological importance of that relationship. One might say briefly that he has become an historical contextualist, taking the cultural epoch as his context, and always asking what principles are in operation therein and what view of Being or Becoming is implied by making one decision rather than another. The fact that he edited Wieman's *The Directive in History* in 1949, only one year after his translation of Tillich's *The Protestant Era,* is more than coincidental.

This concern for historical context, and especially for the relations between theology and social organization, is reflected in the critique of individualistic existentialism which for years has punctuated JLA's lectures. Thus he has viewed Kierkegaard as a one-sided proponent of Christian faith: he centers attention upon personal and interpersonal aspects of piety to the neglect of institutional implications and responsibilities. The Marxists for their part exhibit indifference to personal virtues. What Kierkegaard lacks Karl Marx has, and what Karl Marx lacks Kierkegaard has. To both of them JLA likes to apply the Sainte Beuve maxim that nothing is so much like a swelling as a hole. The Kierkegaardian lack of concern for institutional problems and responsibilities appears today in the ontologism of Heidegger and in the *Innerlichkeit* and "pietism" of Bultmann. Warnings against false securities do not provide any substitute for a positive social theology or for political participation. Adams predicts that the inadequacy of Bultmann "pietism" will become evident the moment the German economic miracle begins to fade. This "pietism" presupposes the stability of the socio-political order, it does little to give shape to that order. In this respect it ignores a basic presupposition of the Bible. This presupposition lies behind the doctrine of the covenant namely, that God is a community-forming power and that man's response to it entails full social and political participation.

The manner of working through the problems of the world are almost as interesting in JLA's life as the problems themselves. For instance, when he becomes wrapped up with an author or problem he cannot sleep. Many students report that his lights burn late into the night. One evening in Chicago, after going to bed he found he could not sleep and, slipping his robe over his pajamas, crossed over to the nearby library to make use of the wakeful hours. He became so involved that he failed to notice the hour and only belatedly started on his way back home. He arrived at the library door just in time to greet the librarian coming to work. Both he and she were embarrassed.

During this period he began to develop a propensity to answer questions with bibliography. It became part of the lore of the school that if one wanted a complete, cross-indexed, annotated bibliography on almost any topic, he had but to capture JLA at the corner of Woodlawn and 57th Streets, on his way home from classes. At Harvard, the same point is made by graduate students, who tell incoming B.D. candidates that Adams has nightmares that somewhere in Widener Library is a book he has not read.

Adams's academic interests are always supplemented by activity. I shall only report a partial, indeed selected, list of organizations and activities in which Adams has been involved, but these should show how seriously he took his own injunctions regarding the importance of voluntary associational participation.

> Member, State Board, Americans for Democratic Action
> Editor, *Christian Register*
> Member, Unitarian Commission of Appraisal
> Editor, *Journal of Liberal Religion*
> Associate Editor, *The Protestant*
> Chairman, Independent Voters of Illinois
> Chairman, National Advisory Committee, Department of Social
>   Responsibility, Unitarian Universalist Association
> Chairman, Admissions Committee, Albert Schweitzer College
> Member, Advisory Board, American Christian Palestine Committee
> Member, Unitarian Commission of Planning and Review
> Associate Editor, *Faith and Freedom (British)*
> Co-Editor, *Journal of Religion*
> Chairman, Advisory Board, Beacon Press

Member, American Committee for Cultural Freedom

Consultant, Legal Defense and Educational Committee, National
    Association for the Advancement of Colored People

Member, Apollos Club

Member and officer, Christian Action, Chicago Chapter

Vice-President, Chicago Chapter, Protestants and Other Americans United
    for Separation of Church and State

Member, Religion and Labor Foundation

Member, American Association of University Professors

Member, Middle West Theologians Ecumenical Group

Member, National Committee to Repeal McCarran Act

Member, State Board, Civil Liberties Union

Member, Unitarian Fellowship for Social Justice

Member, Hyde Park Community Conference

President, Society for the Scientific Study of Religion

Member, International Council, La Société Européenne de Culture

Member, Congress of Racial Equality

Member, National Advisory Board, Northern Student Movement

Member, State Board, American Association for the United Nations

Member, American Society for Political and Legal Philosophy

Member, American Society of Christian Social Ethics

Fellow, American Academy of Arts and Sciences

Member, American Sociological Association

The major trends of JLA's life have been suggested. The dominant, overarching result of his thought has been the development of an associational interpretation of history. The various periods of history and the various philosophies of each epoch are exegeted primarily through, and find much of their importance in, the kinds of social structures characteristic of the period. A typical statement from his lectures is, "If you want to know what a man means by a given set of theological concepts, ask him what his ecclesiology is," although he recognizes that theological meaning is not thereby exhausted. The ways in which power is distributed, authority functions, and institutional requirements are met in the church are the best place to take the pulse of theology. Further, if a man sets forth a political philosophy or a set of moral principles, ask him how he is to implement this in the community—that will give you some notion of what it actually means. But this is not merely a theoretical concern for JLA; it is a quite practical matter. While it is true that it is various refinements on this set of fugues that provide the center of his lecturing concern and the substance of his correspondence, these concerns find their embodiment in his own involvement. He is still active and holds office in a variety of organizations, most notably in ADA and Civil Liberties Union, although the move to Harvard did cut him off from certain channels of inside information and some organizations that he had cultivated for two decades in Chicago.

The impression should not be left, however, that it is only political and parapolitical efforts that occupy him. While these are important, two other areas of activity and sensitivity should be mentioned. Both are interests of long standing, but have come to focus especially since Professor and Mrs. Adams came to Harvard and began spending their summers in the Berkshires. Since his youth Adams had an interest in music, nurtured in his youth even though his parents feared that it might turn to jazz, and at Chicago he participated in lunch-break chamber music sessions with some friends. Also for nearly two decades while Adams was in Chicago, students would gather in the Adams's living room once a week to listen to recordings, discuss composers and compositions, and attempt to relate this art form to other aspects of cultural life. (Adams now has one of the finest hi-fi and stereo component rigs I have seen.) Mrs. Adams had studied at the New England Conservatory and was considered an accomplished pianist. Dr. and Mrs. Adams had been also, respectively, members of the Glee Club and of the Radcliffe Choral Society. (Mrs. Adams attended Radcliffe for three and one-half years, although she actually received her degree from the University of Chicago.) The interest in music has persisted; they then spent their summers only seventeen miles from Tanglewood, where the Boston Symphony plays almost daily, regularly attended these concerts. Also they became interested in Ted Shawn's School for the ballet at nearby Jacob's Pillow. For Adams, this has, characteristically, become a passion. The expression of ecstasy, creativity, and spirit through disciplined form and the body could not but intrigue one of his persuasions.

But the majority of their time in the Berkshires was taken up by their involvement with Gould Farm, a therapeutic halfway house for those who have emotional disturbances and are on their way back to society. Gould Farm is located near Tanglewood and Jacob's Pillow. Frequent weekends and most summers were spent at Gould Farm in working, talking, and discussing with those trying to break free of bonds that inhibit existence by establishing new associations.

His energies were still not exhausted, in the summer of 1952 he was asked to become a member of a Study Tour of the Middle East under the auspices of the American Christian Palestine Committee. During the course of the extended trip he lectured in England and at the Albert Schweitzer College in Switzerland. In 1953 he delivered the Noble Lectures at Harvard, and it was soon thereafter that he was called to Harvard Divinity School. In Tokyo in the summer of 1958, he was a participant in the Ninth International Congress for the History of Religions, an experience that provided the occasion for the development of many friendships in the Orient as well as in Europe. During that summer he also lectured in Rangoon, Calcutta, and Bangalore. In 1960, he delivered a paper at the Arminius Symposium in Amsterdam and had the opportunity to renew European acquaintances.

In the school year 1962-63, he traveled in Europe on his sabbatical, being relieved at Harvard by his former student, James Gustafson of Yale. He delivered the Hibbert Lectures in England, lectured widely in Germany and Italy, and was a guest professor at Marburg University. Perhaps the most remarkable thing about these trips was JLA's ability to sustain the contacts and friendships made during his excursions. From all over the world came letters, manuscripts, and reprints. His daily mail was a funnel through which theologians and ethicists from many countries channeled their products and from which they derived much sustenance.

One could continue and supplement such a chronicle at nearly every sentence, for if one can prevail upon JLA to "repeal reticence," as he says trying to get others to talk of themselves, the stories flow like an artesian well—and with the artistry of a master bard. But space forbids. One can now only ask briefly what is the significance of such a constellation of concerns in the modern theological scene.

In a day when the harsher shouting of THE WORD by self-conscious Neo-Reformation theology is getting somewhat smaller audiences, when the radical existentialism produced by the *anomie* of the post-World War II period is recognized as insufficient for full understanding of modern man, when the Ecumenical Movement within Protestantism and within

Christianity at large is the dominant mood, even if we are not sure why or whither, it is instructive to listen to one who has heard, really heard, many speakers for some time. JLA is a liberal who refused to be intimidated by the attempts of some branches of Neo-Protestantism to shout down a caricatured straw man. At the same time he was sensitive and receptive to the just criticisms against the false securities of a liberalism that was becoming LIBERALISM. While he persisted in unmasking the pretensions of a liberalism that attempted to erect itself into an inverted dogmatism, he continued to demand that the neo-orthodox theologians acknowledge (1) their indebtedness and continuity with certain aspects of the 19th century, and (2) the power that the social situation exerted on their efforts, lest they erect culturally determined temporality into a presumptuous and false eternality.

Hence, he has provided some helpful hints for the new generation that must attempt, as each generation must, to construct a theological and associational framework that is adequate to the understanding, fulfillment, and transformation of the life that we now live interpreted by the faith we know. JLA suggests again and again a possible direction for what appears to be an emergent, chastised neo-liberalism.

The critical-comparative approach with which we started our tale is one that is necessary not only for understanding his life nor only for suggesting his significance for theology at large but also for understanding his students. For it is in the theologically sensitive social witness of pastors trained under him and in the theses and books of his graduate students that the seminal, if diffuse and sometimes even fragmented, ideas of Adams are worked out systematically. Yet it must be said that any student who has tried to grasp the depths of these efforts has felt frustrated at the inability to measure up to the standards set by Adams. And while, working under JLA, the student becomes sure that he will never really be a scholar, that he will never be able to box the intellectual compass in a comparable way, he also becomes sure that he will henceforth know a scholar when he sees one.

Again, his style of teaching is as interesting as the subject matter and the results. He strides into his 9:00 a.m. class, having just come from a committee meeting or from two hours of dictating correspondence. He greets the brethren as he takes off his hat and coat, which, after class, he will invariably forget to recover until the next class is about to start in the same room. He opens his briefcase, and hauls forth voluminous notes and often several books to which he plans to make reference. Then, like an old evangelical who has memorized the Bible, he consults the pages before him only long enough to trigger his mind. Stalking around the room, he then delivers himself of his lecture.

The lectures themselves have been variously characterized, partly, I suspect, because of the variation of the lectures from year to year. While the main concerns remain the same, surrounding these is an ever differing way of painting the picture. The concerns are the perennial efforts of humanity to discern the realities of the situation under God and in history, but the treatment is ever changing. If one reads the lecture notes of students ten years ago and compares them with one's own, one finds the outline strikingly similar, but the interlinear excursuses are a catalogue of what Professor Adams has been reading or experiencing, a chronological account of alternating sensitivities that occur in the literature on the subject under discussion.

But his teaching is not confined to the classroom, nor has it ended. His teaching long has reached as far, one is tempted to say, as the mails will carry.

It is not inappropriate that we speak of his correspondence when we speak of his writings. His letters flow with incredible volume and scope to every corner of the globe. For innumerable theologians, philosophers, former students, friends, politicians, and acquaintances, James Luther Adams has served as a one-man clearinghouse of information, knowing where the research on such and such topic is taking place and where one might find a bibliography on a given subject, and also often knowing the wives and children and private interests of most of the correspondents. Perhaps, thus, it is appropriate to close with a quotation from a letter that could be duplicated a dozen times from as many countries.

Franklin Littell spoke for us all when he wrote, on hearing of the preparation of this biographical sketch:

The thing I hope you will emphasize is his extraordinary generosity to scholars everywhere. For example, I have never taken any classes with him. Nevertheless, he has sent me reprints, bibliographical notes, etc., for all these years (since 1938) and taken the most direct personal interest in helping me learn.

During the years I spent in Germany, nearly a decade, he was my best correspondent and advisor on what was happening in intellectual circles here, what books to read and so on. This generosity of spirit is typical—the most typical thing about Jim besides his encyclopedic knowledge.

From *Voluntary Associations: A Study of Groups in Free Societies*, Essays In Honor of James Luther Adams edited by D. B. Robertson (John Knox Press, Richmond, Virginia, 1966.)

Harvard Faculty Memorial Minute

By George Kimmich Beach

James Luther Adams—"JLA," as he came to be affectionately known—was born in Ritzville, Washington, in 1901, the son of James Carey Adams, an itinerant Baptist preacher and farmer, and Leila Mae Bartlett. When his father, who later joined the Plymouth Brethren, went on his Sunday preaching circuit, young Luther (as he was called in the family) often went along, taking his violin to accompany the hymns. His childhood experience of fundamentalist Christianity and of farm life deeply influenced his development, and became a source of the storytelling for which he later became renowned. At age 16, when his father fell seriously ill, he dropped out of high school in order to help support the family. Among other jobs, he worked for the Northern Pacific Railroad, acquired speed shorthand, and soon rose to the position of secretary to the regional superintendent. To his boss's astonishment, he turned down the lucrative offer of promotion in order to further his education—his "deprovincialization"—he often called it. In 1920 he entered the University of Minnesota, while continuing to work nights in the railroad yards.

After a phase in which he radically rejected all religion, Adams came to recognize it as his passion and ministry as his calling. He entered Harvard Divinity School in 1924, with the intention of becoming a Unitarian minister. In his autobiographical essay of 1939, he recounted his transitions from the "premillenarian fundamentalism" of his youth, to "scientific humanism" (as expounded by John Dietrich in Minneapolis, during his college years), and then to liberal Christianity. He recalled the words of an influential teacher, Dr. Frank Rarig, who once told him that his problem was that he had never heard of a "self-critical religion." The entire quest of Adams's professional career may be seen as transformative responses to his childhood religion in two basic respects: first, his quest as a theologian for "an examined faith"—a faith subject to self-criticism and growth—and second, his quest as an ethicist for a faith that "takes

George K. Beach, former student and long-time friend of James Luther Adams, is Minister *Emeritus* of the Unitarian Church of Arlington, Virginia, and editor of these books by Beacon Press, Boston: *The Prophethood of All Believers*, 1986; *An Examined Faith: Social Context and Religious Commitment*, 1991; *The Essential James Luther Adams*, 1998; *Transforming Liberalism: The Theology of James Luther Adams*, 2005.

time seriously"—a faith that seeks to embody its ethical commitments in history.

In 1927 Adams was ordained and installed as minister of the Second Church (Unitarian) in Salem, Massachusetts In the same year he and Margaret Ann Young, an accomplished pianist and graduate of the New England Conservatory in Boston, were married. Margaret went on to study social work and actively promoted social reform movements. In their more than fifty years together they raised three daughters and shared musical and other interests. They hosted weekly informal evening gatherings in their home, a place for communal support and discussion among theological students, during his years of teaching theology. Margaret died of cancer in 1978.

During his pastorates in Salem and, subsequently, in Wellesley Hills, Massachusetts, Adams pursued graduate studies in comparative literature at Harvard; for several years. He also worked as an instructor in the English Department at Boston University while continuing in ministry. Among the Harvard professors whose influence he warmly remembered were Irving Babbitt, Alfred North Whitehead, George Lyman Kittredge, and Willard Sperry, Dean of the Divinity School.

In the course of several extended trips to Europe between 1927 and the late 1930's, he sought out intellectual and church leaders such as Martin Niemoeller, T. S. Eliot, Karl Barth, Karl Jaspers, and Rudolf Otto. He was especially attracted to Otto, the Marburg University professor and avowed anti-Nazi, and to Peter Brunner, a Lutheran pastor and theological teacher. Brunner, who some years before had become a close friend of Adams at Harvard, was at this time a leader in the anti-Nazi Confessing Church movement. Adams's personal encounters with Nazism, including being detained for questioning by the Gestapo, deepened his sense of global political and cultural crisis, a crisis he believed demanded spiritual renewal and social-ethical commitment. It is this sense of historical urgency and engagement that underlies one of the most characteristic accents of his thought.

Adams credited Rudolf Otto with insights into the origin and meaning of Jesus' announcement of the kingdom of God, insights which gave fresh relevance to eschatology as a psychological and historical (if not cosmic) phenomenon. Jesus, he learned from Otto, proclaimed the kingdom of God not as a future event (hence, a failed prediction) but as paradoxically sent and yet to come. As a religious "root metaphor" (a concept favored by Adams) drawn from the political realm, the kingdom of God signifies "the pull of the future" toward fulfillment; it is an image of hope in dark times. The present, then, becomes a time of courageous and hopeful decision, a creative thrust toward meaning in history. Socially relevant decision, however, will necessarily involve engagement in groups, and especially voluntary associations, which seek to influence communal, national, and even global, life.

These ideas and concerns formed the central thrust of Adams's life-work in the church and the university. He developed them with great rhetorical force and charm, as writer, lecturer, raconteur, and conversationalist.

In 1937 Adams joined the faculty of the Meadville Theological School, a Unitarian seminary in Chicago, as professor of religious social ethics. (Since the Unitarian Universalist merger, the school has been renamed Meadville/Lombard Theological School.) From 1943 he was also a member of the newly formed Federated Theological Faculty of the University of Chicago. In 1956 he returned to Cambridge to become the Edward Mallinckrodt, Jr. Professor of Christian Ethics at Harvard Divinity School. There he taught courses on modern era social reformers, voluntary associations, the Radical Reformation, the thought of Ernst Troeltsch, and the theory of natural law. These were hardly typical fare for seminary course offerings in the field of ethics, but reflected the breadth and depth of his erudition.

By the force of both his personality and his ideas Adams deeply influenced a generation of students for the ministry (in many denominations) and doctoral students in ethics and society. Always an advocate of interdisciplinary studies and inter-professional discussion, Adams—together with Professor Harold Berman of the Law School—conducted for several years a seminar on religion and law, and with Professor Arch Dooley of the Business School, a seminar on religion and business decisions.

In 1968 he retired from Harvard, becoming Professor *Emeritus*, and accepted temporary appointments to the faculties of Andover-Newton Theological School and, subsequently, Meadville/Lombard Theological School. In 1976 he and Margaret again returned to their Cambridge home on Francis Avenue, within the precincts of the former Shady Hill, originally the estate of Andrews Norton and Charles Eliot

Norton. He continued to be active in church life, serving as Minister of Adult Education at the Arlington Street Church, Boston. At the 350th anniversary of Harvard in 1986, he was awarded a medal for distinguished service to the University.

Through his last years Adams experienced continuous discomfort and often intense back pain due to the progressive disintegration of his vertebrae. For several years he wore a back brace which, like a turtle shell, encircled his chest with a steel arm. He ultimately cast the brace off as more trouble than it was worth. He continued during this period to maintain voluminous correspondence and to entertain a stream of visitors at home. Colleagues and former students formed the James Luther Adams Foundation to promote his thought and enable continuation of his work. Secretarial service provided by the Foundation enabled him to dictate and edit more than a thousand pages for his autobiography; which was posthumously published—cut by half—as *Not Without Dust and Heat: A Memoir* (Chicago: Exploration Press, 1996). Adams died on July 26, 1994, at the age of 92, having maintained his full mental faculties into his last year of life.

Adams was a major transmitter and translator of the work of the German theologians and historians Ernst Troeltsch, Karl Holl, and Paul Tillich. In 1948 the University of Chicago Press published his translations of early essays by Tillich, *The Protestant Era*, with a major afterword by Adams. His doctoral dissertation at Chicago became the basis of his major work on Tillich, *Paul Tillich's Philosophy of Culture, Science, and Religion* (New York: Harper and Row, 1965; New York: Schocken Books, 1970; Washington, D.C.: University Press of America, 1982). Tillich, who became his colleague at Harvard, once said—probably without exaggeration—that Adams knew more about his work than he did himself. Adams published several major essays interpreting Tillich's thought; the last and definitive of these appeared in *The Thought of Paul Tillich* (New York: Harper and Row, 1985), edited by Adams, Wilhelm Pauck, and Roger L. Shinn. He translated and wrote introductions for two other books by Paul Tillich, *What Is Religion?* (1973) and *Political Expectation* (1971). It would be fair to say that he was less enamored with Tillich's later work (on depth psychology and systematic theology) than his early work on the theological interpretation of history and the history of Christian thought (especially Augustine and Luther).

Adams wrote an introduction to Ernst Troeltsch's major work, *The Absoluteness of Christianity and the History of Religions* (Richmond: John Knox Press, 1971). With Professor Walter F. Bense of the University of Milwaukee, he translated and introduced a volume of essays by Troeltsch, *Religion in History* (Edinburgh: T. and T. Clark, and Minneapolis: Fortress Press, 1991). Also with Bense, Adams edited and introduced several volumes of essays by Karl Holl, an initiator of modern Luther studies and a critic of Troeltsch, including *What Did Luther Understand by Religion?* (1977) and *Reconstruction of Morality* (1979).

Many of the hundreds of published and unpublished essays, reviews, introductions, lectures, and sermons of James Luther Adams have been published in several books: *Taking Time Seriously* (Glencoe: The Free Press, 1957); *On Being Human Religiously*, edited and with an introduction by Max L. Stackhouse (Boston: Beacon Press, 1977); *The Prophethood of All Believers*, edited and with an introduction by George K. Beach (Boston: Beacon Press, 1986); *Voluntary Associations: Socio-Cultural Analyses and Theological Interpretation*, edited by J. Ronald Engel (Chicago: Exploration Press, 1986); *An Examined Faith: Social Context and Religious Commitment*, edited and with an introduction by George K. Beach; *The Essential James Luther Adams: Selected Essays and Addresses*, edited and with an introduction by George K. Beach (Boston: Skinner House Books, 1998).

Two videotapes, *No Authority But From God* (28 minutes) and *Religion Under Hitler* (26 minutes) with Adams and George H. Williams commenting on figures and events in Germany, along with original films taken in Germany by Adams in the 1930's, were produced by The James Luther Adams Foundation (First and Second Church of Boston, 1990). Another videotape featuring Adams as storyteller, *JLA at Home: A Conversation in Six Parts with James Luther Adams*, was produced by George K. Beach (Unitarian Universalist Church of Arlington, Va., 1988). A Festschrift volume was published at the time of his retirement from Harvard, *Voluntary Associations: A Study of Groups in Free Societies, Essays in Honor of James Luther Adams*, edited by D. B. Robertson (Richmond: John Knox Press, 1966). The book includes a foreword by Paul Tillich, a biographical sketch by Max L. Stackhouse, an interpretive essay by James D. Hunt, and a bibliography to date.

Adams's name is most closely associated with the study of voluntary associations and their role in a free society. He practiced what he preached. Adams founded groups for study and devotional discipline (The Greenfield Group, Brothers of the Way), participated in a therapeutic community (Gould Farm), and was active in church life and reform (as a founder of the Unitarian Commission of Appraisal in the 1930's). He served as president of the American Theological Society and of the Society of Christian Ethics; he was a founder and president of the Society for the Scientific Study of Religion, and president of the Society for the Arts, Religion and Contemporary Culture. He founded and edited *The Journal of Liberal Religion*, and served for various periods as editor of *The Christian Register* and *The Protestant*.

In the 1940's Adams was a founder and leader of the Independent Voters of Illinois, a grassroots organization in Chicago. Later, for the American Civil Liberties Union (Massachusetts branch), he served for fifteen years as Chairman of the Committee on Church and State. He helped found FREE, the Fellowship for Racial and Economic Equality, which continues today as the Southeastern Institute.

A listing of the voluntary associations that engaged his energies over the decades hardly conveys the intensity of his activities in the struggles against racism, poverty, anti-Semitism, and the violation of civil liberties and rights. For example, he tells of an all-night vigil in a new federal housing project in Chicago from which whites were excluding blacks: "A brick thrown at the police paddy wagon in which I was riding demolished the windshield." He tells of representing race-relations organizations before officials of the Red Cross in Washington, D.C., to demand an end to the racial segregation of blood for soldiers in World War II. He tells of being ejected from a ministers' meeting in South Chicago, in the midst of racial hostilities, on grounds that he was an "outsider" from the University of Chicago. He tells of carrying on a project of "aggressive love" to bring blacks into the First Unitarian Church of Chicago (Hyde Park) — "and to insist that they be given responsibilities other than that of ushering on Sunday morning."

Each experience has its story, lending drama to the message within Jim Adams's many messages: In the struggle for social justice the prize will be won, in John Milton's phrase, "not without dust and heat."

Respectfully submitted,

George Kimmich Beach, S.T.B. '60, Th.M. '65

A Celebration of life

By Max L. Stackhouse

Delivered at a Celebration of Life at The Arlington Street Church in Boston on October 23, 1994.

James Luther Adams dictated two letters when one of his many strokes forced him to ponder his own mortality with a new urgency. In the first letter, he specified that a memorial service be held here at Arlington Street Church (rather than in an academic setting), that it be on a Sunday afternoon so that his daughters and the clergy could come, and that we have particular pieces of music.

His wishes in death extended his commitments in life: he loved the church and called academia to attend to its importance in the souls of individuals and in the destiny of civilizations, even though he was often impatient with it. He loved his family, in spite of the fact that he knew that he often neglected them because he was preoccupied with a multitude of adopted sons and daughters, represented by the many ministers and professors here today.

And he loved the arts, holding that true beauty also shows itself to have a "heart of service," one that can reveal "the nature of existence and the character of the transformed life," as a marvelous article of homage to him states in the new issue of *Arts*.

Music was his labored art. Although he was a student and teacher of literature, and although he introduced theological students to the importance of sculptors and painters from Giacometti and Cezanne to Bosch, his early training on the violin and his half century marriage with his beloved Margaret, herself a musician, prompted them to explore the glory and anguish of life through the harmony and dissonance of composed sound. Their first date was to hear Bach's *St. Matthew's Passion*, a piece to which he never referred without noting Soderblom's comment that it should be called the "fifth gospel;" but I always suspected that the "other" evangelist of his life was really Margaret, not Bach.

In his letter, he is very specific about the music he wanted. Mozart's *Ave Verum*, Brahms' *How Lovely Is Thy Dwelling Place*, and Berg's *Concerto for Violin and Orchestra* were his choices. His comment on the Berg is the most extensive. It was written, says Adams, to commemorate

Gustav Mahler's relationship to his daughter, and it involves a Bach-like statement of a transcendent care that remains even when death triumphs over life.

The letter reveals, however, not only his commitment to the classical tradition and to its capacity to reveal the depth of meaning; but his awareness that truth and beauty are tied to social justice and commitments. Thus, his next sentence asks that those gathered today sing the Black National Anthem, *Lift Every Heart,* as was done also at Margaret's memorial service.

There is a second letter supplementing the first. This one specifies the biblical texts he wanted us to include. Again, his choices are revealing. The first is the Good Samaritan, perhaps the key parable for teachers of ethics with an ecumenical bent of mind. As everyone knows, its focus is on the compassion of a stranger for the victim; but not everyone knows, as Adams did, that the stranger belonged to a reviled people who were not only viewed as ritually impure, but as a sect who, like the early church, refused to follow the established religious authorities. Both his early Baptist roots and his later Liberal instincts warmed to that. In contrast to self-important but morally blind leaders of sacramentally-preoccupied religion, here is a hero who got the ethical point of the common tradition—and knew that justice and care for the neighbor cost, effort, personal engagement and financial support for healing institutions.

Second, Adams wanted selections from the story of Hosea the prophet and his wife, Gomer. Here we see the betrayal of relationships as the expression of the perpetual crisis between God and the People of God. Gomer, image of the chosen people of all generations, races, sexes and life-styles, always wants to return to the wanton life, and Hosea represents both the legalistic impulse that wants to hedge her in with thorny laws and the wrath of God that judges her waywardness. But God calls Hosea to remember the power of forgiveness that can overcome faithlessness and restore righteousness. Many of us here have felt a forgiving spirit in Adams; some, mostly people not here, only his judgmental side. Whether he selected this passage as his own final statement of contrition and request for forgiveness, or as a statement about the kind of divinity he affirms, is between him and God.

Interestingly, Adams also wanted some readings from Proverbs—passages, he said, which reflect hellenistic thought. Now, how much hellenism is in Proverbs is a matter of scholarly dispute, but the dispute is revealing. Throughout his life in the Unitarian Universalist movement, he pressed the members of his denomination to remember their rootage in the biblical and classical theological traditions. We can see this in his involvement in the Unitarian Universalist Christian Fellowship, and in the wonderful new collection of *James Luther Adams Papers* they published.

But in the face of hyper-revelationists of all stripes, he was also a natural law theorist. He felt deep affinities to those classical and Enlightenment philosophers who believed that all humans could know something of true wisdom and of the principles of justice without biblical revelation. Indeed, this motif of his thought caused him to prefer the philosophical approaches of Tillich and Whitehead to the proclamatory styles of Barth and Bultmann. And it both connected him to Roman Catholic natural law teachings and drove him into conversation with secular theories of sociology and jurisprudence.

Even more, in a century divided by nationalistic, ideological, cultural and racial hostilities, he emphasized the universality of humanity. Many know of his encouragement of opponents of the Nazis. Fewer know that he and Lewis Mumford were the first Americans to join the Societe Europenne de Culture, an organization that called intellectuals and artists to the tasks of reconstruction after the war. He was invited to join the very year that Albert Schweitzer also joined. In a recent tribute to Adams, Madam Michelle Campagnolo Bouvier, the International General Secretary of the Societé, said that he was a "living example of an *homme de culture engage*, who for forty years shaped the society, "conveying (his) precious judgment on many important issues of our day to colleagues all over Europe East and West and the Americas."

How did all these themes fit into a life that extended from the meager beginnings of a country preacher's kid at the beginning of this century through an energetic life as student, preacher, scholar, teacher, and activist to the cosmopolitan brink of the next century? We have heard the stories of his life, and we suspect that most of them are true. We know that he was elected president of some of the most distinguished academic societies of the land, editor of many more than a dozen books, journals and collected papers, co-founder of even more than a score of advocacy organizations, author of enough essays to fill, so far, seven volumes of essays edited by others, and the inveterate correspondent with hundreds of acquaintances. We know that he and Margaret fought racism and sexism in pioneering ways, and he struggled personally and politically to find how intimacy and ultimacy could be embodied in affectional bonds and social institutions. It remains a mystery how all this fit together with such integrity and charm.

We have tried to capture some of the rich texture of JLA's contributions by asking representative friends, disciples, editors and colleagues to select favorite readings: from his early student, George Huntston Williams, now Hollis Professor of Divinity, *Emeritus*, at Harvard University, to Professor Stephen Mott, who just these last weeks has helped Louise Des Marais do the final editing of the forthcoming volume of JLA memoirs entitled, *Not Without Dust and Heat*. We invited non-clergy and non-academics to join in this memorial service to indicate the range of his influence. In all, we see a complexity of soul that only "chaos theory" could begin to chart.

Clearly, he early chose not to follow Aristotle's advice that virtue is the gentleman's sober, cool habituation into a middle path that avoids extremes and controls the passions. Instead, here is a life full of dust and heat that knows reason, yet agrees with Pascal that the heart has reasons that the mind knows not of; who loves virtue, yet believes that true morality involves identifying opposite virtues and occupying all the space in between; who joined warm humor and disciplined living to passionate commitment.

Perhaps when all is said and done, it is better to remember Adams as a "charismatic sage," one sent to us in the midst of a century desperately seeking for ways to love and live justly and walk humbly and confidently with God, even when much signaled the resurgent worship of Mars, Baal, Mammon, Pan and Whirl, not to mention the twin idols of Fundamentalism and Secularism. Not all of his message got through; not all of us were prepared to receive it; not everything in it was completely valid. But we have been touched, deeply, personally, and repeatedly by what he brought to us. The world is better for it.

We should not be surprised that the term "charismatic" is applied to a Liberal. It is a term already in use before the rise of the pentecostal movement and before journalists began applying it equally to any rock star who draws crowds or to any religious fanatic who draws federal agents. In re-reading files of his class notes from 1960-1965, I found that the term "charisma" appears prominently in every class, along with "vocation," "covenant," "association," and "responsibility." Adams introduced the term to his students by pointing to the rise of the prophetic tradition and the formation of the early church. He frequently referred also to the Radical Reformation's pluriform understanding of the gifts of the Spirit, to Rudolph Sohm's theory of the Holy Spirit developed in the late nineteenth century, and to Max Weber's understanding of a "called" individual who, as Weber writes, "is set apart from ordinary men and endowed with exceptional powers not accessible to the ordinary person, but is regarded as exemplary, and... is treated as a leader."

Specially gifted people sometimes exhaust their friends and try their loved ones, but it can surely be said that he labored well; he used his gifts for others; he often, more than most of us, transcended his limitations; he illumined a stormy century; and he was a blessing to our minds and souls. And so, with deep gratitude for his charismatic wisdom, we commend its gifts not only to the future, but also to God from whence comes every good and perfect, even every imperfect, gift.

We pray that you, James Luther Adams, beloved husband, father, friend, teacher, and presence, may rest in peace. We will remember you.

II.
James Luther Adams at 75

Introduction by the Editor

In the lead article on "James Luther Adams and the Unitarian Denomination" in the January, 1977, issue of the *Andover Newton Quarterly,* George H. Williams, Hollis Professor of Divinity at Harvard University, concludes his historical portrait with this sentence:

> JLA will in due course be fully recognized as one of the great triumvirate with Channing, the minister, Bellows, the continental denominational promoter, and with Adams as professor of professors and minister to ministers: one dominating personage for each of the three half centuries of the denomination, 1825 -1975.

Professor Williams's article was originally an address delivered in celebration of the publication of JLA's new book *On Being Human Religiously: Selected Essays on Religion and Society*, edited by Max L. Stackhouse (Boston, Beacon Press, 1976). In his introduction to the volume, Professor Stackhouse locates Adams's social ethics in comparative relation to America's late prophetic theologian, Reinhold Niebuhr, and to the Harvard social philosopher of justice, John Rawls.

The final section of the JLA book contains essays on five great figures. Together these five may partly symbolize JLA's unique role—extending over six decades—of fostering religious and secular dialogue between European thinkers and American thinkers. In addition to essays on Karl Marx and Rudolf Sohm, there is another on Max Weber, whose *Sociology of Religion* is one of a host of works now in print in this land due to the editing (and often also the translating) of JLA. A fourth essay may well stand as a sign of the Ernst Troeltsch revival in American social and religious thought which he pre-eminently fanned. The essay on the now world-renowned theologian and philosopher, Paul Tillich, may symbolize the fact that this thinker's entry into the mainstream of American culture was directly due to JLA's superb translating, editing and interpreting of Tillich essays in *The Protestant Era* (1948). Equally noteworthy is the classic study of Tillich's early thought, *Paul Tillich's Philosophy of Culture, Science, and Religion*. This book was Adams's doctoral dissertation at the University of Chicago, the community where he taught for 20 years before going to Harvard in 1957.

Although there is no space here for me to speak of other writings by JLA, it must be noted that John Wilcox, a Roman Catholic teacher of religious studies, developed a bibliography of more than 400 articles, reviews, papers, and books by Adams. This was part of the work he did for his doctoral dissertation at Union Theological Seminary, "James Luther Adams: His Contribution to Christian Ethics." Wilcox's dissertation was the second doctoral thesis on JLA, the first being, "James Luther Adams and His Demand for an Effective Religious Liberalism," by James D. Hunt, Syracuse University, 1965. The Wilcox bibliography was an extension of a labor of love begun when friends and former students of Professor Adams issued a 1966 *Festschrift* in his honor, *Voluntary Associations: A Study of Groups in Free Societies.*

The foreword to the JLA *Festschrift* was written by Paul Tillich and deserves to be known by those who will never meet the tome. Note these lines introducing "this book which is dedicated to the life and work of my dear friend, Jim Adams:

> Without him I would not be what I am, biographically as well as theologically. He... studied my thought so thoroughly that he knew more about my writings than I myself...
>
> Beyond this personal support, his thought and work have given me a deeper understanding of American Christianity. First and most important is the truth of which he is a living witness, that agape, Christian love, is not dependent on trinitarian or anti-trinitarian or other dogmatic traditions (he is a Unitarian), but on the divine Spirit...
>
> The second thing I have learned from him was the emphasis on the practical, social as well as political, application of the principle of agape to the situation of the society in which we live. In this respect he represents the prophetic element in Christianity which much teaching in the churches badly neglects...
>
> The third point in which he gave me an example is his extraordinary knowledge of facts and persons and the preciseness and conscientiousness with which he works in all his theological, sociological and psychological investigations. There is humility in this attitude which I deeply admire. It is ultimately an expression of agape, which cares for the smallest, without becoming small itself.
>
> But there is the other side of him which is equally astonishing: the largeness of interests and involvements in all sides of man's cultural creativity: in the arts as well as in the sciences...
>
> James Luther Adams is a living proof of the ultimate unity of eros and agape and for the possibility that this unity becomes manifest, however fragmentarily, in a human being.

With respect to the theme of this JLA *Festschrift,* his distinguished peer in the field of social ethics, Walter George Muelder, states in the second article in the same issue of the *Andover Newton Quarterly:*

> No contemporary theologian has contributed more or stimulated as much thinking and research about voluntary associations as Professor Adams has. Their origins, types, conflicts, pathologies, and promise have all engaged his attention.

JLA's thesis concerning the indispensable role of autonomous groups, standing midway between the individual and the state, is exemplified through all six decades of his professional life, as well as through his corresponding action as a world citizen in relation to both secular and religious societies, from the twenties through the seventies. A few examples must now suffice.

Dr. Adams, with Leo Szilard and sixty other professors, released the first public protest against the atomic bombing of Hiroshima and Nagasaki. This despite the fact that he was no pacifist but, rather, was part of the anti-Nazi underground. He was one of the founders and a president of the Society for the Scientific Study of Religion, as well as a president of the American Society of Christian Ethics. He lectured at the World Center for Buddhist Studies in Rangoon, as well as at the congress of the International Association of the History of Religion at Tokyo and at the universities of Oxford, Manchester, Liverpool, Marburg, Bern, Mainz, Berlin, and Padua. He was a Protestant Observer at the first session of the Roman Catholic Church's Vatican Council II, representing the International Association for Religious Freedom. He served as Chairman of the Board of FREE, the Fellowship for Racial and Economic Equality formed by some of his former Harvard Divinity School students to combat white racism by "uniting psychotherapy and social change." In addition to service as President of the American Theological Society, Chairman of the Committee on International Organizations, the American Academy of Arts and Sciences, he was Chairman of the committee on Church and State of the Civil Liberties Union of Massachusetts (ACLU). He and Lewis Mumford were the first Americans to be invited to become members of the International Council of La Société Européenne de Culture, and he was the first theologian to become a member of the Society for Political and Legal Philosophy.

For us to sound merely this associational theme, however, is an act of injustice to JLA. His scope is much broader. For example, in 1940 the American Unitarian Association published a classic pamphlet by Adams, "On Being Human—the Liberal Way." My first acquaintance with him came through this pamphlet, as well as through hearing him speak concerning "A Faith for Free Men" at a gathering of the Channing Club of the First Unitarian Church of Chicago when I was a student in the College of the University of Chicago at the end of World War II. For three decades I have been stirred and delighted by his invigorating, dramatic union of prophetic pronouncement and philosophical depth, provoking commitment to the liberal religious way of life. More specifically, the years of his life, from the mid-twenties to today, elicit a continuing imperative, which four words may suggest: *liberal Christian humanists, unite!*

JLA is a liberal who for half a century has identified the crisis of our culture and actively helped to develop and to evaluate relevant strategies of reconstruction. In the pages which follow, you will first find his call to unite in action, embedded throughout his autobiographical address, "The Evolution of My Social Concern." This self-portrait was drawn, by request, for the January, 1962, Louisville, Kentucky, meeting of the American Society of Christian Social Ethics. The transcript—which is here published for the first time—identifies JLA's early prophetic labors to unite liberals in the fight against Nazi rule. It also discloses his early awareness of the poverty of liberalism, the contradictory readiness of German liberal Christians to join not the resistance but the National Socialist Party of masses shouting, *"Heil Hitler!"*

The first of the six hitherto unpublished JLA papers—each representing one of the six decades of his professional life—is entitled "Pessimism and Optimism in Religion." Not to go unnoticed in liberal circles is the fact that even before the rise of fascism in Europe, even before the Wall Street crash of 1929, Adams was publicly declaring the necessity for, and the positive value of, liberal religious pessimism. Delivered as a sermon to the congregation of the Second Church in Salem, Massachusetts on January 17, 1926, the manuscript was then submitted to the student preacher's homiletics teacher, Willard L. Sperry, the beloved dean of the Harvard Divinity School, who was also both the Plummer Professor of Christian Morals at Harvard and the Preacher to the University. Dean Sperry's critique of this effort is included with the text since it has documentary worth with respect to persons of the period and holds sheer human interest. In the address itself, you will meet the remarkable mind of JLA in the middle of the 1920s. It is well to recall that the message came from one whose fundamentalist-millenarian ("Christ is about to come from the clouds") preacher-father exclaimed when he heard that his son was going to become a Unitarian minister, "I shall pray that you will be a *failure.*"

An imperative which I suggest is implicit in these JLA papers of six decades "*liberal Christian humanists, unite!*" most fully discloses its humanist dimension in the essay, "Christianity and Humanism." Delivered at the University of Iowa in 1937 to a group of Irving Babbitt admirers, it not only intimates Adams's participation in the Harvard cultus of literary humanism associated especially with Babbit and Paul Elmer More, it also explicates JLA's own dialectical, critical affirmation of Western and Eastern, classical and Chinese quests for mature humaneness. Through diverse forms of culture, "humanism aims to achieve the development of the self toward human maturity and proportionateness." Babbitt and More inducted Adams and hundreds of others into "the religious ideas of Plato, the Buddha, Jesus and Christian theology," making the ancients come alive.

This humanist motif in JLA's thought is complemented by his paper on "The Stabilizer and Shatterer." An oracle of professional experience, this address was delivered as the Charge to the Minister at the service of ordination of a prized student, George H. Williams, the Church of the Christian Union, Unitarian, Rockford, Illinois in 1940. Listen to the warning: "It is doubtful if any profession occupies a more ambiguous position in the esteem of men than does ministry." The reason given is that the liberal minister represents both the stabilizing and the disturbing forces of history. Here is a new enunciation of Adams's unifying principle of liberal religious living: "Realism is as blessed a word as idealism."

For the decade of the fifties, the paper selected is "The Liberal Christian Looks at Himself." Delivered in 1955 at All Souls Church, Unitarian, in Washington, D. C., it was part of a series known as the Foundations of Liberal Christianity Lectures. Appropriately enough, JLA uncovers the vibrant roots of Liberal Christianity and its ally, secular democracy, in the Radical Reformation—the precise area of concentrated research chosen by the Reverend George H. Williams when he became

Professor of Church History at Harvard. In this JLA paper, we face the fact that Adams is by no means merely a modern theologian; truly—though some religious liberals find it incomprehensible—James Luther Adams, Unitarian Universalist, is quite unambiguously a *Biblical* theologian. Here the sometimes hidden center of Adams's mind is revealed:

> [Liberal Christianity is] a faith that finds its classic expression in the Old Testament prophets and in the being, the character, and the mission of Jesus. In that faith we find the generating spirit and the norm of norms for Liberal Christianity.

"Festschrift: Presentation to Paul Tillich," the paper chosen to represent the 1960s, was delivered in the Braun Room of the Harvard Divinity School in 1960, but it also speaks for a much vaster span of Adam's attention. The reader is hereby warned, however, that this distinctly special occasional piece stands apart from the other JLA papers published here. Despite its almost private character, it is included because it classically conveys the master-disciple relation.

When Adams first went to Germany in 1927, he became acquainted with Tillich's thought. Before a decade had passed, such formative Tillichian concepts as "theonomy" were operative elemental categories of interpretation in Professor Adams's teaching and writing. By the end of the second decade of deep knowledge by acquaintance with the architectonic mind of the German intellectual who was part of a great migration to America, Adams was recognized as the foremost interpreter not only of "Tillich's Concept of the Protestant Era," but also of Tillich's philosophy and theology. Now, after a half-century—when not a few have put their hands to the task of interpreting Tillich—JLA still stands as the unweary interpreter, but by no means uncritical champion, of Paulus Johannes Tillich.

Our concluding paper, "The Body and Soul of Learning," was Professor Adams's commencement address at the Meadville/Lombard Theological School on June 13, 1976. It is designed for celebration of the golden anniversary of the affiliation between the school and the University of Chicago, initiated fifty years ago. It should come as no surprise to find here once again his insistence on a union of opposites: body and soul. The institutional pole of realistic religion is emphatically affirmed. Without the body, there is no soul, no reality, no religion. Without the social disciplines of freedom, there is no learning, no possible passion for excellence; indeed, there is no self.

The heretofore unpublished papers of James Luther Adams presented in this issue of *The Unitarian Universalist Christian* not only represent six decades of his life, they remind us of a multitude of JLA manuscripts awaiting the permanence of print. Even as we honor JLA at 75 for the fullness of the years of his life and thought as a liberal Christian humanist, we acknowledge that he is still much too much the unknown theologian in our midst. When, we must ask, will the corpus of his own thought be readily accessible to the next generation? When will the varied JLA papers, including the many which were published in fugitive journals, be gathered in such a way that we may see the development of his distinctive mind?

In 1939, after *The Christian Century* published a series of weekly articles on "How My Mind Has Changed in the Past Decade," written by eminent churchmen and theologians, editor Charles Clayton Morrison concluded with an overall analysis and summary. Reflecting on the piece by the 37-year-old Adams, Morrison confessed: "I am bound to say, at the risk of losing my position as impartial umpire, that few if any testimonies in this series have so fascinated me as has the testimony of Mr. Adams."

JLA at 75 retains his fascinating hold on our minds through his own dramatic exemplification of the union of opposites, a union experienced in the daily battle of faiths both within us and without us in history. Through these papers representing six decades of his ministry, we are mindful of continuing imperatives:

Unite pessimism and optimism in religion.

Unite Christianity and humanism.

Unite your social roles as stabilizer and shatterer.

Unite the Liberal Christian movement for peace with justice and freedom.

Unite the mystery which is *theos* and the understanding which *is logos*.

Unite the body and soul of learning.

Unite—or perish!

The Evolution of My Social Concern

By James Luther Adams

I was reared in a Plymouth Brethren home where the name of Darby was a household word and where the Scofield Reference Bible, with its *heilsgeschichtliche* footnotes on the dispensations was the daily food. Indeed, the food at table always followed the spiritual repast of the Bible-reading. In accord with Scofield's footnotes, my father's constant attention was devoted to interpreting apocalyptically the signs of the times. This whole apparatus, and even the interest in the Bible, disappeared from my consciousness for a time when evolutionary humanism and then classical humanism (under Irving Babbitt) took their place.

Considering the early training, I find it no accident that following upon my student years at Harvard in theology my experiences in the face of Naziism assumed crucial significance. I would like to ask your indulgence here as I relate an incident of some importance for me. In the summer of 1927, six years after Hitler became head of the movement and six years before the Party came into power, I visited Nuremberg just at the time when thousands of people, young and old, were in the city for the annual Nazi festival. On the day of the great parade in the streets of Nuremberg, history as it was being made at that juncture gave me personally a traumatic jolt. Standing in the jostling crowd and watching the thousands of singing Nazis with their innumerable brass bands as they passed along the street, I inadvertently got into a conversation with some people who turned out to be Nazi sympathizers. Out of curiosity as to what they would say, I asked a bystander the meaning of the swastika that was everywhere evident. Within a few minutes I found myself in a heated conversation with more and more people joining in, particularly when the discussion turned to the Jewish question. As I bore down in the argument against these defenders of Nazism, asking more and more insistent questions, I was suddenly seized by the elbows from behind, and pulled vehemently out of the crowd. No one made an effort to help me. I immediately thought I was being taken into custody. I could not see who it was—who, after extricating me from crowd, marched me vigorously down a side street and then turned up into an alley. On reaching the dead end of the alley, my host, a young German workingman in his thirties, wheeled me und and shouted at me, "Don't you know that when you watch a parade in Germany today you either keep your mouth shut or get your head bashed in?"

My palpitation mounted even higher at this moment, and I was all the more puzzled when my captor smiled and said, "Don't be frightened. I have saved you."

"Saved me from what?"

"From being sandbagged. In about five minutes more of that argument on the curb, they would have knocked you out, flat on the pavement."

This man was an unemployed worker and an anti-Nazi. He immediately invited me to take dinner with him at his home. I accepted gladly. Then came the second shock: the walk into the slums, the trudge up four flights of a rundown tenement house, where some of the stairs were missing, and even some of the bannisters. The dinner was just as far from normal. In the few hours I spent with this man and his family I learned at first hand about the *Sitz im Leben* of the rising Nazism.

The experiences in Germany during that summer became crucial for me, but they did not assume full significance in my consciousness until in the middle Thirties I spent some months in the so-called "underground" movement of the Confessing Church in Germany. Meanwhile, I had resumed graduate studies at Harvard. These were years in which my acquired religious liberalism came under the scrutiny that we associate with that period in American Protestantism. The awareness of the thinness of its theology was in part stimulated by the Whiteheadean concern for metaphysics, by Irving Babbitt's vigorous attack upon Romantic conceptions of human nature, and by von Huegel's emphasis upon the theological, the historical, the institutional, and the devotional elements in Christianity. The depression and the early Roosevelt years, along with a markedly unideological interest in the writings of Marx, an increasing interest in the problems of unemployment and of the labor movement, participation as a minister in the activities incident to the great textile strike in Salem, Massachusetts—all these things conspired to develop a social concern, both theoretical and practical, which had previously been relatively peripheral. At the same time, the awareness of the fissiparous individualism and the unprophetic character of conventional middle-class, humanitarian religious liberalism served to increase my concern for the nature and mission of the church and especially for the *ecclesiola in ecclesia* as indispensable for the achievement of significant and costing consensus relevant to the historical situation.

Some of us Unitarian ministers initiated a study group just before I went to Germany in 1927. The group undertook a vigorous year-round discipline of reading, discussion, and the writing of papers. We collectively studied major literature of the time in the fields of theology, Bible, historical theology, social philosophy, art, liturgy, prayer, ever seeking consensus and seeking common disciplines whereby we could implement consensus in the church and the community. During one entire summer, for example, we read thoroughly and discussed at length Troeltsch's *Social Teaching of the Christian Churches*. Reinhold Niebuhr and Karl Mannheim, of course, figured largely in our study. Such groups have increased through the years, they continue in several parts of the country. I speak of this group discipline here, because in my conviction the concern for group participation and group responsibility became increasingly crucial in the quest for identity.

These multiple concerns were brought to a convergence by my second, more prolonged visit to Europe, a year of study of theology, of prayer and liturgy, of fascism and its persecution of the churches. During a period of several months at the Sorbonne, also at the Protestant theological faculty, and at the Catholic Institute, I lived in the home of a retired professor of the Sorbonne. Another paying guest in this home was a right-wing nationalist student. Many an hour we spent arguing the issues between democracy and fascism. I soon became aware of the fact that he would hesitate not a moment to shoot me down in cold blood if his wave of the future came to flood tide. I cannot enter here into detail about the experiences of those days. Listening to lectures daily at the hands of a liberal theologian, of an orthodox Calvinist, and of the principal Parisian Barthian—none of them making any analytic effort to interpret the signs of the times, signs that were the chief interest of the secularists—the Fascists and the Marxists. Meanwhile, I was also under the tutelage of an eminent Jesuit spiritual director at the Roman Catholic Seminary of Saint-Sulpice. Each week I posed my questions on prayer, and the following week he answered them. But always I felt the gap between the cultivation of mental prayer and the bludgeonings of a period of history that was swiftly moving into the storms of our time.

I recall an experience not dissimilar to the one of 1927 in Nuremberg. Early one morning I went to the Pantheon to watch the formation of a United Front parade. When it began to move, I could not get out of the jam. Willy nilly I marched; no escape was possible. Every cross street was filled with crowds of people, obstructed also by a police cordon. For two hours I marched, pushed along as if I had been seized by the elbows and at every moment seeing people giving the Communist salute from the lows of the buildings. On the day when Hitler marched into the Rhineland, I was in the home of Edgar Ansel Mowrer. We stayed up all night.

It is perhaps not surprising that soon after this in Geneva I adopted the counsel of the young Visser ët Hooft. "You are to study in the German universities? I hope that is not all! I am going to give you the advice that I constantly give to churchmen going to Germany. But none of them takes my advice. I say you should get into the underground of the Confessing churches and learn the meaning of the Synod of Barmen."

I took his advice, though I also attended the lectures of Bultmann and Heiler, of Jaspers and Barth and Brunner, of Heim and even of Wilhelm Hauer, the founder of the German Faith Movement. I cannot here narrate the melodramatic experiences of the underground, largely in company with or under the auspices of a former Harvard friend, Peter Brunner, who had served time in the Dachau Concentration Camp and who is now Professor of Theology at Heidelberg. For several months, during an interim, I spent two or more hours a day with the retired Rudolf Otto at Marburg, at the same time taking the lectures of Bultmann and others in the University. In view of my connections with leaders in the Confessing Church, Rudolf Otto saw to it that I should get acquainted with German Christians, Nazis among the clergy whom he deemed to be insane.

It is extremely difficult to pass over a description of the maelstrom of this whole experience in Germany, an experience that brought fearful encounter with the police and even a frightening encounter two years later with the Gestapo. The ostensible charge made by the Gestapo was that I was violating the law by walking on the street with a deposed Jewish teacher and by visiting a synagogue. The word existential came alive in those hours of bludgeoned questioning and of high palpitation. It is difficult, I say, to suppress giving an account of incidents in connection with the Nazis, the anti-Nazis, and the hidden underlings. It is even more difficult to determine how to compress into brief statement what all this did for the evolution of my "social concern."

One way to do this is in terms of the ideological battles, specifically in terms of symbols. The ideological battle, as Schelling would say, was a war of the gods, a war between myths. Here I express indebtedness to Paul Tillich, whose reputation and writing I began to encounter at this time, seeing in him a German counterpart to Reinhold Niebuhr. I wish I could pause here to speak of the lectures of Jaspers and Heidegger and Bultmann. But let me hasten on. As between Bultmann and Otto, I was the more greatly attracted to Otto. The gnostic existentialism of Bultmann, despite his heroic stand against Hitler, did not speak directly to my condition. Like others in the Confessing church, he possessed only an abstract conception of concreteness and decision with respect to *positive* action in history. Indeed, his aversion to concern for the historical Jesus and his preference for *kerygma* alone seemed to me to be part and parcel of a really inchoate non-historical outlook, despite the frequent admonition of openness to the future. His concern for anthropology to the exclusion of ontology seemed to me to urge the cart without the horse. The increasing criticism of Bultmann today, even among his quondam disciples, insists on a more historical understanding of history, on the resumption of the quest for the historical Jesus, and the centrality of ontology.

What gave focus to the whole experience in Germany was Rudolf Otto's *The Kingdom of God and the Son of Man.* The conception of kingdom as more than judgment, as redemptive dynamics, as seed that grows of itself in struggle against the demonic powers, Son of Man as suffering servant, the kingdom as both present and future—all of this represented a turning point away from the eschatology of Schweitzer. In the course of studying simultaneously the anti-prophetic organic symbolism of the Nazi myth, I like everyone else, became more vividly aware than hitherto of the role of myth in religion and culture, but more specifically I became aware of the *types* of symbolism. Later on I was to recognize the ontological significance of myth, particularly at the hands of Schelling, Tillich, and Heidegger. Later on, too, I was to see the anthropological significance of symbolism—the view that language was a decisive medium for the expression of the freedom of man. But at the time I was particularly frustrated by the pietistic, individualistic symbolism of Kierkegaard and of American individualism. Heinrich Frick of Marburg (whom I saw a great deal) suggested in his *Vergleichende Religionswissenschaft* a distinction between symbols drawn from history—dynamic symbols oriented to time—and symbols drawn from nature—static symbols oriented to space. The pertinence of dynamic symbolism had earlier been impressed upon me by the study of Whitehead.

But more significant than this sort of typology was the distinction between symbols that relate the concept of the kingdom of God to the inner life or the life of the individual and that relate the concept of the Kingdom of God to institutions, that is, to the church and to other institutions. Quite decisive for me was the recognition of the *political* character of Biblical symbolism. As political, this symbolism, particularly in the Old Testament, expressed the sovereignty of God over all of life, including the institutional structures. From this time on I saw, with the aid of Troeltsch, the narrowing of Christian obligation which in Lutheranism resulted from the two-kingdom theory—a bifurcation of political symbolism which makes a dichotomy between the church and culture and thus reduces tension between them.

In conjunction with a doctrine of vocation oriented only to daily work, the two-kingdom theory released the eschatological tension and also prevented the doctrine of vocation from including dynamic political obligation. Likewise, the merely interpersonal emphasis on the priesthood of all believers crowded out dynamic functioning of a doctrine of the prophethood of all believers in the face of institutions. In contrast to this institutional orientation of political symbolism, one can readily observe the merely interpersonal orientation of the doctrine of justification by faith or the doctrine of forgiveness. I still offer a prize to students in my classes if they can bring in a report that the Sunday morning Lutheran Hour on TV finds any symbol of the power or the demand of God other than the power and the demand of God to forgive. It is difficult to work out a social ethics on the basis of a doctrine of forgiveness. Toward this end, the doctrine must be related to political symbolism. One must emphasize, of course, that both the personal and the institutional belong together in soteriology and in a theological anthropology. To separate them is to violate the sovereignty of God. One sees these two corresponding forms of distortion in Kierkegaard and Marx. Both of these thinkers are unthinkable without the Bible, but in their reduction of ethics exclusively to the personal or to the institutional they are both of them unbiblical. Looking at them, one must say there is nothing so much like a swelling as a hole. Kierkegaard, despite his astute attack upon so-called Christendom, is in Christian circles a form of infidelity to the sovereignty of God over institutions, a sophisticated form of pietism, that is, a form of political and ecclesiastical irresponsibility. In industrial society, pietism tends to support by default the primacy of the economic life over the political.

These considerations underscore the fact that Christians possess almost infinite capacities of dissolving the political symbolism of covenant and kingdom. These forms of dissolution include the reduction of Christian ethics to personalism, systematic theology that has no reference to institutions, psychotherapy that possesses no sociological framework, abstract existentialism that talks about concreteness and decision but does not drive towards actualizing concreteness and decision in the social-historical situation.

Why is it so extremely easy for Christians to become pietistic, in the sense that they see little connection between Christian ethics and structural institutional analysis or between Christian ethics and responsibility for the character and influence of economic and political institutions? One reason for this is the ease with which pietism can appeal for sanction to the Gospels. The first sentence of Troeltsch's *Social Teaching of the Christian Churches* asserts that primitive Christianity was not a social movement. In one of his long essays, *The Social Philosophy of Christianity,* he argues that primitive Christianity had no social philosophy, no articulated theology of social institutions which could provide a critical and positive interpretation of ongoing economic and political institutions. Accordingly, he asserts that early Christianity turned to pagan natural-law doctrine in search of a basis for a social philosophy. I do not need to examine this issue here. I would like to say only that the angelology and the doctrine of Christ the King recently under debate among New Testament scholars offers some challenge to Troeltsch's view. A masterly essay by G. Dehn on the doctrine of the Kingship of Christ appeared in the Barth *Festschrift* of 1936; through the years I have asked my students to familiarize themselves with my translation of this essay. According to this view, the state, for example, is seen to be in a fallen condition and under the aegis of fallen angels; under Christ the King, it and other social forces are the end to be restored to their essential nature. Thus salvation is for society as well as for the individual. In a recent essay, Amos Wilder has suggested that the doctrine of the Kingship of Christ could serve as a new Christian theological basis for Rauschenbusch's Social Gospel. I mention this here only in order to suggest that a continuing problem for Christian ethics is the place of political symbolism. The Nazi movement and the Communist movement have given new urgency to the explication of the political symbolism of the Bible and of later articulations of Christian ethics. It is striking to observe how little the Bultmann School has contributed to contemporary understanding of the political symbolism of the Bible. One must question the adequacy of the Heideggerian anthropology as a framework for demythologizing the Gospel.

I must now return to consider another aspect of the impact of Nazism upon my social concern. This consideration, if fully set forth, would entail the discussion of the sociology of religion, the philosophy of history, the relations between Christianity and democracy, as well between Christianity and capitalism and religious socialism. But I must spare you the full rehearsal of those themes. I must be highly selective.

Let me repeal reticence so far as to say that the experience of Nazism induced a kind of conversion. I recall a conversation with Karl Jaspers at his home one day in Heidelberg in 1936. I asked him what he deemed to be the contemporary significance of liberal Christianity. He replied with unwonted vehemence, "Religious liberalism has *no* significance. It has *Zwang*—no costing commitment."

He was thinking of the liberals who had become German Christians (Nazis), the while overlooking the impotence and silence of orthodoxy and neo-orthodoxy in the burgeoning period of Nazism, overlooking also the collaboration of the Catholic Center Party and the Vatican with Fascism and Nazism—a collaboration that is now at last receiving candid discussion precisely in Catholic circles in Germany. So Jaspers now offered me some advice. "If I were a young man of liberal preferences today, I would return to the most orthodox branch of my heritage."

Immediately I asked him if he planned to do this himself. He flushed, he blushed, and replied, "I am not making a personal confession. I am giving you a sociological judgment." So spoke the pupil of Max Weber!

I did in those days recover a sense of the centrality of the Bible and of the decisive role in history of both the sacramental and the prophetic elements. I mention only in passing here the influence of Christian art, and especially of Bach, upon me. In addition, I pressed upon myself the question, "If Fascism should arise in the States, what in your past performance would constitute a pattern or framework of resistance?" I could give only a feeble answer to the question. My principal political activities had been the reading of the newspaper and voting. I had preached sermons on the depression or in defense of strikers. Occasionally, I uttered protests against censorship in Boston, but I had no adequate conception of citizen participation.

I must now turn to this theme. The German universities, supposedly independent entities, had been fairly easily Nazified. My American acquaintance, Edward Yarnall Hartshorne, later killed in Marburg when serving as American Military Government director of the universities at Hesse-Nassau, wrote a well documented account of the Nazification of the universities: *The German Universities and National Socialism* (Harvard University Press, 1937). Hitler also liquidated the trade unions. The persecuted Confessional Seminary I attended in Elberfeld occupied an abandoned Masonic building. The order was forbidden to hold meetings. Repeatedly I heard anti-Nazis say, If only 1,000 of us in the late twenties had combined in heroic resistance, we could have stopped Hitler. I noticed the stubborn resistance of the Jehovah's Witnesses. I observed also the lack of religious pluralism in a country that had no significant Nonconformist movement in the churches. Gradually I came to the conviction that a decisive institution of the viable democratic society is the voluntary association as a medium for the assumption of civic responsibility. Ernst Troeltsch's treatment of voluntarism of associations, his account of the free-church movement and of the associational creativity of the Calvinists began to flood back into memory. I read Max Weber's *Proposal for the Study of Voluntary Associations* and his typology of Associations. In his "Proposal" Weber said it had been the genius of the Prussian government to drain off the national energies into Singing Academies, thus diverting attention away from public policy and from civic responsibility. More than Troeltsch, I, the former sectarian (Plymouth Brethren), began to appreciate the role of the aggressive sect in Western history and of its grandchild, the secular voluntary association concerned with public policy.

You will forgive me if I mention here quickly the important ingredients of this development of social concern. I plunged into voluntary associational activity, concerning myself with race relations, civil liberties, housing problems. I joined with newly formed acquaintances in the founding of the Independent Voters of Illinois, I began to learn at first hand about *Moral Man and Immoral Society*. I traveled to Washington fairly often to consult with men like Adlai Stevenson, Jonathan Daniels, and Harold Ickes regarding Chicago politics. At the same time I participated in precinct organization, becoming a doorbell ringer and also consulting with party leaders in the back rooms. There is nothing intrinsically unusual about all this. It was only unusual for the Protestant churchman or clergyman. Equally significant for me was the new motivation for sociological understanding. The social sciences acquired an existential quality; and increasingly they figured in my thinking, in my associations, and in my courses.

Moreover, this combination of impulses conditioned my historical studies. I turned to the history of the Radical Reformation, to the influence of English Independency and Quakerism on the rise of democracy. From Bourgeaud I first learned to appreciate the epic sweep of what Whitehead had called the diffusion of opportunity and what I called the dispersion of power, the capacity to participate in social decision. Here with considerable excitement I pursued the theme through modern history— the transfer of radical concern from the Independents and the Levellers to the initiation of rationally devised public agitation and to the initiation of political parties, the spread of this voluntarism into education, and under Methodist leadership the rise of the British labor movement, and so on. In a memorable address by Whitehead before the American Academy of Sciences in 1941, he spoke of the *gap* between Statesmanship and Learning, between the processes of social coordination and the activities of the vocations and professions. The voluntary association in manifold ways fills in these gaps. Indeed, voluntary association stands between the individual and the state, providing the *opportunity* for achievement and implementation of consensus. It provides, alas, other opportunities, depending on the goals, the constituency, the internal organization of the association. I can mention here the American Medical Association, the name of James Hoffa, or the Board of Trustees of a suburban church in captivity.

Max Weber adumbrated a philosophy of history in terms of his typology of authority—traditionalist, rational legal, and charismatic (relying here in part upon Sohm's *Kirchenrecht).* Troeltsch offered a typology of religious associations—church, sect, and mystical type— which became the basis of a philosophy of church history. He has also offered a typology of Christian political theory, arranged according to the degree of reliance upon individual spontaneity or upon the external shaping disciplines. In a general way, all of these philosophies of history may be traced back to Joachim of Flora's theory of the three ages of the church, but more immediately the father of this associational theory of history and its periods is Otto von Gierke. In his magnum opus *Genossenschaftsrecht,* we may recognize a special kind of anthropology. Men are associating beings. Their differences may be determined by observing the associations they form, and by observing the relations between their voluntary and their involuntary associations, the types of participation they give to these associations. Accordingly, Gierke offers a theory of the periodization of Western history from the time of Charlemagne to the eighteenth century, a theory that characterizes the periods in terms of the dominant types of association.

Now the ramifications of associational theory are of course manifold. Maitland and Jenks have traced the history of England in terms of associational theory and practice. Gierke and Fred Carney have shown the great significance of the Calvinist Althusius for Protestant theory. Troeltsch and Weber really presuppose Gierke in their works. H. Richard Niebuhr in his neo-Troeltschean work on the *Social Sources of Denominationalism* traces the development of Protestantism in terms of the structure and dynamics of associations.

I would like now at the end to list some theses and some problems. First, some theses very briefly put.

Considering the associational character of human existence, we may say that the social meaning of a theological idea is to be determined in a crucial way by the type of association it calls for in the minds of the believers. Here we have a special application of the pragmatic theory of meaning. By their groups, their associational fruits, shall ye know them. If the theological or the theological ethical commitment does not issue in associational preference or transformation, it is to this extent not yet clear or meaningful.

Let me give two illustrations. R. B. Braithwaite, the British linguistic philosopher, in his book *An Empiricist Approach to Religion* argues that we can determine the meaning of Christianity by observing its consequence for behavior. To be a Christian, he says, means that one is committed to an agapeistic way of life. This view, like Bultmann's openness to the future, is extremely abstract. A Roman Catholic, a Presbyterian, and a Quaker might provisionally agree with Braithwaite. But consider the wide breach of differences they exhibit in their doctrines of the church. We can most quickly determine the meaning of a theological outlook by examining its doctrine of the church.

A second illustration. H. Richard Niebuhr has offered a typology of the relations between Christ and Culture. Here he gives the now familiar rubrics Christ Against Culture, Christ Over Culture, Christ Transforming Culture. The rubrics are scarcely sufficient. Within each of these classifications one can find a considerable variety of associational theories, and in several of the classifications one can find thinkers who would hold very similar associational theories. This fact shows us, on the one hand, that no timeless associational theory may be taken as definitively normative for the Christian. On the other hand, one does not know enough about a particular type of Christian ethos at a given time if one does not know the type of associational arrangements that are preferred. From this perspective man from Mars could be misled if he accepted William Adams Brown's claim that the Protestant and the Catholic worship the same God. The man from Mars would do well to look into Sohm's *Kirchenrecht* or into K. Barth's *Christengemeinde und Buergergemeinde.* At the same time we must say that the Christian ethos can appear in a considerable variety of types of association. To this extent and by this means the Christian ethos is differentiated. It is also differentiated by the types of non-ecclesiastical associations in which the Christian participates. Associational theory contributes to the analysis of meaning by reminding us, "By their groups shall ye know them." Here the social sciences have their contribution to make by assisting in the study of the types, the structure and dynamics, and the pathology of associations. So much for the pragmatic theory of meaning when applied to associations.

A second thesis I do not need to spell out. Christian vocation extends beyond the job to the church and the community. The means by which the church goes into the world is through the voluntary associations. That is, the responsibility of the Christian is to participate in the associations that define and re-define the actual situation, in the associations that give utterance and body to prophetic protest, and to social change or to social stability in associations that provide the occasion for the Christian and the non-Christian to enter into dialogue and even to achieve a working consensus—in short, in the associations that contribute to the shaping of history. Indeed, it is from these associations that the Christian can carry back to the church experiences, significant facts, informed concerns, insights demanding interpretation at the hands of the *koinonia*.

Now for some problems.

We do not have, and we probably shall not be able to get, an adequate study of the history of voluntary associational activity in the various countries, including our own. Arthur Schlesinger, Sr., following the lead of de Tocqueville, has outlined the history of American associations under the title of A *Nation of Joiners*. Great changes with respect to associations have come about in the twentieth century. Many of the changes that were implemented during the nineteenth century within the context of voluntary philanthropic activity have been taken over by the welfare state. There yet remain thousands of associations in the United States. Some of them, like labor unions and the American Medical Association, are scarcely voluntary, and their internal structures exhibit Michel's iron law of oligarchy—the tendency of political organizations to come under the control of a small group of "eager beavers." Doctors who deplore the tight bureaucratization despairingly say that in order to break the hierarchy, they would have to expend more energy than they can afford—they trained to be doctors and they want to be doctors. Some of the associations provide the opportunity to cross racial and class lines, in order to work for the general welfare. The NAACP, which has lost some of its dynamic, has done much to elevate the status of the Negro and to extend democracy. Many civic associations function to bring about minor reforms or to serve as watchdogs. On the other hand, many associations serve only special and narrow interests. Pressure groups with enormous budgets enter into collusion in state legislatures and in the national legislature, to promote or obstruct legislation. On the whole, participation in associations concerned with public policy is a middle class phenomenon, and even then in special interest groups. Philanthropic associations in large degree have this middle class constituency. Rev. Robert Cowell of Denver, in his study published in the *Harvard Business School Bulletin* shows that business and professional people, so far from breaking through class and race barriers, more deeply entrench themselves in their own perspectives by participation in philanthropic and service organizations. Like the churches, voluntary associations of this sort shape the society into isolated grooves or channels. Mirra Komarovsky, in her studies of associations in New York City, shows that the average membership in associations apart from the church is less than one per person. Some indication of the trend in the USA is revealed by the fact that from 1892 to 1948 the percentage of eligible voters who participated in national elections declined from 87 per cent to 57 per cent—hardly credible. This fact alone reveals the character and extent of the opportunity for the operation of the political machine. Komarovsky has suggested that nonmembership and nonparticipation in associations concerned with public policy is the criterion for the appearance of the mass man. Add to these facts the structure and power of the American business corporation community, and the largely centralized control of the mass media of communications, and we see the dimensions of domination in American society; we see the measure of the impotence of the churches in face of the principalities and powers.

I share the conviction that Christian ethics must be promoted in direct confrontation with these principalities and powers. These principalities and powers have to be analyzed with the assistance of the behavioral sciences, which in turn are promoted by persons who, like us, are under the grip, even under the spell of the principalities and powers. From certain quarters we hear the term "the end of the ideologies." This term itself bespeaks an ideology. If we observe the confusion brought to a focus by the indictment of General Electric, Westinghouse and other corporation executives; if we observe the extreme difficulty one encounters in the attempt to secure basic information regarding poverty in the United States; if we ask the question as to the contribution of the United Fruit Company to the rise of Castro; if we ask the question how the mass media are to be freed from their bondage to the processes of marketing, we should be brought to an awareness of the epochal structural dimensions of our economy, and thus to an awareness of demands that the Lord of history places upon us at this time and in this place.

III.
James Luther Adams Papers:
Six Decades

1. Pessimism And optimism In Religion

Delivered at The Second Church in Salem, Massachusetts,
on January 17, 1926.

The story is told of an old minister in a mill city in New England who used to preach annually a long sermon on the year's discoveries in astronomy. His people—cotton brokers, bankers and weavers—bore this ordeal with patient resignation. Someone asked him, "What the is the use of this sermon on the stars and astonomical space?"

He replied, "My dear boy, it isn't any use, but it greatly enlarges my idea of God."

It is just such a motive that prompts me to talk to you today upon the subject of pessimism in religion. The cry is often rightly made that religion is not a sad affair, that it is something to be enjoyed, but it is very doubtful if the person who makes such a contention has a religion worth enjoying if it has not had another side—a pessimistic side.

In Ecclesiasticus, we have a happy and optimistic view of life:

> All the works of the Lord are good, and he will supply every need in its season. And none can say, This is worse than that: for they shall all be well approved in their season. And now with all your heart and mouth sing ye praises, and bless the name of the Lord. (Ecclesiasticus 39:33-35.)

Then, in the very next verse, comes a correspondingly gloomy outlook upon life:

> Great travail is created for every man, and a heavy yoke is upon the sons of Adam, from the day of their coming forth from their mother's womb until the day of their burial in the mother of all things. The expectation of things to come and the day of death trouble their thoughts and cause fear of heart; from him that sitteth upon a throne of glory even unto him that is humbled in earth and ashes; from him that weareth purple and a crown even unto him that is clothed with a hempen frock. (Ecclesiasticus 40:1-4.)

In that great storehouse of human experience, the Psalms, there can be seen throughout these two distinct outlooks on life. One is represented by the song of the joy of living: "Sing aloud unto God our strength; make a joyful noise unto the God of Jacob. Take a psalm and bring hither the timbre!, the pleasant harp with the psaltery."

Then, but turn the page and find: "Save me, O God, for the waters are come in unto my soul. I sink in deep mire, where there is no standing; I am come into deep waters where the floods overflow me."

This alternation of attitudes towards life is found in every great religion. One can hardly imagine happier poetry than that of the old blind Homer; indeed, he is called the poet of the rosy-fingered dawn.

Nevertheless, we occasionally see indications that even in the golden age, all was not well. Listen to this from the Iliad, "For there is nothing more wretched than man of all things, as many as breathe and move o'er the earth."

Now, unless we deny the name of religious experience to these gloomy attitudes, we cannot call religion wholly optimistic. This does not mean that the religious person cannot believe in optimism; in fact, he must believe in it, but "no optimism is worth its salt that does not go all the way with pessimism —and arrive at a point beyond it."

There are several effects which pessimism has upon the religious and moral experience of the individual, good effects which cannot be otherwise secured, and therefore strong arguments for the encouragement of a certain kind of pessimism.

The first of these effects is a searching out of *all* the facts of experience—I say "all the facts," because a hasty optimism is usually based upon a *part* of experience. The important facts which this healthy pessimism searches out are those facts dealing with our own inner or our own outer life. We call the poet who can do this a realist. Indeed, the great spiritual message of poetry (and this is especially true of modern poetry) is in its discovery of the conveniently forgotten facts—unpleasant facts. The poet sees more clearly and feels more profoundly. His mind is a sensitized plate on which the world of nature and the spirit records its faintest impress. He is the true psychologist—not by analysis and experiment but by imagination and feeling, by putting himself in the place of another, feeling with another, thus interpreting life hidden from the common eye. Thus he gives us revelations of life that are sometimes disagreeable, but that are convincing and cleansing. As an example of this realism which reminds us of the conveniently forgotten facts, listen to this stanza from one of our own Western poets, Carl Sandburg:

A bar of steel—it is only
Smoke at the heart of it, smoke and the blood of a man.
A runner of fire ran in it, ran out, ran somewhere else,
And left—smoke and the blood of a man
And the finished steel, chilled and blue.
So fire runs in, runs out, runs somewhere else again,
And the bar of steel is a gun, a wheel, a nail, a shovel,
A rudder under the sea, a steering-gear in the sky;
And always dark in the heart and through it,
    Smoke and the blood of a man.
Pittsburgh, Youngstown, Gary—they make their steel with men.

We have here an insight that gives us a vivid picture of the whole industrial process, both material and human; this is what pessimism can reveal in its fearless realism.

But the pessimism that comes much closer to each one of us is that which gives us a true view of what we really are. George Frederick Watts, the eminent English artist, painted a portrait of a well-known Englishwoman of society, and she was startled in seeing revelations of the inner life in the eyes, which she thought well hidden in her own heart. One of the things which impressed one most in the recent exhibition of John Singer Sargent pictures at the Museum of Fine Arts in Boston was the poverty of soul in some of the portraits. The drawing of Eleanore Duse was one of the few faces in the group which showed that the artist had something besides externals to portray. One felt in looking at this picture that here Sargent had a reason for making a portrait other than the fact that the subject could afford to pay for it. The great artist searches the Real, revealing the deeper and unknown self, the very secret of the life. Such must be the aim of religious vision—it must include *all* in its horizon. This requires insight and unflinching honesty with one's self.

This insight into human nature was probably never revealed so fully as in the teaching of Jesus. Like all of the prophets of Israel, he fought the optimistic complacency of his people. He showed them that it was not only mistaken, but sinful; that true virtue is found in the righteousness

---

From *Smoke and Steel* by Carl Sandburg. Copyright 1920 by Harcourt, Brace & World; copyright 1948 by Carl Sandburg. Reprinted from *Carl Sandburg Complete Poems* (New York: Harcourt Brace Jovanovich), copyright 1950 by Carl Sandburg. Used by permission.

which exceeds the righteousness of the scribes and Pharisees. H. G. Wells has given us a virile figure in his picture of Jesus of Nazareth in *The Outline of History:*

> He was too great for his disciples. And in view of what he plainly said, is it any wonder that all who were rich and prosperous felt a horror of strange things, a swimming of their world at his teaching? Perhaps the priests and the rulers and the rich men understood him better than his followers. He was dragging out all the little private reservations they had made from social service into the light of a universal religious life. He was like some terrible moral huntsman digging mankind out of the snug burrows in which they had lived hitherto. In the white blaze of this kingdom of his there was to be no property, no privilege, no pride and precedence; no motive, indeed, and no reward but love. Is it any wonder that men were dazzled and blinded and cried out against him? Even his disciples cried out when he would not spare them the light. Is it any wonder that the Roman soldiers, confronted and amazed by something soaring over their comprehension and threatening all their disciplines, should take refuge in wild laughter, and crown him with thorns and robe him in purple and make a mock Caesar of him? For to take him seriously was to enter upon a strange and alarming life, to abandon habits, to control instincts and impulses, to essay an incredible happiness... Is it any wonder that to this day this Galilean is too much for our small hearts?

The value of pessimism, then, is that it makes us see ourselves as we really are, and, conversely, wherever one finds a religion that is wholly optimistic one may be certain that it is blind to some of the facts of life. The optimism that does not face evil has brought the criticism in recent years that religion is an escape from life—an opiate for the people, as Karl Marx would say. Sigmund Freud has suggested this interpretation of religion. He says that when the child gets into trouble he runs to his mother, in an attempt to escape the evil. During the early years, the child thus acquires the habit of dealing with evil by evasion. When he grows older he can no longer run to his mother's arms, so he runs to God.

This is a fair criticism of the religion that is optimistic only, that will not face and fight the evil. The same indictment is often made in calling religion otherworldly, the kind of religion that says: "I am a stranger here, heaven is my home." The history of asceticism is largely a history of withdrawal from active life here, avowedly for the purpose of living closer to God. But experience has taught us that if there be literally no other interest in life than God, the outcome is an empty and barren worship as well as a weakening of normal life. Communion with a God who is wholly of another world cuts the nerve of life in this world.

"No, I thank you," said a recent writer, "religion is like a sleepwalker to whom actual things are blank." None of us can help feeling that this man is more religious for, after all, his is the mind whose demands are greatest, the mind whose criticisms and dissatisfactions are, in the long run, fatal to a shallow optimism. Indeed, how can a religion that is only optimistic be anything more than a means of escape from the crassness of reality? It was probably some such thought as this that caused William James to say that "since the evil facts are as genuine parts of nature as the good ones, the presumption should be that they have some rational significance, and that systematic healthy-mindedness [James's word for narrow optimism], failing as it does to accord to sorrow, pain and death any positive and active attention whatever, is formally less complete than systems that try at least to include these elements in their scope. The completest religions would therefore seem to be those in which the pessimistic elements are best developed."

This brings us to the second good effect of pessimism in religion, namely, that it causes one to see the real values of life. This thought was in the mind of an acquaintance of mine who said recently, in speaking of a certain statesman, "I can trust that man because he has suffered. Such a soul must have been purged of all that is petty." The very pessimist is himself a witness to man's higher destiny. He is afflicted with goading and repining. He is disgusted, because he sees the seamy side, or rather he sees beyond it, and therefore revolts. "Do you call this a perfect world?" he cries. That of itself is a kind of prophecy. He calls in question all our ideals. Religious pessimism need not be a doctrine of despair. Rather does it breed hope. And right there is the great contribution that Jesus made to true religion. Pessimism had caused the pagan poets to place the golden age in the far past, it made the Hebrew prophets refer it to the distant future, but Jesus dared to say it might be here and now—"the kingdom of God is within you." Pessimism thus makes one an interpreter not only of actual life, but also of possible life.

Here again we have a parallel between religion and poetry. The poet is not only the realist; he is also the idealist. He knows that realism must be crowned with idealism if he is to portray the whole truth. The poet

Presses on before the race,
And sings out of a silent place.
Like faint notes of a forest bird
On Heights afar that voice is heard;
And the dim path he breaks today
Will some time be a trodden way.

Jesus, the great realist and idealist, saw in the corrupt publican a poverty of spirit, but he also saw a hunger for a better life which was to make of him a great disciple. This was knowledge of the actual crowned by insight of the possible. This is truly the divine discontent. But such noble depression cannot be known to the religion that is only optimistic. It must first have gone all the way with pessimism. It must have experienced a painful realization of the actual. If we suppose the power of sight to be given for a week to a man born blind, and then suddenly taken away, can we say he is restored to his former condition? Yes, in one sense, for he is put back into precisely the same darkness as before. But there is this terrible difference. Now he knows what darkness is. He has tasted one of the fruits of the tree of knowledge and the result is sorrow. The vision of the better life refuses to leave him.

It must be admitted that although the force which raises life to a higher level is a form of pessimism, a religion with such a foundation is not, as a system, a consistent pessimism. If it were that, it would have to end in despair. Christianity is not a consistent pessimism. This is what gives it its claim to superiority among world religions. It has gone all the way with despair and ends in a point beyond it. In the bedrock of its gloom there are veins of the pure gold of optimism. Christianity has not only preached of the depravity of man but also of the kingdom of God. It wishes and hopes for a transformation of man and the world. Graeco-Oriental piety, Plato, the mystery religions and ascetic Christianity all alike have said to man, "Free thyself from the world by detachment." Jesus said, "Get free from the world by conquest, in order to work in this world in the spirit and in the love of God." This is a noble kind of otherworldliness. It is a warning against what Wordsworth called the world that is too much with us. The God of Jesus is an active God, who works in man, and the religion of Jesus is thus a mixture of pessimism and optimism. In this peculiar tension between these opposite poles lies its uniqueness. This constitutes its greatness, its truth, its depth, its strength. Jesus' significance for us is that he fights against the spirit of the world, forcing us to abandon the level on which we move, even in our best thoughts and inspiring us to rise to the height from which we may judge things according to something in us still higher. Jesus calls this the will of God active in us.

As a contemporary example of an optimism that has gone the whole way with pessimism let us notice for a moment the philosophy of life expressed by the English thinker, Bertrand Russell, in his essay called "The Free Man's Worship." "Only," he writes, "only on the firm foundation of unyielding despair can the soul's habitation henceforth be safely built. The life of man viewed outwardly is but a small thing in comparison with the forces of thoughtless Nature. But great as they are, to think of them greatly, to feel their passionless splendor, is greater still. And such thought makes us free men; we no longer bow before the inevitable in Oriental subjection, but we absorb it, and make it part of ourselves. To abandon the struggle for private happiness, to expel all eagerness of temporary desire, to burn with passion for eternal things—this is emancipation, and this is the free man's worship."

Mr. Russell sees no hope, no future for the race, as "slow doom falls pitiless and dark." Nevertheless in man there are ideals, noble thoughts, and it is man's business to cherish these. It is difficult to remember that we are supposed to be in the world of pessimism, but what do we actually find here? Out of the darkness visible flash the outlines bold and austere. The great features of man's inheritance stand out only the more distinctly. "Here," as one writer has said, "we have sympathy and self-sacrifice, love and duty, beauty and eternal truth. Assuredly we would leap to the side of such a pessimism in contrast with an over-hasty optimism."

By examining the pessimistic side of the shield, the optimistic side has become more intelligible. We must not let ourselves be pushed to the point of choosing the one or the other. If we want our religion to apply to all of life, we must tenaciously cling to what one writer has called the "both and" attitude. Religion must have contrasts if it is to have depth. If our optimism is given a true schooling in pessimism, it will shine through us and illuminate all we touch. But if we have either one alone we will, like a rower with only one oar, be unable to progress.

There is no need of apology for pessimism in religion. It helps us see life as it really is, and thence it leads us onward until we receive the

Perfect, stretching on beyond the limits of sight, and fling us forward to possession....

CRITIQUE

Dear Adams,

I am glad that you are preaching in this general direction. In a set of essays which I happen to have, there is a terrible indictment of Chesterton under the caption, "The Blasphemy of Optimism."

The attack on Chesterton is a bit too severe. But the title is a good one and takes a fair shot at one of the weaknesses of liberalism. The older more melancholy theologies were nearer the facts than our Pollyanna-ism. I have never been quite sure whether it was cowardice or too much comfort—or what—in our general complacent Christianity that made us so superficial. I am inclined to conclude that it was the inevitable and natural reaction from the too gloomy Puritanism of the past. But I never get over a sense of something essentially dishonest in the "cheerio" mood of a great deal of our supposedly emancipated and scientific theology.

Hence my personal pleasure at finding your mind matching mine in the matter. Do you know George Tyrrell's definition of Christianity as "an ultimate optimism founded upon an immediate pessimism"? It is a fine ringing phrase. But you have the feel of that definition, if not its actual quoted form.

One could pile up suggestions as to more material by way of illustration. Look up some time in Huxley's *Life and Letters* what he says about his Romanes Lecture on "The Ethics of Evolution." There is a fine scientific apologia for an initial pessimism.

Then, didn't you yourself quote me those essays of Middleton Murray about the realism of Siegfried Sassoon and his kind, with reference to the Russian realists, who always set the grim fact in its whole milieu. If you don't know those essays perhaps I can get you the reference. But they did a good deal to help me clear up my mind as to why Sassoon as he stands isn't true, in the sense of being wholly true.

I think you are probably wise to rub in the pessimistic streak in thinking, over so long a period at the outset of your sermon. You have to disabuse the blasphemers in the name of a too cheap optimism.

But the fact remains, as is so often the case in a sermon of this sort, that you have left yourself rather scant time to stress the ultimate optimism. I think you could have picked up a few ringing examples of what Wordsworth calls our "great allies,—thy friends are exultations, agonies, and love, and man's unconquerable mind." The passage from Bertrand Russell seems to me to furnish the transition from one idea to the other, and would have been more effectively placed if you had used it just a page earlier. It gets you across, very admirably, from one consideration to the other. Where it stands it is a bit of an afterthought.

Would it be out of place to suggest that you keep your eyes open for great symbolic stories? Your mind is well stocked with poetry and with quotations from the books of the philosophers, psychologists, and the like. You use this material well and wisely. Like myself you will have to be perpetually conscious of the liability of scissors and paste—and I know how bad a seduction that may be. But, heaven knows, better a man whose mind buzzes with living and appropriate reference, than a man whose mind reminds you of a dried pod in autumn in which a couple of attenuated peas rattle about aimlessly. I agree to the peril of too much quotation, but I would rather be guilty of it than of the lean and hungry look of so many sermons.

To get back to the stories. If you will patch out your reading, as a preacher, with a third kind of book—perhaps novels, perhaps books of travel, adventure and the like—that will give you still a third source on which to draw.

Take the story of which I am so fond, that of the *Nan Shan* in the middle of the Typhoon—at the moment when the narrator fights his way to the bridge and bellows in the captain's ear that the boats have gone—and he hears from very far off the sound that will be heard when the heavens fall and the earth dissolves—a human voice saying, "All right, all right." A thing like that gets you by the throat and preaches itself. In your general reading have an eye and ear for such passages as that. They are often the very making of a sermon, and become its occasion, the preacher in his own mind, backing up and starting for them from the outset.

I find that it makes all the difference in the world if when you sit down to write you have a definite idea of the particular form of the conclusion at which you arrive.

Most sermons fade away or peter out because we do not see the end from the beginning. I am not in favor, personally, of making an indefinite skeleton outline and then patching on bits of flesh here and there. But

I am in favor of getting the objective clearly in mind, and then actually taking it as a man takes a high jump, measuring the steps and the take off all the way, with the eye, while the writing runs along, so that everything is paced and timed for the actual goal of the thought.

As ever,
WILLARD L. SPERRY

2. Christianity and Humanism

Delivered at The University of Iowa in 1937

The world of scientific thought and speculation presents today a remarkable spectacle. After four hundred years of vaunted promising to bring in the kingdom of man through the knowledge that is power, we now find that the sovereignty of man that lieth hid in knowledge, to use a phrase of Francis Bacon, is being threatened by the relentless and brutal application of sheer racial and national power. The blind Samson of power has stalked into the temple of man and is now recklessly tumbling it to the ground. In the face of impending disaster, heresy hunters are rising on all sides and attempting to identify the demon that is taking us down the Gadarene slope. Mr. Mortimer Adler says it is the professors who are to blame, and especially the scientists; Mr. Archibald MacLeish blames the irresponsibles among the novelists and poets; John Haynes Holmes blames governmental leaders who do not carry out the wishes of the populace; Mr. Earl Browder says it is the capitalists; M. Ortega y Gasset says it is the revolt of the masses; and the Pope says it is the refusal of modern man to accept the guidance of Rome.

Whatever the cause for the present debacle, we are all rapidly coming to fear that civilization today possesses more of memory than of promise. As we approach the abyss, the feared eclipse of all that is dear to civilized man, we echo the words of the prophet, "Watchman, tell us of the night." But whatever the outcome, we are all being forced to ask the question as to what it is that we would have. Like Macbeth we appreciate the dignity of man only when we have become aware that we are losing it, only when we realize that we are in the twilight that may precede death's dateless night.

In such a situation as this, a discussion of the subject "Christianity and Humanism" acquires a more than academic significance, for there are not a few people who, like Abraham pleading for Sodom, will say that if only two good things, Christianity and humanism, can be shown to be still alive among us, our modern Sodom is still worth saving. Even the news commentators of the radio, men who run as they read, are occasionally to be heard appealing to the enduring values of both

Christianity and humanism. And yet, it is doubtful if these two concepts represent anything very definite for a large proportion of those who appeal to them. They are merely blessed words for anyone who wants a prayer-wheel. What it is that would be saved if our civilization were, in the outcome, to be able to transmit Christianity or humanism to another generation is not very clear. Moreover, it is equally unclear what elements in Christianity or humanism would be able to help save civilization. There is something pathetic about the tardy discovery that Christianity is not something for the masses alone and that humanism is not merely an optional luxury for the cultivated few. Indeed, it is difficult to avoid also the impression that there is a note of condescension in the voices of those who in passing give lip service to either Christianity or humanism. We detect the unstated presupposition that if we can only get out of our present predicament with the aid of Christianity and humanism, we shall in good time be able to return to the condition in which we shall not have to be disturbed either by Christianity or by humanism.

The cause of the vagueness that attaches to the average educated man's references to Christianity and humanism is not mere indolence or the love of catchwords. Christianity and humanism are not easy to identify. Their supporters are themselves divided. Moreover, both movements have had a long history in which a great variety of ideas and activities have appeared. The result is that there are as many types of Christianity or of humanism as there are of anti-Christianity or of anti-humanism. Yet it is not necessary to delineate all of the types of Christianity or of humanism in order to arrive at a working definition of either Christianity or humanism. To delineate adequately all of the types of Christianity or of humanism would be tantamount to classifying most of the types of religion that have appeared in the West within the past thousand years, and to delineate the types of humanism would require that we take into our purview movements of thought that are entirely beyond the boundaries of Western civilization. At all events, we shall assume that neither of these tasks is necessary for our present purpose, and we shall instead attempt to bring into relief only the basic characteristics of these two movements.

First, let us attempt a general definition of Christianity. Christianity is a religion of salvation from sin and death, a salvation ultimately effected by a loving Creator-Redeemer God as the result of the response of man, the child of God, to divine historical revelation. This response takes the form of repentance and conversion, of faith and charity, all of which are signs of the breaking of the kingdom of God into history. Hence, it may be said that thinking in Christian terms means thinking in terms of creation, revelation, and redemption. In other words, all of the categories of Christian theology are theonomous: they point to an Other that is the Beginning and End of all being. Salvation is of the grace of God, not of man. Here, then, we find the leitmotifs of the Christian religion. This religion has come into contact with many other tendencies, religious and secular; it has adjusted itself to the supposed needs of different times and places. As a result, it has successively (and) even simultaneously manifested itself in a great variety of ways. But in spite of this variety it has always aimed to take the primitive Christian faith with its Jewish *praeparatio evangelica* as in some sense or other normative. It is, therefore, a religion oriented not only to the transcendent but also to events in history. Hence, its character cannot be properly dealt with without reference to a salvatory history.

Humanism is not a religion, nor is it, like Christianity, a unique historical movement with a historical figure at its center. Like generic religion it possesses certain general features, but it is always conditioned more by the environing culture than by any particular and decisive historical event. There is no such thing as humanism in general. There is the humanism of Confucius, conditioned by the special historical circumstances and world-views which surrounded it. There is the humanism of Greece and of Rome, colored by the general world-view and religious outlook of paganism. There is a Christian humanism that was not only conditioned by the fact that it developed on Christian soil but also by the fact that it has been openly allied with Christianity, both Protestant and Catholic. The Christian elements within the various types of humanism that are to be found in modern Western civilization are in some cases difficult to isolate, but all forms of modern humanism depend upon Christianity as well as upon Hellenism. This is equally true for Christian humanism, for the revolutionary humanism of the seventeenth century and of the late eighteenth century, for the romantic humanism of the twentieth century. Now, although there are Christian elements in all of these types of humanism, there is also in every humanism something that distinguishes it from Christianity. What are these distinguishing features of humanism? That is, what is the essence of humanism? It is the tendency to view human existence without reference to the religious transcendent, that is, as self-sufficient and self-enclosed. In place of salvation as a goal, humanism aims to achieve the development of the self toward human maturity and proportionateness. It seeks to achieve these qualities by means of methodical self-reflection, by taking direct cognizance of the self-enclosed human situation, by maintaining through pedagogy a creative, intuitive relation to the past. Whereas the distinguishing feature of the Christian ethos is humility or creatureliness, the distinguishing feature of the humanist ethos is the poise of mature humaneness. Hence, whereas Christianity aims through the power of God and through fellowship in the church of Christ to effect man's overcoming of his fallen condition of "living well." In both Christianity and humanism the necessity of pedagogy is, to be sure, recognized, but in Christianity this pedagogy is theonomous; that is, under the guidance of the Holy Spirit in and out of the church, whereas in humanism this pedagogy is from man to man under the guidance of intuition. Moreover, the pedagogy of Christianity has for its material content Christ's revelation of God's purpose for man, whereas the pedagogy of humanism gives instruction to man concerning himself, that is, concerning his essence and the perfecting of this essence.

Although modern humanism, as distinguished from ancient humanism, is largely dependent upon Christianity, we may identify certain elements as common to Christianity and ancient humanism. An example is belief in the dignity of man, though Christianity emphasizes the dignity of each individual, and ancient humanism emphasizes the dignity of the rational human essence in general. One may also recognize a certain similarity between Christianity and ancient humanism as, for example, in the Christian concept of conversion, the Platonic concept of becoming like God, and the Aristotelian concept of the divine life in man. But we cannot dwell on these similarities here. Indeed, to do so might give the erroneous impression that the ethos of Greek humanism and of Christianity are more nearly similar than they actually are. It must suffice here to say that there is a fundamental difference between the decisive concepts of the Greek ethos and of the Christian ethos, a difference that is usually symbolized by the terms Eros and Agape.

We must turn our attention to the similarities between the modern forms of humanism and Christianity. This procedure finds its justification in the fact that even when the modern humanist appeals to ancient humanism, he tends to select elements that are compatible with his own conscious or unconscious adherence to certain Christian presuppositions. Indeed, the similarities between modern humanism and Christianity are for the most part the consequence of the dependence of modern humanism upon Christianity, due to the fact that the humanists of the Middle Ages and of the modern era were nurtured on Christian soil.

SIMILARITIES BETWEEN CHRISTIANITY AND HUMANISM

Let us now turn to a consideration of those elements of the Christian world-view that are shared in varying ways by all major forms of modem humanism, but here confining our attention to the Christian humanism in the Renaissance and the type of modern humanism represented by Irving Babbitt. What are the principal similarities between Christianity and this tradition of modern humanism deriving primarily from the so-called Christian humanism of the Renaissance?

1. First, there is the similarity of attitude towards nature, an attitude that is either implicit or explicit in modern humanism. The Christian attitude towards nature may most succinctly be characterized by reference to the Christian doctrine of *creatio ex nihilo,* a doctrine that depends ultimately upon an attitude characteristic of the Old Testament. The Christian attitude towards nature grows out of the view that God is the Creator of nature, as well as of man, that the heavens and the hills declare the Glory of God. In substance this view implies a repudiation of the pagan view that the world of nature is demonically hostile to man or basically resistant to the power of God. Here we discover immediately a difference between modern humanism and pagan humanism. The latter, for example in the thought of Plato and Aristotle, views nature or matter as resistant. In their view God in nature has to deal with a recalcitrant material, a material that must be subjected to form. In the Christian view of *creatio ex nihilo,* on the other hand, matter is itself the result of God's creative act. Hence, it is asserted in the book of Genesis that God looked upon his creation and saw that it was good. This same view is, of course, to be found also in the New Testament. It is true that nature in the Jewish-Christian view is believed to exist now in a fallen state. Yet, matter is not in itself evil. For this reason the Christian contrast between flesh and spirit does not imply a derogatory judgment of flesh as such. As Augustine and Luther point out, flesh in the Christian view is a perversion of spirit due to man's corrupt will. Now, it is largely because modern humanism adopted this general attitude towards nature that it must be distinguished from paganism. And that is also the reason why it eschews asceticism. Modern humanism, no less than Christianity, is thus opposed to Manichaeanism and to any view that considers the body the prison of the soul. Hence, we may say that modern humanism accepts the this-worldly implications of the Christian view of the resurrection of the body. Indeed, it is likely that it was largely because of Christianity's positive estimate of nature that Christians, both Protestant and Catholic— aside from fundamentalists—have so readily adjusted themselves to the scientific method of the investigation of nature. For the Christian as well as the modern humanist, there is no fundamental taboo with regard to nature. Here we find, then, the basis for a certain optimism shared by Christianity and humanism in contrast to a pessimism and melancholy so common in pagan humanism. For in Christianity and humanism there is no fear of nature.

2. The second similarity between Christianity and humanism arises from the fact that modern humanism has taken over the Jewish-Christian idea of monotheism. The basic significance of this idea, a significance that is implicitly recognized today far beyond the confines of the Christian Church, is that it asserts the unity of meaning of all existing things. On this basis, and only on this basis, can the unity of the knowledge of the natural order and the unity of ethical activity directed towards changing the world be maintained. In Christianity and in Christian humanism, all attempts to divide the world up into various spheres that confront each other with absolute claims is rejected. Both the humanist and the Christian reject any interpretation of existence that involves a conflict or a dualism between divine powers. They deny that there is any ultimate demonic enemy. The demonic is subordinated to the ultimate unity of meaning. Hence, the spiritual and social idea of unity as held in the Occident derives from the Christian doctrine of the unity of God. Here, again, we find a motif in modern humanism that weights the balance on the side of optimism and that resists the pessimism and melancholy of pagan humanism.

3. And yet, though nature is not a demonic power for either Christianity or humanism, it is also not worthy of man's highest interest if he is to be saved or if he is to achieve his human maturity. This brings us to a third similarity between Christianity and humanism. We may characterize this similarity as a common acceptance of a sort of doctrine of incarnation. Whereas the Christian's salvation involves his becoming a member of the body of Christ and sharing in the new being that comes from living *en Christo,* humane maturity requires that man shall enter into his inheritance through considering mankind as the proper study of man, and through submitting himself to the general norm derived from this study. Through acquiring the habits that will turn him from triviality to seriousness, from the preponderance of single elements to proportionedness, from eccentricity to highly serious normality, he will ascend to meet his fellow men in the common sharing of the humanly significant. In opposition to Burckhardt's emphasis upon individualism as the central characteristic of Renaissance humanism, we must recognize that in the Christian humanism of the Renaissance, in the tradition of the courtier and the gentleman, and in the methods of literary and artistic production, a large place was given to the idea of imitation. Thus the Christian idea of the imitation of Christ finds a parallel in the humanist idea of imitation of models. Consequently both humanism and Christianity are opposed to naturism, and they are also opposed to ethical relativism. This means that human destiny is from the humanist and the Christian points of view not to be fulfilled through any immediate coming to terms with the environing reality, as is the case with scientism and naturism. Both views aim to transcend the present moment and to bring about an experience of "filled" or "enriched" or "interpenetrative" time. The past is consciously and selectively carried over from moment to moment in the collective consciousness of the church or of the humanist society. All of these ideas are implicit in varying ways in both the Christian doctrine of the incarnation and in the modern humanist doctrine of imitation.

4. The fourth similarity between Christianity and humanism is an aspect of the attitude toward history that they share. It is also an implication of their common antipathy for naturism. Ultimately the source of this attitude must be traced back to Hebrew prophetic and Persian eschatological thought. It constitutes one of the basic differences between Greek and Christian ways of thinking, as Augustine so clearly points out in the twelfth book of *The City of God.* In paganism, reality is viewed unhistorically. Its decisive concept is physics and not history. The conception of nature as eternally repeating itself in cycles is viewed by Augustine as characteristic of this pagan attitude towards the world. In contrast to this attitude, Christianity views the world as historical, as involved in a process of directed time rather than of cyclic time. Man is moving towards a goal. Thus the idea of fate in paganism is replaced by the ideas of the fall, of providence and of the Eschaton in Christianity. Howard R. Patch's study of the goddess Fortuna in medieval literature provides an instructive account of the gradual subordination of Fate to Providence. It must be conceded that the Christian idea of Providence and of directed time has been carried to an extreme in the pre-millenarian sects of evangelical Protestantism. And likewise we may concede that this sense of the significance of the directedness and meaningfulness of history has received naïve expression in the secular idea of progress. Yet in large measure the optimistic attitude towards human history found in modern humanism is an inheritance from the Christian view of history as the theater of salvation. This element in modern humanism and in Christianity along with the first idea mentioned—namely the idea that creation is fundamentally good rather than demonic or resistant—goes far to explain the world-affirming character of Western civilization, a feature that is a constant source of surprise to the Orient.

5. The fifth similarity between Christianity and humanism is in their estimate of human nature. On this point the various types of humanism differ. Revolutionary humanism possesses an undialectical concept of human nature which is bound up with the idea of human perfectibility. Romantic humanism, as represented by German idealism, overstresses the likeness between the structure of the human mind and that of the absolute mind. It tends thus to minimize the difference between man's essence and his existence. Christian and modern classical humanism, on the other hand, restates the Christian doctrine of the Fall by asserting and emphasizing a fundamental and enduring difference between man's essence and his existence. Man has two natures, a higher and a lower, and never the twain shall meet. Thus both classical and Christian humanism are on principle opposed to all forms of Utopianism. The vision of the greatness of man never blurs the vision of the littleness of man. As Professor Douglas Bush says, "It is that simultaneous double vision of man which gives the literature of the English Renaissance its ethical strength and centrality, its heights and its depths of tragic emotion. The Christian religion exalted man's sense of his divinity and deepened his sense of bestiality; the distance between the two extremes is greater than it is in the most religious and philosophic of the classical authors."

Consequently, Christianity and Christian humanism place great emphasis upon the need for discipline and upon the primacy of the will over the intellect. For the same reason, they both favor an aristocratic view of human nature. For the humanist, this natural aristocracy depends upon the ethically disciplined will. For the Christian, it depends upon the redemptive love of Christ. Hence, rank, class, vocation, inheritance, race are all deprived of decisive significance. The distinction between the Greek and the barbarian is transcended in this modern humanism as well as in Christianity. Even the formal equality of all men with regard to rationality, as asserted by Stoicism, is transcended. In their place we find in humanism the concept of humanity and in Christianity the distinction between the regenerate and the unregenerate. Here we have another implication of the idea of monotheism. The criterion of meaningfulness cuts across all artificial or natural boundaries that separate human beings. The basic frame of reference or definition of value is valid for all. And no man is justified except through the grace of God or through the exercise of will.

In this connection, we must mention one other aspect of the Christian-humanist conception of human nature, namely, the assertion of the infinite value of the individual personality. This attitude is expressed in the distinction between man's external possessions or situation and the quality of his inner life. Hellenism tended to neglect this opposition between inwardness and external situation. And even Roman Catholic Christianity has blunted this distinction by replacing the Jewish law with a church law and a demand for external works (in the sense of ritual). Radically Protestant Christianity and Christian humanism both aim to transcend legalism, the one by asserting the supremacy of the Gospel of love over law, the other by relying upon intuition rather than upon mere convention or external decorum. Something of this attitude is to be discerned in Confucian humanism, with its emphasis upon inner propriety. This general attitude involves the affirmation of the dignity of the individual soul. In radical Protestantism it takes the form of respect for individual conscience (in the fellowship of believers), of denial of the necessity for hierarchical intermediaries, and of the doctrine of the priesthood of all believers. This radical laicism passes over into modern classical humanism and assumes the form of an individualism, disciplined according to a universal norm. In the Christian scheme this individualism is subordinated to charity and in humanism it is checked by the ideal of proportionateness or of complete humanity.

It should be clear from this analysis that all forms of modern humanism share in varying degrees and ways in the Christian heritage. It is definitely inaccurate, therefore, to associate Christianity in a narrow way with Hebraism or to associate humanism exclusively with Hellenism. In Christian and in modern classical humanism the Hellenic elements are transformed into something non-pagan, and where there is no transformation there is at least subordination to a Christian ethos. It may be added in this connection that it is misleading to speak of the spirit of religion and the spirit of the gentleman as if they were entirely distinguishable. We see also that the familiar characterization of naturism, humanism, and religion as representing three different levels of experience may also conceal as much as it reveals. If not in accomplishment, at least in attitude, modern culture—and especially modern humanism—have absorbed certain important features of the Christian world-view and ethos. Indeed, so deeply have Christian ideas affected modern humanist society that it would require a miraculous self-conscious atavism for it to return to Hellenism. The Christian attitude toward nature, toward the unity of meaning, toward interpenetrative time and directed time, and toward personality, seem rather to be on the verge of destruction at the hands of a post-humanist and post-Christian barbarism of blood and class. Of this we shall speak in our conclusion.

DIFFERENCES BETWEEN CHRISTIANITY AND HUMANISM
Autonomy vs. Theonomy

Let us turn now to the differences between Christianity and modern classical humanism. The fundamental difference between Christianity and humanism is in their attitude toward the transcendent, toward what might be called the vertical dimension of existence. In the parlance of theology, Christianity is fundamentally theonomous, and humanism is autonomous. As we have already indicated, Christianity with its goal of the salvation of man, relies ultimately upon grace, whereas humanism with its goal of human maturity relies ultimately upon the intuition and ethical will of self-sufficient and independent human nature. It has often been asserted that Christianity is heteronomous and that the humanism that accepts Christianity must also become heteronomous by submitting to an authority "anterior, superior and exterior" to itself. In this connection, a very important distinction must be made, a distinction often overlooked by Roman Catholics and orthodox Protestants and also by many exponents of humanism. The Christian movement arose as a protest against heteronomy, i.e., as a protest against rabbinical legalism and the heteronomy of the Jewish law. It did not call men to the absolute obedience of any earthly authority, any institution, or any man. It confronted men with the necessity of recognizing the inbreaking kingdom of God through its herald, Jesus Christ, and also with the demand for a change of heart in order that this kingdom might be fulfilled. Both the heteronomy of Jewish legalism and the autonomy of the self-sufficient creature were replaced by a relation to the dynamic transcendent action of God in history through His herald, Jesus Christ. The history of Catholicism and of orthodox Protestantism represents a deflection from primitive Christianity through the revival of legalism and heteronomy, through the incursion of the heteronomy of the church in Catholicism and of the church and the Scriptures in orthodox Protestantism. Primitive Christianity with its orientation to the suprahistorical kingdom of God had again cast the light of the divine upon all things finite, breaking them in their self-enclosed power, and revealing their inevitable ambiguity in the existential order. The theonomous view of man and nature thus locates the absolute beyond time rather than in time, and consequently it denies all absolute claims that may be attached to nature, man, institutions, books, and even to events in history. Jesus himself asks a disciple to call no man good, not even Jesus himself.

In the light of these distinctions, we must say that both Christian theologians and humanists have erred in characterizing Christianity as essentially heteronomous. Heteronomous Christianity is a perverted Christianity. It is a form of idolatry in the sense that it presupposes that something finite can exhaust reality. It gives to a finite object the status that belongs only to the transcendent, to God. Hence, any humanist that says he cannot accept Christianity because he cannot surrender his autonomy needs to learn that the real battlefront between himself and Christianity is at another point. In refusing to accept heteronomy, he is actually refusing to accept a perversion of Christianity. The fundamental line of the cleavage between strict humanism and Christianity is thus the difference between autonomy and theonomy. This does not mean, however, that Christianity denies autonomy to man. Rather it only denies absolute autonomy to human nature. It asserts that whether he recognizes it or not, man's basic power to exist and to fulfill his essence is something given. And it asserts also that this power to exist and to fulfill the human essence is infected with a perversion, a contradiction, that permeates all existence and separates it from its essence. On the other hand, so long as man or anything exists, it manifests in some degree the divine power of being and of integration. If this divine power were not present, existence would itself come to an end. And, conversely, existence can be brought nearer to its essence only through the meaningful incursion of the creative and re-creative power of the transcendent.

Hence, the human essence is not the ultimate and creative ground of temporal existence. Man is a creature, and in all meaningful activity he manifests the divine tendency toward integration or re-integration. In other words, man is the *Schauplatz* of cosmic forces, and not a self-contained, self-sufficient essence. Hence, it would be erroneous to suppose that there obtains a simple opposition between theonomy and autonomy. It is true that formerly this concept of theonomy was used to express divine determination in contrast to self-determination, but this usage presupposes a radical dualism between the divine and the human. In contrast to this usage, we employ the term only to express a transcendent qualification of self-determination. Theonomy is, in opposition to heteronomy, the fulfillment of self-determined forms with transcendent import. Theonomy does not involve the renunciation of autonomy, as does heteronomy in the Catholic theory of authority; it involves, rather, the deepening of autonomy in itself to the point where it goes beyond itself. In other words, theonomy involves the transcending of the autonomous forms of culture and society. It reorientates these autonomous forms to a religious principle that both supports them with the power of being and breaks into them, opening them to transcendent judgment and fulfillment. It does not repudiate autonomy, but it does assert that human nature is not self-sufficient and independent of the creative powers of the cosmos and, also, that the independence or self-sufficiency of humanism eventually brings about the loss of its own creative power and suffers the nemesis of emptiness and blindness. In both of these aspects of theonomy, we find, then, a corrective for humanistic pride.

We must remember, of course, that if the besetting sin of humanism is a pride in humanistic possessions and a consequent tendency to be terribly at ease in Zion, the besetting sin of Christianity is a pride in divine possessions that leads either to fanaticism or to heteronomy. Therefore, the Christian, or at least the radical Protestant, would assert that the only cure for either of these besetting sins is the spirit of penitence which is elicited by a vital theonomous relationship. Although there is a similarity between the besetting sins of Christianity and humanism, the humanist tries to find the cure within himself, but the Christian finds salvation in the new being emanating by grace through Jesus Christ.

There is also another besetting sin of historical Christianity and of humanism which should be mentioned, for it will serve to bring into relief another aspect of the fundamental difference between Christianity and humanism. We have already spoken of the history of Catholicism and orthodox Protestantism as a history of heteronomy overcoming theonomy in religion. This same tendency is to be found in humanism. In its denial of the transcendent, our modern civilization has been largely influenced by secular humanism, but it must be noted that modern civilization, like modern humanism, has not been able to remain strictly secular. Many humanists, recognizing the need for a transcendent relationship, have, instead of accepting a theonomous view, surrendered to Roman Catholic heteronomy. But a still larger number of modern secularists and even of nominal Christians have surrendered autonomy through accepting still other heteronomous authorities. They have become idolators of imperialism, capitalism, Marxian socialism, racism, nationalism. The emptiness of a humanistic society has become intolerable, and as a compensation, there has emerged a frantic attack upon autonomy and an attempt at demonic fulfillment through heteronomy. These repudiations of a humanistic society, then, are to be explained at least in part as deriving from an inadequacy, a besetting sin, of humanism, namely, the tendency to develop first into a state of emptiness and then into a disguised religion of a heteronomous character. We are suggesting that the corrective for this tendency of both Christianity and humanism to become heteronomous is the conception of theonomy, a conception that transcends both heteronomy and autonomy.

Humanist and Christian Views of Institutions

We have characterized a fundamental difference between Christianity and humanism as a difference between theonomy and autonomy, yet, we must make reference to three other major differences between Christianity and humanism.

The second major difference is the difference between the Christian and the humanist attitudes toward the role of institutions in human life. In general, we may say that humanism, because of its academic character, tends either to interpret the institutional problem in a narrow way or to give it only slight emphasis. It interprets the role of institutions in a narrow way by confining its attention primarily to the school. This means that although humanism has emphasized the necessity of both doctrine and discipline, its disciplines are specific only for the youth who are in school and at best very vague and individualistic for the adult section of the community. Growth in grace for the Christian is not possible apart from the fellowship of believers, a fellowship that aims to establish standards and practices that will nourish the individual (and the group) from childhood to old age. These standards and disciplines touch the domestic vocational, political, and social life. The disciplines aim to educate and nourish all sorts and conditions of men, both youth and age, both educated and uneducated, both privileged and underprivileged. And they aim not only to affect the mind but also the ethical will. Not that humanistic education does not affect the will. The point is rather that Christian nurture provides a close-knit community in which ideals and conduct are regularly brought under scrutiny by the group, and in which the disciplines of prayer, worship, and social action offer channels for the exercise of the will. Since humanism, apart from the church, does not possess this close-knit community with its disciplines, its adherents have only a furtive relation to each other and are thus deprived of the constant mutual support that alone can make reason and the will of God prevail. In this respect, humanism possesses a tendency similar to that of pietism: it emphasizes the "tending" of the individual soul to the neglect of communally supported social interests. It would be a gross exaggeration to assert that Christianity has achieved an adequate equilibrium between doctrine and discipline, but we are justified in saying at least that organized Christianity has more fully recognized the problem and more adequately dealt with it than has secular humanism.

Attitudes Toward the Psyche

The third difference between Christianity and humanism is a difference of attitude concerning the nature of the human psyche. It is a difference that is closely related to the one that we have just been discussing. Humanism, and with it much of Liberal Protestantism, has tended to attach great significance to the conscious intellectual life. This is a consequence of the humanist and the liberal Christian concept of personality, a concept that neglects the large role of emotion, association, and imagination in individual and social life. Indeed, the phenomenal rise of the new heteronomies of communism and national socialism, not to speak of the power of nationalism ("man's other religion"), is partly due to the imaginative and symbolic power of these movements. So great has been this symbolic power that many people from both the humanist and the Christian traditions have been won over. One reason for this mass conversion is to be found in the appeal of these movements to deeper levels of the human psyche. There is a limit to the weight of the burden that can be placed on the human consciousness.

Christianity has not failed to recognize this fact, and it has from the beginning been rooted in something deeper than the human consciousness. Indeed, the doctrine of the Holy Spirit may be cited as an integral part of the significance of the forces beneath and beyond the human consciousness. This is only one example. Christianity in both doctrine and discipline has utilized the symbols and institutions—for example, the ideas of the kingdom of God, the doctrine of the body of Christ and the practice of the Lord's Supper, not to mention the power of song and the regular discipline of public worship, as well as the symbols and disciplines that enlist the whole man rather than only the mind. In this connection, Irving Babbitt emphasized the large role of the imagination in the human psyche, but it seems to me that the problem of the imagination was left by him to be solved by the individual. At all events, we may assert that secular humanism has not developed imaginative symbols that are generally recognized by humanists to be decisive or constitutive for the transmission or practice of humanism. It might be argued, of course, that the ideal of the gentleman, or of the *honnete homme,* represents an appeal to the imagination, but this is obviously the sort of symbol that is powerfully effective for only one group in society. Moreover, it has even among gentlemen lost its former spontaneous and decisive force.

Humanist and Christian Attitudes Toward Culture

This brings us to the final difference between Christianity and humanism to be given special mention, the difference between their attitudes toward culture. Here again the relationship is not a simple one. Just as theonomy does not represent an orientation which replaces or exists alongside that of autonomy but rather one which goes through and beyond it, so Christianity does not demand a repudiation of culture but rather a deepening and transcending of it. Christianity does not essentially oppose culture, it only radically disputes its self-sufficiency. Hence, there is no basic feud between Christian theology and culture as such. Christianity is not ascetic, and it does not despise the forms and meanings that are associated with culture. Its quarrel with culture is the same as its quarrel with autonomy: culture in a humanist society is viewed as self-contained, self-sufficient, and at best an expression of man's orientation toward particular, finite, meaningful objects. It fails to see the transcendent meaning of the finite and thus becomes unaware of the transcendent threat that confronts every self-enclosed entity, the threat to overweening security and self-assurance. It is because of this tendency in humanism that we may say that urbanity kills Christianity.

The disastrous consequence of humanist self-sufficiency may be better observed if we turn to the sociological area. The general effect of autonomous humanism in modern civilization has been to shunt religion into an area by itself. The religious group has become a separated sociological group in which something different is at stake than in the other sociological groups. Religion is associated with its socological bearers: the institution of the church, the priesthood, the officers and members of the church, the sacraments, and the special disciplines of the church. Then these sociological bearers of religion are repudiated and the humanists make the claim to offer a more palatable substitute. The heteronomous churches have only assisted in encouraging this attitude by claiming to have in their possession peculiar and exclusive media for the dispensing of grace or for approaching the transcendent.

The theonomous point of view that has been suggested in this paper represents a radical denial of both of these views. It denies that religion is one thing alongside others, that the transcendent is accessible only in certain areas of life and that the other areas of life may maintain independence. More than that, the theonomous point of view carries with it a denial that God himself is merely one Being alongside other entities; it is a qualification of the conditioned and finite objects of the world of nature and man. The world and all finite objects point beyond themselves to some unconditioned aspect of reality in which they participate and from which they are at the same time separated. The theonomous consciousness does not hold that there is a separate transcendent world, but rather that all finite objects possess a transcending character, and that when they have entirely lost this character they have also lost their power to exist or to fulfill their essence.

This loss of the sense of the transcending character of all things is the precise cause of the atomism of modern civilization and of the defeatism and emptiness that is in our day making a desperate attempt, through the surrender of autonomy to heteronomy, to regain a vivid and dynamic sense of meaningfulness.

Professor Douglas Bush, in his book on *The Renaissance and English Humanism,* indicates that he believes "it will be impossible for us to bring back a general belief in a supernatural world," but he does suggest that something like it will have to be appealed to if we are to avoid the loss of the values of Christianity and humanism incident to the rise of the new religions of nationalism, capitalism, communism, national socialism, and the vitalistic psychology of the unconscious. It would seem that man is incurably religious in a much more ominous fashion than M. Sabatier originally meant to suggest. The choice that lies before man is not Christianity or humanism, but rather Christianity or paganism. The power of humanism derives in the long run from the transcendent orientation of Christianity, and when this power is weakened, one form or other of idolatry will take its place, the idolatry of academic isolationism, or erotic or material possessions, of class, race, or nation.

I recall a conversation I had a few years ago with the famous German philosopher, Karl Jaspers in Heidelberg. I ventured to ask him his view concerning the significance today of humanism and liberalism. I asked the question partly because of the general assumption that he thinks of himself as a humanist and a liberal. His reply was shockingly emphatic for a man of poise and vision. He replied, "Humanism and liberalism have no longer any significance. The only group that in our world has the positive courage of its convictions is that of the orthodox Christians. My advice to any young man is that he return to orthodox Catholicism or Protestantism. Only in these groups is there to be found the *Zwang* that can resist the rising tide of barbarism in the world." But it is worthy of note that Dr. Jaspers has not himself returned to orthodox Christianity. I pointed this out to him, and he replied that he was speaking as a sociologist and not giving a confession of his personal faith.

There are many such men of good will around us today who see that the values cherished in common by humanism and Christianity are not eliciting the loyalty needed for their survival, and yet they cannot accept Christian supernaturalism. It is my conviction that they are justified in making this refusal, but they are themselves partially to blame for the stalemate. They have supinely accepted the statements of the supernaturalists and of the authoritarian churches as to the nature of religion and even of God. Having done this, they labor under the erroneous impression that the only alternative to a secular humanism is a heteronomous supernaturalism. What is actually needed is a group of Christians and of humanists who will humbly take up the task of working out a religious conception of life that will at the outset repudiate the projection of an objective divine world behind and alongside the objective natural-human order, who will together take up the hints in this direction that have been thrown out by Christian theologians from the early Middle Ages down through Nicholas of Cusa, Schelling, and Friedrich von Huegel and thus make possible the overcoming of those modern idolatries, political, ecclesiastical, and academic, that are attempting either to bring in the kingdom of heaven by violence or are pining away with anemia. The power of God is not to be despaired. Our sin is that old devil *Accidie*. Dark night and chaos are upon us only because we cannot hear the summons: Repent ye! The kingdom of heaven is at hand.

3. The Stabilizer and The Shatterer

The Charge to the Minister at the Ordination of George Huntston Williams at the Church of the Christian Union, Unitarian, Rockford, Illinois, on November 14, 1940.

We have often heard him spoken of with extravagant praise. We have heard him mentioned also with contempt. We have heard him castigated as an agent of anachronism, of sluggish cultural lag. From the lips of two of our university professors, I have heard him characterized as having practically no significance for good or for evil. Of course, I am referring to the minister.

It is doubtful if any profession occupies a more ambiguous position in the esteem of men than does the ministry. What with the writings of Chaucer and Isaak Walton, Emerson and Robert Ingersoll, such an anthology would not only include some of the greatest writers; it would also be as largely compounded of satire and criticism as of praise and adulation. But we do not need to go to literature and history for these paradoxes. Even ministers themselves are not always confident of the necessity or value of the profession. I have known young ministers who even consider it a compliment to be told that they do not look or talk or act like a minister.

Not so with the other professions, like the law, medicine, and science. Some men may doubt their own fitness for one or other of these professions, yet they seldom, if ever, question the significance of these professions themselves. In a mass culture like ours, the artist and the teacher may not be held in such high esteem as the lawyer, the doctor and the scientist, yet both are generally conceded to have some proper role in the scheme of things. The minister belongs in a class by himself. In many quarters, he is on the defensive precisely because he is a minister.

What is it about the ministry that makes it appear to some people as the highest calling and to others as the lowest, most contemptible? Various are the answers we might offer to this question. To be sure, some people would deny that the ministry does occupy this ambiguous position in the minds of "right-thinking people." Hence, they are prone to say that only sinful and irresponsible men, only men estranged from God and church, doubt the significance and value of the ministry. There are others who say that the minister may once have played a proper role

109

in society, but that religion must now yield to science (or something else) in order that it be no longer a drag upon human progress. Harold Laski, for example, insists that the ideal society to be worked for will be the completely secularized society.

I am not so much concerned now with what people of this sort say, but with what the minister himself feels. The average minister not only knows that he is both respected and despised in the world, but he even views himself in this ambiguous fashion. And we ask, why?

The answer is: because of the very nature of the profession. For the minister—or at least the liberal minister—plays a dual role in society. He is, or is supposed to be, both a priest and a prophet; he is the representative of both the stabilizing and the disturbing forces of history. He is devoted to the task of proclaiming the divine imperative that men should give the forms of love and justice to human life and encourage those who are engaged in this universal endeavor. But he is also committed to the divinely demanded task of criticizing and shattering certain of the forms of meaning and meaninglessness in society. He is the apostle of both divination and prophecy. He celebrates the joys and sacrifices of the common life, he is the professional guide for Christian nurture; but "under the great Taskmaster's eye," he is also bound by duty radically to criticize the frustrations and perversions of "Christian" nurture and even of the "Christian" ministry. He is called upon to produce the social cement of human association, and yet if he is true to his prophetic function, he is also bound to stand beyond merely human associations, to be a man of conscience—a dangerous creature—and thus to be a pulverizer of encrusted forms and barriers. He is called to follow the Master of those who love by being the friend to all, but he is called also to follow that same Master right into the Temple of respectability and become seemingly the very enemy of society and religion.

Because the liberal minister must in love and in good conscience play this dual role among us, his profession by its very nature inevitably makes him elicit the scorn of certain of his contemporaries, for the minister cannot by any means whatsoever avoid arousing the scorn of men. If he does not wish to be scorned among men, he should be warned not to enter the profession. Indeed, he will bring more scorn upon the profession if he possesses an undue love for appreciation. Like it or not, the profession of the ministry is made only for those who expect to be despised and rejected.

Let the minister be more of a priest than a prophet. Does he thereby make his path easier? Not one whit. He still has his conscience to deal with, he has to square himself with the traditions of prophecy; and if neither of these forces is active, then he will have to meet the scorn of sensitive and responsible people both inside and outside the church. This scorn from outside the church is not always the sign of a hostile secularism; it is often the expression of a prophetic spirit that the world may have caught from the prophets. No doubt Emerson reflected this spirit when he wrote his lines:

> I like a church; I like a cowl;
> I love a prophet of the soul;
> And on my heart monastic aisles
> Fall like sweet strains, or pensive smiles;
> Yet not for all his faith can see
> Would I that cowled churchman be.

Emerson did not shrink from wearing the cowl because he had a distaste for piety, but rather because he thought the besetting sin of the ministry is its artificial and hollow conformity. We learn from his essay on "The Preacher" that it was the scorn of ministerial cant and insincerity and pretense, the using of big words for trivial ends, that he feared. "What sort of respect," he asks, "can these preachers inspire by their weekly praises of texts and saints, when we know that they would say just the same things if Beelzebub had written the chapter, provided it stood where it does in the public opinion?"

✳✳✳

Let the minister be more of a prophet than a priest, even then he will not escape those who sit in the seat of the scornful. Far from it. Let him detach himself from the immediate demands of the age, let him substitute "Thus saith the Lord" for "Thus saith the age." Let him refuse to be the hireling priest for the age, let him inspire the church to fulfill what Dean Inge has called its major function—the refusal to cooperate with the spirit of the age—and he will only find himself again confronted with scorn, scorn of a different sort but of an equally bitter taste with the scorn of the hireling priest. Let him bring universal truths down to their application for the age, let him call by name those forces that make men terribly at ease in Zion, and (even if he is both justified and tactful and even if he speaks in love), he will find that he is not wanted, that he has stepped beyond the boundary of permitted detachment.

Even at his best and truest, then, the complete minister is a marked man, urging others also to be marked men, urging them to be wanderers as well as sojourners on the earth.

Why then is the minister in this precarious position, why always to be despised or rejected whatever he does? It is because he is called to be the proclaimer of the living Word of God, of the Word that is at the same time a consuming fire and an inflaming love, a shattering *and* a creative power. He is the proclaimer of a kingdom that is *in* this world but not *of* this world. Thus, if he fulfills his calling, he must expect derision from one group, and if he does not, he must expect it from another. The question is not whether the man of God will be despised and rejected. The question is, By whom?

In all this the minister is, of course, subject to no peculiar fate; he shares the fate of all, the fate and the privilege of living in a world in which the promise and the splendor of life find their ingression into history only through the cross. For the cross is not merely a beautiful ornament on a watch fob or merely an adornment for the altar. It is at the heart of all meaningful living. It is, in short, the one indispensable means of grace.

4. The Liberal Christian Looks At Himself

Delivered at All Souls Church, Unitarian,

Washington, D.C., in 1955

One of the recent developments of research in the area of biology has been the study of social organizations among the animals, and particularly among the fowls. Some of the social scientists have been studying, for example, how long it takes a group of fowl to form a social organization. As I recall the findings, only eighteen to twenty-four hours elapse before a group of chickens hitherto unacquainted with each other form a tightly structured social organization, a flock.

The social organization turns out to be a rigid hierarchy. At the top is one chief hen who by dint of pecking the other hens has established her prestige: she is able to peck any other hen and none other dares peck back. Immediately beneath her in pecking rank will be three or four hens who are second in command; they have established their power and "right" to peck all the other hens in the yard except Number One. And then gradually the hierarchy broadens out to *hoi polloi*, the common hens, who may be pecked by any of the hens in the higher echelons but may not peck back. Food and other privileges become accessible in accord with these rankings. This hierarchy is called a "pecking order."

A hierarchy of this sort is to be found also among other animals. Among horses, for example, there are "kicking orders." Squirrels, monkeys, and even cows establish comparable pyramids of authority. And we all know that something similar is to be found among human beings, a social organization in which authority is centralized at the top and in which some kind of patterned obedience is required of others.

Liberal Christianity, in its religious and social articulation, might be defined as a protest against pecking orders. It began in the modern world as a protest against ecclesiastical and political pecking orders. Protest in the economic sphere also soon appeared. One of the principal sources of Liberal Christianity is what is today called the Left Wing of the Reformation or, as Professor George Williams calls it, the Radical Reformation, a composite movement that in part originated as a protest against the authoritarian organization of the churches that were ruled from the top down. Another source is the Enlightenment with its demand

113

for individual, rational self-determination. (Subsequently, Romanticism emphasized individualism still more, and uncovered something deeper than reason—intuition and feeling.)

In interpreting the character and source of Liberal Christianity in this way, I presuppose that in order fully to understand any religious movement — and indeed, any secular ideological movement — one must include the answer to the question: What consequences do the ideas held by the group have in the sphere of action? A belief is effective when men are prepared to act in accordance with it. "By their fruits shall ye know them." We are accustomed to apply this pragmatic test to the behavior of *individuals*. The test may be applied also to group behavior, and specifically to religious movements. We can extend the test to religious groups by raising the question: What difference do the ideas of the religious movement make in social organization? What kind of social organization do the "believers" prefer? How do they want authority articulated? Do they favor a pecking order or some other kind of "association"?

Although there are other tests of meaning, this pragmatic test is revealing when applied to theological doctrines. We determine in part the meaning of belief in God or in Christ as held by any group, by answering the question: What does the believer in God want changed in the society around him? And what does he want retained? The questions raised by this pragmatic sociological method do not imply that a belief that claims to be an index to the way of salvation will provide important perspectives for all aspects of life and thus also for institutional structures. It is not appropriate to interpret religious ideas in terms of their effect upon the individual as an isolated entity. In fact, such an entity is a myth. Everything must be understood in terms of its relations, and so also the human individual. One determines the meaning of a religious idea, then, by examining its implications for individuals in their relatedness, that is, for their institutions, family, church, state, economy, and voluntary associations.

Let us take an example. Belief in God for a Roman Catholic involves belief in the church allegedly established by that God through Christ and Peter; it involves belief in the infallibility of the Pope, the "Vicar of Christ." One who denies the belief in papal infallibility also denies the true God (from the Roman point of view). Moreover, the word "God" here denotes a superhuman reality supporting the hierarchy of the cosmos; it carries with it belief in the church as a sacred hierarchy.

The same pragmatic method of interpreting the meaning of religious ideas can be applied to other branches of Christianity. It can be employed also in interpreting non-Christian religions. We do not understand what a Muslim believes if we have become familiar only with his conception of God as an isolated entity, for the God sanctions certain types of relatedness—between man and God, between man and man. We have to discover how the Muslim believes that in the name of God the Muslim society should be organized or should be changed. A doctrine of God that has no bearing upon social organization is to that degree irrelevant in face of man's search for meaning in his relations with others. Accordingly, the believer in a doctrine of God which has no institutional implications would have to say that whether the Nazis, the Communists, or the Vatican were in control of society is a matter of indifference in his religious belief. In any conflict between ideologies, this sort of believer would himself be a matter of indifference. He would belong to any master who could gain control.

In this connection we should observe an illusion that is entertained by some people who believe themselves to be favorable to piety. We sometimes hear it said that the problems of society would take care of themselves if people would only return to belief in God. People making statements such as this often overlook the fact that beliefs about God vary greatly and that the social-institutional implications vary accordingly. In the early centuries of the modern era, internecine wars were fought over religion. In these struggles, people on *all* sides believed in God. But the conceptions entertained of the character of God and of God's demands upon men in society were vastly different. The God of the Left Wing of the Reformation was different from the God of the Right Wing; moreover, conceptions varied widely in the Left Wing and the Right Wing. Likewise, the Left and the Right Wing of the Reformation were opposed to Roman Catholicism. Today we cannot in any strict sense assert that Protestants and Roman Catholics worship the same God. If they did, they would share the same or similar perspectives on the organization of church and society.

Liberal Christianity, as we have noted, has its roots partially in the Radical Reformation. The Radical Wing in England—the Independents, the Friends, and the shapers of congregational polity, for example—rejected the notion that the cosmos is a hierarchy and that society must be organized on the pattern of hierarchy controlled by priest and monarch. They insisted that the state should not use coercion in matters of religious belief and that the ecclesiastical authorities should not interfere in the political order. Accordingly, proponents of the Radical Wing demanded the separation of church and state. They offered various theological defenses for this position. A typical anti-hierarchical view appealed to the belief in the freedom of the spirit: "The Spirit bloweth where it listeth." The Radical Wing also insisted that the church is a layman's church; it is not to be controlled by the clergy. Every child of God has his own individual conscience, for the Holy Spirit is available to every child of God. As applied to church order, this view has been called the principle of radical laicism. Indeed, the Friends have held that there should be no "hireling priestcraft." Every layman is a clergyman. In various ways the Radical Wing found a sanction in the New Testament for their conception of the Holy Spirit and of church organization.

In the Radical Reformation one finds also the view that religious fellowship does not require uniformity of belief. A religious fellowship should rather be the place where the members, respecting each other in mutual confidence, will hear from each other and will test what the Holy Spirit prompts; thus the fellowship, and also each member of the fellowship, is to be enriched. As Rufus M. Jones says in *Mysticism and Democracy in the English Commonwealth,* "There is something more in each individual than there would be if he were operating in isolation. He becomes in a real sense *over-individual,* and transcends himself through the life of others." In this fellowship, a minority position was to be protected in the very name of the Holy Spirit. According to this view, God works in history where free consensus appears under the great Taskmaster's eye. Thus the sanction for the maintenance of freedom was held to be a covenant between the people and God. The idea of the covenanted fellowship with a high degree of local autonomy is the essence of what is called congregational polity.

Out of these ideas and others like them, political democracy was born. Basic to this whole development was the demand for co-archy in place of hierarchy. This demand was first applied to the church and then also to the state. Thus some proponents of the Radical Wing considered their free church to be a model for a democratic state. The political conceptions were drawn by *analogy* from the conception of the free church. What were originally elements of a doctrine of the church appeared now as ingredients of a political theory: the consent of the governed, the demand for universal suffrage, the rule of law over the executive, the principle of the loyal opposition. The conception of the democratic society, then, is in part a descendent of the conception of the free church.

In the Enlightenment of the eighteenth century, new influences affected the emerging Liberal Christianity. Here a vigorous anti-traditionalism, a belief in the perfectibility of man and in human progress, in freedom of inquiry, and in the test of reason were characteristic emphases.

From these sources, Liberal Christianity gained its major thrust. In face of the traditional pecking orders, liberalism developed its characteristic feature, namely, the conviction that human beings should be liberated, indeed should liberate themselves, from the shackles that impede religious, political and economic freedom and which impede the appearance of a rational and voluntary piety and of equality and justice for all. Here we can discern vigorous reformist (and even utopian) elements that were already strong in certain branches of the Radical Wing.

There are, of course, other ways in which Liberal Christianity's origin and development could be described. One could, for example, stress liberalism's confidence in man and his capacities. Here one would need to expound its protest against the doctrine of total depravity. One could stress its promotion of tolerance. Here one would need to recall its thrust against sectarianism, its demand for universality, a demand that has engendered a new attitude of sympathy and openness toward other religions. Or one could bring to the fore its passion for rationality and rational discrimination. Here one would recall its battle against rigid and arbitrary traditionalism and against obscurantism, a battle that has brought historical understanding of the tradition and especially of the sacred literature. Here one would stress also its eager encouragement and appropriation of the values of culture and science. All of these things have belonged to Liberal Christianity. In earlier days before the outlook had lost some of its luminous glow, they were summed up in the magic symbol "progress." A concurrent theological symbol was "progressive revelation."

***

But Liberal Christianity has its blemishes. These blemishes have appeared not merely because its performance has fallen short of its intensions. Some of its blemishes have issued from its character. One must add, however, that criticisms of Liberal Christianity have come not only from hostile critics. They have been made also by the liberals themselves. Indeed, in our undertaking here to hold the mirror up so that the Liberal Christian may look at himself critically, we aim to vindicate the method of liberalism. Liberalism lives partly from its criticism of itself.

Before we consider some of the criticisms of Liberal Christianity, we should note certain ambiguities that attach to its definition. These ambiguities arise from the fact that a tension inevitably develops within Liberal Christianity and within liberalism in general. This tension is an aspect of the morphology of ideas and of social movements. Alfred North Whitehead has pointed out that when we examine the intellectual agencies that function in the adventures of ideas, we find a rough division into two types, one of general ideas, the other of highly specialized notions. As an example of a general idea he cites the ancient ideal of the intellectual and moral grandeur of the human soul; as an example of a highly specialized notion he cites the ideals of early Christianity. The distinction is pertinent for an understanding of the tensions and ambiguities within liberalism and within Liberal Christianity.

An analogous distinction may be made between the general idea of liberalism and the more highly specialized notions of liberalism worked out in the eighteenth and nineteenth centuries. Liberalism's "general idea" has been to promote the liberation of men from tyranny, provincialism, and arbitrariness, and thus to contribute to the meaningful fulfillment of human existence. This aspect of liberalism we may call its progressive element: it is critical of the status quo, and seeks new paths of fulfillment. A "specialized notion" of liberalism has developed during the last two centuries, namely a doctrine of pre-established harmony coupled with the laissez-faire theory of society. Under the conditions of early capitalism, this doctrine was vindicated in economic progress, but beginning a century ago, progressive liberalism became critical of this "specialized notion." From the point of view of progressive liberalism, the laissez-faire society was producing new pecking orders that frustrated both equality and justice. Accordingly, the more general idea of liberalism has come into conflict with a specialized version of it. Progressive liberalism has criticized laissez-faire liberalism as closely bound up with the narrow interests of the middle class, and also with their dogma of political nonintervention in the economic sphere. Progressive liberals have protested against the status quo that was defended by laissez-faire liberals. In support of the crescent labor movement they demanded a more responsible society—a political intervention for the sake of the disinherited. So great has been the tension between the general and the specialized forms of liberalism that the strategies of progressive liberalism (working in the direction of the welfare state) have become almost the opposite of those of laissez-faire liberalism. We see, then, that there is an ambiguity in the meaning of the word *liberalism,* and that it is the consequence of a tension between two related versions of liberalism. Indeed, the ambiguities are even more complex than we have indicated. New tensions and ambiguities have appeared in recent years as progressive liberalism has moved on to become critical of an exclusive devotion to the pattern of the welfare state. Here progressive and laissez-faire liberalism have moved nearer to each other. Thus the ambiguities in terminology continue to appear.

But there are still other ambiguities to be taken into account. Liberal Christianity is not identical with liberalism considered either as a generalized or as a specialized notion. Liberal Christianity is explicitly oriented to the ultimate resources of human existence and meaning discerned in the Old and the New Testaments and in Christian experience. At the same time, Liberal Christianity has been associated with several kinds of liberalism both generalized and specialized. Indeed, because of its intentional entanglement in the secular order (in contrast to orthodoxies that claim to remain aloof), Liberal Christianity is never in its actuality easily to be distinguished from one or another of these forms of liberalism, except perhaps in terms of its ultimate orientation. Accordingly, Liberal Christianity has aimed to be critical of these forms of liberalism. The relationships of creative involvement and of critical tension are roughly analogous to those which Paul Tillich takes into account in his conception of the "Protestant principle," a principle that is creative but that also brings under judgment every actualization of Protestantism. Thus Liberal Christianity may be understood as a continuing dialogue not only between these and alternative non-liberal outlooks. The very persistence of these dialogues is indispensable for the viability of Liberal Christianity. But it also gives an inner tension and an ambiguity of direction to any Liberal Christianity or any liberalism that is not single-mindedly and piously driving towards self-destruction.

***

In order to consider some of the criticisms of Liberal Christianity I want to employ a somewhat pedestrian analogy. Every viable social movement or philosophy requires several dimensions, for it must have body—amplitude of form or shape. In short, it must have the dimensions of depth, breadth, and length. I shall interpret the criticisms of Liberal Christianity in terms of these dimensions.

First, then, we shall speak of depth. Liberal Christianity, in the initial forms emanating from the Radical Reformation, placed great emphasis on the sovereignty of God, the view that the whole of life—not merely the inner life, not merely the life of the individual, but the whole of life including social institutions—is to be brought under obedience to the righteous, sovereign God and in response to the promptings of the Holy Spirit. We have noticed already how these conceptions, as articulated by the Radical Reformation and by the Enlightenment and Romanticism involved the rejection of the hierarchy of being and of the traditional church and society based upon this hierarchy of being.

In the nineteenth century there appeared new conceptions of historical development and new knowledge at the hands of the sciences. The earlier ideas of progress were merged with the idea of natural and the social evolution. Here the Liberal Christians made a laudable effort to take seriously the new insights emanating from Darwinian biology and from other historical research. The Bible was subjected to a new criticism. Previously the idea of miracle had been rejected. Now the history of religion and society was seen to be in constant evolution. Partly from this insight came one of the great accomplishments of modern times —the higher criticisms of the sacred literature.

At the same time, however, a misreading of the Gospel ensued, and with it the loss of depth in the religious interpretation of God, man, and history. The conception of God became purely immanental, man was believed to be gradually becoming better and better as God unfolded

120

himself in evolving humanity, and history was viewed as the arena of unilinear progress. Enlightenment conceptions of man as a rational being and the Neo-Darwinian view of human evolution "onward and upward forever" were alleged to be implicit in the New Testament. These ideas, seen in succession, were taken to be evidences of "progressive revelation."

Father George Tyrrell, the Catholic modernist of a generation ago, indicated cryptically the error in this modernization of the Gospel when he said that the Liberal Christian looks down the deep well of higher criticism, sees his own image, and calls it Jesus. This particular form of modernization of the Gospel was not only objectively false, it issued in a reduction of tension between the Gospel and "the world," between the Gospel and the natural man. The overweening confidence in the natural propensities of human nature and in the upward grain of history was a superficial view, and it could not be maintained before the facts of life.

Much has happened to call in question this optimism about man and history. In our century of re-barbarization and of the mass man we have witnessed a dissolution of values and the appearance of great collective demonries, the nihilism that Nietzsche predicted. Progress is now seen not to take place in the moral and spiritual realm merely through inheritance. Each generation and each person must anew win insight into the ambiguous nature of man and must in changed circumstance give new relevance to moral and spiritual values. This renewal does not take place in the manner of technical progress—with each succeeding generation standing on the shoulders of previous achievement. It requires a realistic appraisal of man's foibles and a life of continuing humility and repentance. At the depths of human nature there are potential divine resources, but there are also ever-powerful forces working for perversion and destruction. In the New Testament view, the Kingdom of God brings man under judgment; it is not sanction for what Thoreau called "improved means with unimproved ends." Albert Schweitzer, near the beginning of the present century, showed the wide distance between certain modern conceptions of progress and the New Testament conception of the Kingdom of God. Since his time and particularly through the New Testament studies of Rudolf Otto, contemporary Liberal Christians have discovered new depths in the Biblical teachings regarding history and the Kingdom of God. The tragic dimensions of history were missed by those Liberal Christians who interpreted history as unilinear progress. The appreciation of the depth of perversity, as well as of the resources available to men, lies beyond the purview of the "modern" doctrines of progress.

A corresponding loss of depth is to be observed in a related aspect of Liberal Christianity as it has come to us from the nineteenth century. Under the influence of utilitarianism and also of Kantianism, Liberal Christianity in wide sectors has tended to identify religion with the good life. Here we have the thinning out of Liberal Christianity into moralism. Other forces, to be sure, were operative in Liberal Christian thought— for example, the heritage from Schleiermacher which emphasized the transmoral character of religion and specifically of the Christian religion. But from Kant and also from the "practical" bourgeoisie, many Liberal Christians have learned to reduce religion to the observance of ethical precepts. Thus again the depth dimension was lost. Moralism replaced the deeper relatedness to the divine source of and judgment upon our moral "values." In the old Liberal Christianity, Jesus was viewed as primarily a moral teacher and model. Thus the divine ground and source of meaning as disclosed by Jesus and the Old Testament prophets were lost sight of. The protest against the Christ of the creeds was a justifiable protest against a dehumanized Christ, and it was also a justifiable attempt to give Christianity a new ethical relevance. But the ignoring of the problems dealt with in Biblical theology and in Christology could only lead to a narrowing of sensitivity. This reduction is to be observed also in the interpretation of Jesus' parables as primarily ethical parables, whereas modern liberal scholarship has reminded us that they point to the more-than-human resources of human existence, to the Kingdom of God "that grows of itself" and not ultimately by human divising. Here again the writings of the Liberal Christian scholar, Rudolf Otto, have been of signal importance.

Something further must be said regarding the loss of the depth dimension consequent upon the waning of interest in theology. In addition to the influence of forces already mentioned, this tendency has been promoted by scientism, an illiberal imperialism of method. It has been promoted also by the implausible conceptions of God that have been entertained not only by the orthodox but also by merely traditionalist Liberal Christians. Whatever the cause and whatever the justifications of these tendencies may be, the outcome in some circles of Liberal Christianity has been deplorable. A whole range of perennial problems for the religious consciousness has been ignored. In effect some Liberal Christians have said in response to those concerned with theological inquiry, "We must tell you that you are dealing with pseudo-problems. You are an orthodox Christian, perhaps without knowing it. Liberal Christianity has emancipated itself from concern with these pseudo-problems." The paucity of thought and of piety here is blatantly evident today in the lack of a theological interpretation of the great social issues. This kind of "religion" is neither liberal nor Christian. It is a superficial provincial backwash of "progress," impotent to deal intellectually and responsibly with the deeper, ultimate issues of life. Happily, there are countervailing tendencies among Liberal Christians, hinted at in our previous incidental references to certain Liberal Christian leaders.

✳✳✳

In some respects we have already anticipated the discussion of the dimension of breadth. One of the characteristic features of Liberal Christianity has been its intention to maintain familiarity with and participation in the best thought and practice of the secular world. This feature of Liberal Christianity has roots not only in the idea that Christian faith is more than a repetition of traditional words and practices. It is rooted also in the conviction that God's truth is by no means restricted (if granted) to those who praise His name. This conviction is not of recent vintage among Liberal Christians. We now know, as we did not a generation ago, that the relation between religion and science two and three centuries ago was not one of mere hostility ("warfare" was John Draper's description in his long-familiar book). The Protestants, and particularly the liberals, long ago defended and protected scientists whose findings were at first blush believed to be inimical to Christian faith or to Biblical revelation. The methods and findings of the natural and the cultural sciences are of concern to the Liberal Christian. For him these methods and findings must take their place within the integrity of knowledge. Moreover, literature, the fine arts, and philosophy offer him interpretations and criticisms of life which contribute to self-understanding and must be evaluated. They are media through which the meaning of existence and the frustration of this meaning are clarified and interpreted in their interrelatedness. The Liberal Christian holds that he can better gain a sense of the full import of his faith by confronting the insights and questionings that are provided by these disciplines. In the nineteenth century, Matthew Arnold stated this aspect of the Liberal Christian outlook when he said that he who knows only his Bible does not know even his Bible. Shailer Mathews two generations ago shocked some of the pious among his contemporaries by editing a book on *The Contributions of Science to Religion*. The dialogue with these disciplines is necessary if Liberal Christianity is not to become arbitrary, obscurantist, and irrelevant. It is necessary also if the interplay between Liberal Christianity and the generalized and the specialized ideas of liberalism is to be fruitful in the changing historical situation.

But breadth has its hazards. It may be misinterpreted to mean the acceptance of a little bit of this and the rejection of a little bit of that, and with little sense of the whole. "Breadth" of this sort may be tantamount to irresponsibility with respect to religious belief; it may prevent the achievement of integrity. To many people the attraction of Liberal Christianity has been its openness, its tolerance, its freedom. But these qualities can spell the loss of character.

This loss of character in the pursuit of breadth is the more threatening in a society where change is rapid, where there is a multiplicity of norms, where the mass media of communication exert pressures that constitute a form of psychic violence. Within the churches themselves one can encounter a bewildering variety of outlooks. Freud and Jung, Adam Smith and Marx, Schweitzer and Toynbee, Whitehead and Russell, are only a few of the names that may be cited to exemplify the variety of motifs that receive a hearing. One could mention other motifs that have a less distinguished character. These motifs, taken together without some explicit abiding unities, can lead to confusion—interesting confusion perhaps, but confusion nevertheless.

There is nothing more debilitating than sheer variety—a synonym for chaos. Carlyle once said of Tennyson that he was always carrying a bit of chaos around in his pocket turning it into cosmos. Properly understood, Liberal Christianity is not an invitation to fissiparous freedom or to trivialized freedom. It seeks orderliness of mind, and it seeks it in and through fellowship. That is, it seeks consensus. This does not mean that it seeks fixed creedal uniformity. But it seeks a center; indeed, it is worthy of respect only when it lives from this center.

This center is not jeopardized by variety alone. The greater threat to the maintenance or the achievement of a center is accommodation to the idols of nationalism, race, and class. Liberal Christianity in Germany during the period of the Third Reich possessed very feeble powers of resistance. Indeed, many of the "German Christians" and even many of the members of the German Faith Movement were former religious liberals who found in Hitler a prophet of "progressive revelation." To be sure, many of the orthodox Protestants had managed to be irrelevant, if not cooperative, in face of the rise of Nazism. Moreover, millions of Roman Catholics also capitulated to Hitler. Shortly after Hitler's assumption of power and at a time when he sorely needed any scrap of respectability available, the Vatican made a concordat with him. Certain features of the Vatican concordat with Mussolini are still valid in Italy today. The collaboration of many "Liberal Christians" with Hitlerism has made Liberal Christians all over the world newly aware of the necessity of a center along with breadth; indeed, of a center for the breadth. Without this centripetal power, or (to change the figure) without this root, the fruits become a wilding destructive growth.

For Liberal *Christianity* the center is in a faith that finds its classic expression in the Old Testament prophets and in the being, the character, and the mission of Jesus. In that faith we find the generating spirit and the norm of norms for Liberal Christianity. This faith is a response to the sustaining, creative, judging, transforming power that gives rise to a community of love and justice. As we have indicated earlier, it was a special articulation of this faith which initially brought to birth those elements of the Radical Reformation out of which Liberal Christianity and democracy emerged. Without this faith, breadth can become chaos and dark night.

***

This brings us to the third dimension, the dimension of length. If the first dimension is depth—a vertical—dimension pointing to the divine ground, and if the second dimension is a horizontal one referring to the surrounding milieu, then the third is also horizontal it is the time-dimension. One of the distinctive features of Liberal Christianity has been its futuristic emphasis, an emphasis that is found in both the Old and the New Testament and also in the heretical sects of the Middle Ages and of the Left Wing of the Reformation. Liberal Christianity has not been oriented to the past as such, and to tradition. The Bible and the later eschatological movements have served it as a stimulus to continuing renewal. Indeed, we are indebted in part to Liberal Christianity for the modern historical consciousness, a consciousness that has made the modern man aware of the inevitability of change, of the necessity to be critical of the past and the present, and aware also of the possibilities of the future.

But there are hazards in the time-dimension, too. We have already noted the hazard of entertaining false hopes for the future. We must now observe that a sense of the differences between past and present has in some liberal circles issued in an uncritical anti-traditionalism. This anti-traditionalism serves always as a threat to Liberal Christianity's maintaining its historical rootage. It tempts it into a provincialism in time. I can illustrate this danger from a recent occurrence. Not long ago I attended in a liberal church a meeting at which a denominational representative gave an address on religious education. In the spirit of what calls itself "progressive education," he outlined a curriculum in which the emphasis rested upon training the children for living in the present; all of the material recommended for presentation to the children was of contemporary vintage. Nothing even of the modern background of Christianity in general, or of Liberal Christianity, was mentioned. During the discussion that followed his address one of the parents in the audience said, "I am puzzled by your exclusive emphasis on the present and the future. I have been in the habit of supposing that religious education in a liberal church should include a critical appreciation of our past and also a critical appreciation of the Bible." The "religious educator" replied, "I don't mean to say that the Bible has to be excluded. If you want it in the curriculum, I don't see why you should be prevented. We believe in freedom in the liberal church." This cavalier attitude toward the experience of the past, and specifically toward the Bible, can only result in organized religious illiteracy. This kind of illiteracy goes under the name of modernity, but it is simply a form of provincialism and even of rootlessness. It is a provincialism that is very similar to the corresponding provincialism of certain kinds of orthodoxy. The rigid orthodox person of

Fundamentalist persuasion holds that all we need to know is between the covers of an ancient book. The "emancipated" liberal seems to hold that we live only in and on the present and for the future. Both of these forms of rigidity are provincial and dogmatic. Fortunately, higher education for the most part is less provincial.

Nothing significant in human history is achieved except through longstanding continuities. This principle is as valid in the sphere of religion as in the realms of science, politics, and art. In the sphere of religion particularly, the loss of the time-dimension can carry with it the loss also of the depth dimension.

The decisive, substantial features of Liberal Christianity are Christian and Biblical, and the characteristically modern religious elements of Liberal Christianity shall always have been in the Left Wing of the Reformation (though one may rightly question whether the Left Wing as such may be properly considered as definitively normative). Liberal Christianity cannot retain its own character when it severs itself from these roots. A sociological consideration here is almost equally decisive. Without a vital continuing frame of reference, no social movement can make a significant difference for its own constituency or in its impact on the world. One finds in the Bible and in the theological and devotional literature of the Christian tradition the concepts and the structures, the concerns and the insights, that are indispensable for any critical religious interpretation of the meaning of our historical existence and also for the maintenance of those sensitivities that can transcend and be critical of civilization. Indeed, this orientation alone is reliable for maintaining a critical attitude toward Liberal Christianity itself and its fellow-travelers, and toward the general ideas and institutions and the specialized notions and institutions of Liberalism.

***

These criticisms and evaluations of Liberal Christianity do not take into account all important aspects of the movement. For example, the attacks upon Liberal Christianity and upon liberalism in general which have been coming from the so-called New Conservatism or from the more "radical" types of social philosophy, have not been reported. Nor have Liberal Christianity's various attitudes toward non-Christian religions been dealt with. But the types of criticism presented here have been sufficiently influential to have made some Liberal Christians feel uncomfortable under the label of "liberalism." In some quarters, indeed, Liberal Christians now call themselves "Neo-Liberals." Concurrently with these developments the movement loosely called Neo-Orthodoxy has appeared. Actually, there are certain affinities between Neo-Liberalism and Neo-Orthodoxy. Indeed, the significant dialogue going on today in this area is not between the old-fashioned liberals and the old-fashioned orthodox; it is between the Neo-Liberals and the Neo-Orthodox.

In the context of these dialogues, I have here emphasized that Liberal Christianity degenerates when the depth dimension is lost sight of or disappears, that it is not to be identified with any merely ethical outlook but is concerned also with the divine ground for ethics and for the criticism of ethics, that breadth cannot be salutary for Liberal Christianity if the latter does not possess a center-stance that the substance and character of Liberal Christianity are to be understood for the most part in the context of Biblical faith and Christian experience, and that these latter are to be given relevance today only through a continuing openness to criticism and through a continuing effort to give clarity and new formulation to the faith in face of the contemporary situation. Presupposed throughout is the view that the Liberal Christian in criticizing himself aims to confront anew the ultimate demands and to be open to the more-than-human resources that no human tradition or devising can claim to originate or control.

In face of these demands and resources Liberal Christianity must be judged not only in terms of its intellectual depth and breadth and historical consciousness. It must be judged also by the kind of people it produces. And it must be judged by its consequences in relation to the struggle against pecking orders and to the struggle for a community of freedom and justice and love.

These criteria of depth, breadth and length must be understood under the axiom, "By their fruits shall you know them." A decisive test is the consequence in individual behavior and also in group behavior. Depth, breadth and length belong to the integrity of the individual; they impinge also upon the common life. The questions remain, How do these qualities make a difference in face of the pecking orders—in face of the demonic forces and structures of our time? How do they affect our attitudes and actions in the institutional sphere, in the church, the political order, the economic order? The pragmatic theory of meaning in these spheres raises the question, What do we want to remain unchanged there, and what do we want changed in our institutional patterns? What do we work for?

When we look at contemporary society and remember that the Radical Reformation began as a protest against oppression and as an effort in the direction of a new society, we recognize that the Reformation must continue. I need not spell this out here. Instead, I will ask you to take the pulse of a segment of our society today.

A short time ago a black physician in Chicago told me that his regular nightly duty is to treat some black child in the ghetto who has been bitten by a rodent. Recently he responded to an emergency call late at night. The younger of two small girls had been bitten in her sleep. When the doctor tried to give first aid to the younger sister, she was still so frightened that he could not persuade her to stand still to receive the antiseptic and a bandage. She would not quiet down. Finally, the older sister shouted, "Sally, if you don't be quiet, and let the doctor fix you, we'll put you back in the room where the rat is."

A melodramatic episode it is, and grotesque. But it provides a clue to what is meant if we say that at this late date in modern "progress" we still live in tyrannous pecking orders—enhanced by rats. Yes, depth, breadth and length are still in the Valley of Decision.

5. Festschrift: Presentation to Paul Tillich

Delivered in The Braun Room, Harvard Divinity School, 1960.
Among the Essayists: James Luther Adams, Karl Barth, Erich Fromm,
Charles Hartshorne, Karl Jaspers, Charles Malik, Gabriel Marcel,
Reinhold Niebuhr, Welhelm Pauck, and Gustave Weigel

We are here to honor you, Paulus, by presenting to you the *Festschrift*
edited by Walter Leibrecht and given handsome format by Harper &
Brothers.

In the concluding chapter of St. Luke's Gospel we read, "And they
said one to another, 'Did not our hearts burn within us while he spake
to us in the way, and opened to us the scriptures?' And they rose up that
very hour, and returned to Jerusalem."

From Martin Luther comes an equally pungent expression of the
power of words and likewise of the power of the word: "The world," he
says, "is conquered by the Word, and by the Word the church is served
and rebuilt."

On this occasion I want to speak about Paul Tillich as the theologian
of the religious symbol, as the theologian of the classical Christian
symbols, who has made our hearts burn within us and who has shown
again the power of the Word that conquers the world and that serves and
rebuilds the church. Man is a symbol-bearing creature; and the Christian
man belongs to a community that is formed and ever given new life by
virtue of symbols borne by the power of the Word of God. Through
symbols, through words, and through the Word from the living God,
the Christian community, like the fellowship of disciples on the road to
Emmaus, lives and communicates. Through words the church hears its
God-given message, and through them it proclaims the message to the
world. In decisive part the household of faith is formed and reformed and
mediated through words. Out of the abundance of the heart the mouth
speaks.

Paul Tillich has viewed himself as a theologian of mediation. For
him "the task of theology is mediation, mediation between the eternal
criterion of truth as it is manifest in the picture of Jesus as the Christ and
the changing experience of individuals and groups." For him "theology"
implies "a mediation between the mystery, which is *theos,* and the

understanding, which is *logos.*" To be a theologian is to be a theologian of mediation. In order to fulfill this task of mediation Tillich has devoted his life to the search for right words.

Therefore, I speak today of Tillich as the mediator of words with power. In short, I want to speak of Tillich's rhetoric, of his mediation of the Christian mystery through words that are indelibly associated with his name. It is through a Christian rhetoric, as he has revitalized it, that he has mediated not only between *theos* and *logos* but also between the different segments of the Protestant world community, between Protestants and Eastern and Roman Catholics, between Christians and Jews, between Christianity and other world religions, between the Old World of the European Continent and the New World of America, between the church and "the world," between theology and politics, between theology and the economic sphere, between theology and art, between theology and culture, between orthodoxy and liberalism, between theology and atheism. The variety of authorship and of topics in the *Festschrift* bespeaks the composite image of this mediating theologian. Moreover, anyone who knows Paulus knows that he is an itinerant theologian, a circuit rider in the American tradition: he may be expected to appear as a theologian of mediation among not only church groups but also among the artists, the sociologists, the psychiatrists, the architects, and even the proponents of the ballet. I recall discovering years ago an article by Paul Tillich in a German architectural journal whose editorial writer in a footnote to the article identified Paulus as a leading German architect. This editor spoke better than he knew, for is not the architectonic quality of Tillich's whole outlook veritably Aristotelian in its *pathos* for structure? By his mediating rhetoric Tillich has not only assisted in the communication of the Christian message to the churches and to the Gentiles outside and inside the churches; he has also helped to form a new community of self-criticism and of creativity across the boundaries between concern and indifference and between ultimate concern and preliminary concerns, across the other boundaries that separate a fragmented church and a fragmented world. When recently I was in Japan and India, I found myself again and again surrounded by people, both Christian and non-Christian, who wished to pose questions about Paul Tillich the theologian and the man.

Not all of the words of the Tillichian rhetoric, however, strike the hearer as theological. One is reminded of the rhetoric of an earlier eminent theologian of mediation. When Schleiermacher undertook to show to the cultured despisers of religion the inevitableness and indispensability of religion, he confessed at the very beginning of his *Reden* that he belonged to the order of theologians, and then he added: "It is a willing confession, for my language should not have betrayed me; nor should the eulogies of my colleagues in the profession; what I desire lies so far out of their orbit and would little resemble what they wish to see and hear. I am aware that in all I have to say to you I disown my profession, and why shouldn't I therefore confess it like any other misdemeanor?" With greater cause Tillich might well say the same of himself. His writings, as a German interpreter has observed, often delight one in a remarkably untheological, secular way.

This secular element in the Tillichian vocabulary must be understood in relation to an aspect of his mediative rhetoric which I have not yet mentioned: he mediates between past and present, giving new life and new relevance to old symbols. As a mediating theologian, he has recognized that much of our current ecclesiastical rhetoric is lacking in contemporaneousness, because "our intellectual situation" is "different from that out of which the words of the church-proclamation were born."

Old words and symbols therefore require new birth. As Tillich is wont to say, many of the old words are sick; one must "save" words before one can save souls. The core of the Tillichian rhetoric is made up of the key concepts, the root metaphors, which he has "saved" in order to express anew the essential, Christian proclamation. Tillich has explored the thesaurus of the forgotten rhetoric of earlier theologies and philosophies, and he has returned to us with symbols that utter "Open Sesame" to the contemporary mind and that elicit new recognition of the human condition and of its possibilities under God's grace. Changing the figure, we may say that Tillich has thrown his net into the cavernous depths of rhetorical tradition, into the realm of the Mothers; and by dint of the Geiger-counter in that remarkable handle of his net, he has brought to light treasures new and old, thus releasing the latent power of words that speak "kairotically" to our time. Consider, for example, only a few of the terms of the Tillichian vocabulary which already in our time have been in widest commonality spread: the *Kairos,* the New Being, Christ the center of history, the Unconditional, ultimate concern, theonomy, the depth of reason, ground and abyss, the gestalt of grace, living on the boundary, ecstasy, the latent church, the Protestant principle, the Protestant ear, Protestant secularism, and—not least of all—correlation. These are the principal means by which Tillich has mediated between past and present, the means whereby he has become the theologian of *kairos*. Indeed, may we not say that his rhetoric has taken the form of kairology and well as of a theology mediating the Eternal Gospel to our time? By means of this rhetoric of words pulsating with the power of being and with assault upon non-being he has even illustrated an ontology of the Word. He has exhibited the freedom and destiny latent in words, in old words that were covered over with the rusts of time, in new words that spring into immediate currency. As we think of the old symbols to which he has given new life and relevance, we are reminded of the aphorism of Goethe: one cannot inherit, one must earn, a tradition.

These paradigmatic words of Tillich's rhetoric have taken hold even where the total architectonic structure of his thought may be ignored or rejected or not grasped. In every country where there is a Christian community, and even among the emancipated Gentiles, this rhetoric exercises power. Many are the people who listen for and respond to the magic thunder in Tillich's utterance. Many also have been moved to turn towards Jerusalem. By means of the Tillichian paradigm and by virtue of what it points to "beyond itself," new ways have been opened to permit the divine power—the judging, transforming power—to reunite the separated. In the Tillichian version, the old symbols have nothing of the quaintness of the archaic. Far from it. They carry within them and point to the power of the New Being that groweth not old, to the power than conquers the world and rebuilds the church.

In profound gratitude and in festal celebration we, presenting to you a volume of essays issued in your honor, say to you, Paulus, and we repeat to each other, what was said when you were awarded the Goethe Prize of Hamburg: *Wir freuen uns, dass es Paul Tillich gibt.* We rejoice that there is a Paul Tillich.

6. The Body And The Soul Of Learning

Delivered as the Commencement Address,
Meadville/Lombard Theological School, Chicago, June 13, 1976

We celebrate the formal affiliation fifty years ago of Meadville Theological School with the University of Chicago, the University having been founded eighty-five years ago and Meadville 132 years ago in the wilderness of western Pennsylvania. In these events we see ample evidence that the enterprises of religion and of learning require an institutional body, and that without an institutional body neither religion nor learning can have a soul, indeed can scarcely continue to exist.

It is a striking fact, however, that we live in a time when there has been widespread disenchantment with institutions. In some measure radical skepticism has issued from the Watergate scandals, but something deeper than this experience provides explanation not only for skepticism but also for the lack of a positive conception of the indispensability of institutions for meaningful human existence. There are long-standing types of thought and feeling and action which militate against taking seriously an enduring and costing commitment to institutional structures and responsibilities, even though most people gain their livelihood from participation in institutions.

It was perhaps Erasmus who said that humanity is like a drunken sailor on horseback, riding the shaky nag of history, at one jog bouncing in the air and coming down to fall almost in the mud on the one side, and at the next jog bouncing and coming down almost into the hedge on the other side. Sometimes one gets the impression that this sailor lives on the principle that nothing succeeds like excess.

But the excesses are not necessarily forms of deviant, unhuman behavior; they often represent a striving for authentic living. Let me illustrate.

I recall a conversation of several years ago with John Courtney Murray, the Jesuit scholar of Woodstock Seminary, who exercised a major influence on Vatican Council II. In this conversation Father Murray said that among the novitiates in training for entry into the Society of Jesus, the word *institution* was pronounced with scorn. The novitiates wanted personal intimacy most of all, to sit together enjoying directly and simply each other's company. He said in a tone of almost despair that he and his colleagues on the Faculty agreed that the novitiates would probably not be satisfied even if every member of the Faculty were in turn and around the clock to hold one or other student in his lap. To the novitiates it seemed that the preferable sphere of grace is interpersonal, affectional communion. Who would deny the crucial importance of interpersonal communion? But obviously, it cannot take the place of the pursuit of the social purpose of the Order.

Plato had this principle in mind when he said that the family is the enemy of justice, meaning apparently that family loyalty can ignore and even threaten embracing public purposes.

You may rightly say that it is not surprising that this reversal of ethos should appear among the Jesuits, a monastic order renowned for ascetic and almost military discipline, the *militia Christi*. We recall that in certain monastic orders, close, one-to-one friendship was on principle discouraged and even prevented. Close personal friendship was viewed as disruptive and destructive; it was viewed as engendering horizontal loyalty inimical to the vertical loyalty to the hierarchy of the order and the church. Overweening personal friendship, it was held, could become the occasion and the means of dissent or subversion. It has been observed by the sociologists that the vertical organization of the twentieth-century Communist cell to protect against deviation in ideology or strategy was modeled on the vertical organization and loyalty of the monastery. To be sure, these dimensions, vertical and horizontal, need not be articulated in such contrasting, dichotomous fashion. Indeed, these dimensions have been brought into more humane integration in many of the monastic orders, especially since Vatican Council II.

An analogous form of anti-institutional ethos may be observed in an idea equally admirable with that of personal intimacy, the idea that authentic religion is equivalent to inwardness, to inner purity of disposition or motive, a recurrent emphasis in the history of religion in East or West. In the nineteenth century this idea was attributed to Jesus through a mistranslation of a New Testament text: the Kingdom of God is within you. The more accurate translation would be, The Kingdom of God is *among you*—as a community-forming power. I recall a Sermon from this pulpit some years ago by a visiting German theologian who asserted that the uniqueness of Jesus is to be seen in his stress on inwardness, *Innerlichkeit*. Again, who would deny that this inwardness is the root of authentic human existence? We may recall, however, that a generation ago here the late Dean Shailer Mathews of the Divinity School, in protest against this enclosing of Jesus into *Innerlichkeit,* published his book entitled *Jesus on Social Institutions,* wherein he argued that Jesus' teaching leads to a unification of the personality in social and institutional relationships. In short, Jesus' teaching, properly understood, exercises active and responsible impact on institutions, and not only upon religious institutions. The Kingdom of God is bent on social as well as individual purpose.

Let me mention here a third form of hostility to institutions as such, namely a radical critique and rejection for the sake of individual spontaneity and freedom of expression. Professor Amos Wilder and I have served as faculty advisers to a group of students interested in religion and art in the Greater Boston cluster of theological schools, the Boston Theological Union. At the first meeting of the group about half of the members said they wanted to know nothing of the history of religion and art, and nothing of art criticism. These things, they said, would only corrupt their own individual styles. Each student wanted only to do his own thing. At this meeting some of the students countered with such questions as these: If you do simply your own thing without reference to some consensus, how can you expect to communicate? If you wish to operate without recognition of some criterion, how will you know whether or not in doing your own thing you are doing anything having to do with either art or religion? How will you know whether doing your own thing is worth doing? At one point an excited student quoted the judgment of the Athenians on the Melesians: they are not stupid, they only act as if they were.

The problem we confront here is the persistent one of combining order and spontaneity, structure and dynamics, continuity and innovation, and of course also the problem of *standards* of performance. And sometimes we may have to say, the spirit killeth, the letter giveth life.

I recall that over forty years ago, in a meeting here at Meadville of the Unitarian Commission of Appraisal, we were discussing the problem of dealing with overemphasis on the uniqueness of the individual—what we called devotion to uniquity. Walter Pritchard Eaton, a member of the Commission, and the Yale drama critic, asserted that a literary convention is like a religious institution. It requires time and discipline to achieve significant creativity. He said that before Shakespeare there were scores of playwrights working at the forms of tragedy and comedy. At that moment I recalled a lecture I had heard by John Galsworthy, who said that the history of the English novel might be compared to a spinal column made up chronologically of a series of similar, yet unique, vertebrae.

Most important of all, we may say, institutional framework and institutional discipline are indispensable if critical judgment is to be engendered.

I recall reading during my student days a passage in the writings of Dr. George A. Gordon of Old South Church in Boston which has stayed with me when I have been impatient of institutional requirements or of institutional orthodoxy and narrowness. Dr. Gordon writes that by reason of his inadequate preparation he had been admitted to Harvard College as a special student on probation. During his first year he attended Professor William Goodwin's class in elementary Greek. When the time came for the midyear examination he appeared in the classroom with his blue book intending to write the examination. Professor Goodwin told him that since he was a special student he need not take the examination. Dr. Gordon says, "My heart sank within me; I felt precisely as an idiot or an insane person might feel in a lucid moment when he makes the discovery that the community takes no account of what he does so long as he is harmless." Gordon begged for the privilege of being examined, and finally Professor Goodwin assented. "That examination" he says. "I underwent, and it was a turning point in my life. I have come to regard it as the supreme blessing of our life: to live in the presence of high, exacting standards of intellect, of character and behavior, and incessantly to undergo the great testing process of a moral community and a moral world."

What then, is an institution, and particularly an educational institution? It is a socially contrived means of defining patterns of thought and behavior with regard to the perennial problems and conflicts of human beings in society. These patterns involve a definite normative ordering and regulation, "a regulation upheld by norms and by sanctions that are in principle legitimized by these norms." This is the ongoing process of learning, the soul of learning the—search for "exacting standards of intellect, of character and behavior."

But such an institution requires a body, a body not entirely dissimilar to the psychophysical body of the human person with its variety of process and sensitivities. The wife of the former President of the University of Chicago, Mrs. Muriel Beadle, in her memoir of the University, *Where Has All the Ivy Gone?*, reminds us that in addition to the faculty and the students and the board of trustees, this institution requires a whole series of administrators and employees many of whom have no direct connection with the academic enterprise: the office of personnel records, the public relations office, the fund-raisers, the employment office, the legal department, the bursar, the police force, the building-and-grounds department. All of these, and more, are required to make up the body of the learning enterprise. And in the midst of this welter, the crucial process is that wherein teacher and student in both personal and impersonal association undergo examinations in the sense of testing and being tested and defining the standards—all of this for the achievement of freedom and integrity in the search for truth and for authentic human behavior and responsibility, the while trying to shape the spaces for inwardness, for spontaneity and freedom, for meaningful interpersonal relations in this context and in the context of the web of institutions and conflicting ideals that form the society at large.

It was because of the variety and depth of this enterprise at the University of Chicago that Meadville sought and achieved affiliation. Over half a century before moving to Chicago, Meadville offered courses in the natural and social sciences in addition to the conventional theological disciplines. Meadville, moreover, was the third theological school in the world to promote the systematic study of comparative religion, the first being Geneva, and the second, Harvard. The affiliation was effected toward the end of exposing Meadville to and contributing to the broadest range of disciplines, of scholars and their traditions out of Athens, Sinai and Galilee, indeed also out of Benares and Peking and Cairo. The presupposition is that the unexamined life is not worth living, and as one of our colleagues used to say, the unexamined faith is not worth "faithing." This, I repeat, signifies the soul of learning and of religion.

The whole process requires a high degree of specialization—which brings dangers with it. The story runs that one day a visitor at the

University of Chicago was seeking for the office in Cobb Hall of the first President, William Rainey Harper. Encountering a scrubwoman in the corridor, he asked where to find the President. She replied, 'I dunno. I jes' scrub here.' When the visitor repeated the remark to the President, Harper replied, "We are beginning to specialize, you see."

Without specialization a university or a theological faculty has not the soul of learning, of the search for reliable knowledge and standard, but with it the participant may get lost and the student even be ignored. Indeed, there is a kind of isolated inwardness of specialization which can develop in a university as in a theological school. There can be a demonic devotion to isolation from public concern and accountability, a devotion that tempts us to say that some specialists are more dangerous for their virtues than for their vices. I recall the day after the atomic bombs were cast upon Hiroshima and Nagasaki, the atomic physicist Leo Szilard, who with Albert Einstein had persuaded President Roosevelt to sponsor the Manhattan Project, came to me and then to Charles Hartshorne to say that science and religion had too long been separated, that the time had come for them to work together with a new sense of public responsibility for the uses to which their knowledge was put. He acknowledged that he was a little late. We formed an all-University Committee to express protest and penitence. One wonders what might have happened had the cooperation come earlier. As it was, we had traveled what Shakespeare called "the flowery path that leads to the broad gate and the great fire."

Dr. Christie of Meadville, in a sermon delivered at the Divinity School Chapel some years before the formal affiliation took place, reminds us that the usages of the university are efforts to express and to connect with the routine of life that great supernal spiritual reality which is the mother of us all. The University, he said, is a parable of the church, for the Holy Church has its being in a great purpose and a great memory that lives and throbs in that purpose. It is a divine purpose laying hold of men and women to shape them for the life of the Kingdom of God.

The story is told that in the early days of Meadville when it had established itself in the frontier wilderness and drew into its instruction the men and women of the backwoods, a young Harvard classical scholar concluded the final lecture of the year. A sturdy fellow from the farm came forward to express his appreciation. In vigor of admiration he threw his hand to the shoulder of the slender, callow scholar from the

East, causing him almost to lose his balance, and said in a husky voice, "Perfessor, you done noble."

The learning that has not lost its soul does not alienate itself from such sturdy people or from the scrubwoman. It will not give reason for one to say that we must choose between learning and democracy or between religion and social justice.

In this sense the church and the university, the parable of the church, will strive (as St. Paul says) for the sake of one *body* and one *spirit* as we are called for the *one* hope that belongs to our calling.

IV.

James Luther Adams Papers

Introduction By The Editor

James Luther Adams lived in Cambridge, Massachusetts just across from the Harvard Divinity School, where he began teaching in 1956, following his 20 years of teaching in Chicago.

I first met JLA when I was a student in the College of the University of Chicago, and he was Professor of Religious Ethics and head of the Department of Ethics and Society at the University of Chicago. That initial meeting occurred when he spoke at Channing Club, the Sunday evening university student gathering at the First Unitarian Church of Chicago on the edge of the campus. His theme that evening was dramatically expressed in a provocative pamphlet published by the American Unitarian Association, *On Being Human—the Liberal Way.*

Intrigued by JLA's presentation of central working principles of liberal religion, I later met with him when I was exploring study at Harvard Divinity School, which he had attended before he became a parish minister in Salem and then Wellesley Hills, Massachusetts. Since Adams knew Dean Willard L. Sperry, he volunteered to write to him on my behalf. Then, after an invaluable year at Harvard studying religion, philosophy and sociology, I returned to Chicago for study with Adams and other members of the University of Chicago faculty.

At the same time that I was in theological school, I was the Director of Student Work at the First Unitarian Church, and Adams was our Channing Club's university faculty advisor. In 1950, when Dorothy and I were married at that church, Dr. Adams officiated. After our marriage, we lived in an apartment at Channing House, where the Adams family lived. We thus informally got to know Jim's wife, Margaret, as well as their three children: Eloise, Elaine (Miller), and Barbara Jane (Thompson).

During my student years in Chicago, I read all of the James Luther Adams writings then available, including his doctoral dissertation on *Paul Tillich's Philosophy of Culture, Science, and Religion.* I found that this deeply distinctive dissertation superbly supplemented the JLA translated essays and the JLA concluding essay in Paul Tillich's *The Protestant Era* published by the University of Chicago Press in 1948. That Tillich book, which was put together by Adams, was classic enough to put Tillich, a refugee from Hitler Germany, into the very mainstream of American secular and religious thought. Viewed in this context, it seemed to me

143

that JLA's doctoral dissertation on Tillich also deserved to be published. A few years later Adams agreed to let me explore this possibility. When I contacted Melvin Arnold, the president of Harper and Company in New York, who had previously been the director of Beacon Press in Boston, he said he was interested, so we sent him the text. Harper was advised by a prominent scholar that they should not publish the book because Adams had more important things to do than to rework his doctoral dissertation for general publication. Melvin Arnold, who had worked closely with Jim during his Beacon Press years, invited me to present a case to Harper as to why they should publish this book. I argued that Tillich had already become—thanks to Professor Adams—a truly formative figure in American culture and that the Adams interpretation of Tillich's early thought was simply indispensable for any adequate understanding of his thought. Fortunately, the book was published in 1965, and it sold so well that Harper later issued a paperbound edition.

At the time the book on Tillich's philosophy was published, Adams was teaching at the Harvard Divinity School, and my family and I were also living in Cambridge. For some two years the two of us met with some frequency to gather and evaluate papers he had written over the years in order to explore alternative ways of arranging them for publication by Beacon Press. This project finally came to fruition in 1976 when Max L. Stackhouse edited and significantly introduced *On Being Human Religiously: Selected Essays in Religion and Society* by James Luther Adams. That book, which was also later issued in paperback by Beacon, has now been supplemented by three more recent books of additional collected essays. Two of them, published by Beacon Press and edited by George K. Beach, are *The Prophethood of All Believers* (1986) and *An Examined Faith: Social Context and Religious Commitment* (1991). Both volumes have helpful biographical introductions. The third volume of JLA essays was edited by J. Ronald Engel, *Voluntary Associations: Socio-cultural Analyses and Theological Interpretations* (Exploration Press, 1986). Incidentally, the very first book of collected JLA essays, *Taking Time Seriously*, was edited by J. Bryan Allin and published by the Free Press in 1957.

In addition to these publications, there was in 1977 a special double issue of *The Unitarian Universalist Christian* entitled *James Luther Adams at 75*. It was my privilege to serve as the guest editor and to introduce that collection of hitherto unpublished papers which included an autobiographical piece, "The Evolution of My Social Concern," plus one essay for each decade of Jim's professional career, beginning in the 1920s.

Now, through the encouragement of the present editor, Dr. Thomas D. Wintle, we are able to offer this second special issue devoted to James Luther Adams, who has been a Vice President of the Unitarian Universalist Christian Fellowship since 1977. The occasional papers being published here are ones which Dr. Adams released to me for publication. They reach back in time to as early as 1926, but some of them cannot be precisely dated. In certain instances, moreover, there are different editions of the same topic; whereas in other instances, the text is incomplete, but what is available often seemed worthy of publication. Although it is not now possible to provide full documentation with regard to all of the occasions related to the preparation of these JLA papers, here are some specific details:

"Our Enemy: Angelism" was a baccalaureate sermon delivered at the Rockefeller Memorial Chapel of the University of Chicago in 1944.

"The War of the Gods" is drawn from a paper on "The Congregational Idea" co-authored with James Bissett Pratt of Williams College and presented at a pre-World War II Yale conference of Unitarians and Congregationalists.

"Betraying the World with a Kiss" was delivered at Bond Chapel of the University of Chicago Divinity School in 1948.

"Perspectives on the Pluralistic Society" was prepared for a conference on voluntary organizations at Loyola University, Chicago, 1974.

"The Creative Thrust of Conflict" was delivered as a Unitarian Universalist Association General Assembly address at Miami, Florida in 1966.

"By Their Groups Shall Ye Know Them" was a lecture at Baylor University in Waco, Texas around 1970.

"In the Fullness of Time" was delivered at Bond Chapel in 1939.

"Originality" was a sermon at the Second Unitarian Church in Salem, MA in 1926.

"Music, the Language of Hope" (1971) and "Art, Religion, and Utopia" (1975) were delivered at the Arlington Street Church, Boston.

"Archibald Thompson Davison" was delivered *in memoriam* at Andover Chapel, Harvard Divinity School, in 1961.

For those who wish biographical information concerning Adams, beyond what has been previously noted above, I recommend two sources:

"James Luther Adams: A Biographical and Intellectual Sketch" by Max L. Stackhouse in *Voluntary Associations: Essays in Honor of James Luther Adams,* edited by D. B. Robertson (John Knox Press, 1966).

"James Luther Adams and the Unitarian Denomination" by George H. Williams in the *Andover Newton Quarterly* (January 1977).

Note may also be made of other work that is now in process. Under the sponsorship of the James Luther Adams Foundation, an autobiography of JLA is being completed. The title is *Not Without Dust and Heat.* Also, aided by a grant from the Lilly Foundation of Indianapolis, Indiana, Professor George Pickering of the University of Detroit, Mercy, has begun work on an intellectual biography of Adams. A major resource for this project is the JLA archives at the University of Syracuse, some 250 boxes of documents.

Here, then, is the context in which the *Unitarian Universalist Christian* shares with its readers these hitherto unpublished *James Luther Adams Papers.*

1. Our Enemy: Angelism

It is said that when Emerson Hall at Harvard College was being built, the question as to what motto should be carved over the main entrance was vigorously discussed by members of the faculty. Emerson Hall was to house the departments of psychology and philosophy. It was the building in which we human beings were to be studied. At the end of the spring semester, the faculty had presumably agreed upon the Protagorean maxim: *Man is the Measure of all Things.* During the summer a motto was carved in the appropriate place, but when the faculty returned in the autumn, they discovered that President Eliot had authorized a different motto from the one expected. President Eliot had selected a line from the eighth Psalm: *What is man that Thou art mindful of him?* This interrogation, as you might suppose, met with general satisfaction. The essence of the Protagorean maxim was not necessarily denied, but the new motto was properly felt to be a little more in keeping with the humility that befits human beings, even the scholar.

For that matter, scholars have described human beings in many ways. Some have said that we are tool-making animals; others have said we are the laughing animal; others have asserted that we are the political animal, and others have deemed it sufficient to say that we are an animal, with the qualification that we—*homo sapiens*—are perhaps the only species that organizes mass murder of itself. Certainly all these definitions are relevant, though perhaps none of them is adequate.

The first chapter of Genesis would seem to suggest still another answer, that we are a creature who tries to be more than human. Eve was tempted by the serpent to eat the forbidden fruit which would give us the knowledge belonging to God alone. As a result, she incurred the divine wrath and was, with her poor excuse-making husband, expelled from the garden. This primitive story reminds us of the Greek view that humanity is tragic and that our tragedy issues from the fact that we are prone to invade the realm of the gods, thus committing the sin of hubris, the excess exhibited when we try to go beyond mortal bounds. However, the strangest definition in human history is the one the psalmist gives, that we are a little lower than the angels.

Of course, this definition of the human estate sheds little light unless we know what an angel is. Hence we must, in order to understand the

147

psalmist, consider the question, "What is an angel?" Some of you need only to be reminded that when theology was still regarded as the queen of the sciences, one of the branches of this science was called angelology, the science of angels' nature and functions. Many of you may suppose that the study of angelology ended with the Middle Ages. Are we not told that the medieval doctors of the church made a specialty of discussing how many angels can stand on the point of a needle? But angelology has had a part in American higher education also. The Mathers of Boston wrote at length on the subject, and they had distinguished successors. When Timothy Dwight was President of Yale University, he gave a fully course of lectures on angelology to each class of students at Yale.

Perhaps some of you believe in the existence of angels, but those of you who do not believe in angels will inevitably raise the question: Why should I be asked to abandon my mind to the subject of angelology? I hope that you unbelievers will for a moment engage in a willing suspension of disbelief so that I may offer an apologetic for at least a brief consideration of angelology. This science need not, perhaps, be revered, but it possesses at least the value of nonsense poetry. Why does one read *Alice in Wonderland*? Our main reason for reading it is the sheer delight in nonsense, but beyond this I think we may say that there is no better way of coming to appreciate what *is* than by contemplating precisely what *is not*. By seeing the world as it is not, we become aware of the obvious that we have too much taken for granted. Nonsense verse and literature contrive to give one new perspectives. We may say, then, that although the theory that angels exist may be wholly fantastic, yet, like many other fantasies, it suggests something to us about the real world. Perhaps if we consider what the theologians have said about the angels we may the better understand what human beings are not and in this way, be reminded of what we are.

The medieval philosopher was eagerly concerned to find the answer to the question, Who are we?, and one way in which the answer was sought was to determine what we are not. This was done partly through the study of angelology. We need not pause to stress the fact that the medieval philosopher, under the influence of the Neoplatonic doctrine of emanation, believed the universe to be continuous from God to the lowest form of existence. If there were no angels, there would be a great gap in the universe. Moreover, it was thought that God, anticipating our infinite capacity for sinning, had created an innumerable host of angels in order to insure that the universe would always for the most part be good. More significant for our purpose are the attributes assigned to the angels, for example, by Thomas Aquinas. According to Aquinas, four major attributes characterize the angels. (1) They have no bodies. They are disembodied spirits or intelligences. Hence they have no senses. (2) All of their knowledge is innate. By divine illumination it is given them directly by God at the time of creation. Therefore, the angels cannot reason. They do not need to draw conclusions from premises. They have angelic knowledge by divine fiat. (3) There exist no two angels of the same species. Each individual angel constitutes a separate species. (4) The angels exist independently of things. They stand between the pure being of God and our own material and spiritual being. From this general characterization, the medieval thinker brought into bold relief the fact that our knowledge of the world comes through the medium of the senses. Since we must learn by experience and try to remember what we learn, we run the danger of forgetting valuable experiences. Moreover, we must establish community with other members of our species, and we do not live independently of things. We live with other people and we live in and through and with things. We have a mind and a soul, but they are in a body. In short, we are a little *lower* than the angels.

I suppose that most of us would say that all of these propositions about human beings are perfectly obvious. We all know that we live in a community and that we have bodies as well as minds. We know that what we learn is learned from experience in the body and in the world of things. We know that, though our children are at times assigned by the poets the role of little angels coming from heaven, which is their home, trailing clouds of glory, still their bodies need care, their minds need to be developed. We try to show them how to use their eyes, their tongues, their ears, their hands. We do not treat them as though they were pure spirits. We sometimes are even tempted to agree with the Puritan theologian, Jonathan Edwards, who called them "little vipers."

Indeed, through most of our lives we act on the principle that we are a little lower than the angels. We remember that we are dust, that our physical hunger must be satisfied, and that we must maintain social order or perish. To some people, however, these concerns seem to be worldly matters. Hence they speak of a spiritual life that is only beyond the material order. Nevertheless, even our so-called spiritual life depends upon our bodies and requires the resources of the material order. One of the most spiritual things we know is music, but music is heard through the ears, and it requires wood and steel and horse hair and cat gut and finger technique. Bach is not simply a synonym for heavenly and angelic sound.

Nevertheless, when we turn to consider our life in society, we find many people who seemingly forget that we are a little lower than the angels. Religion is thought of as being something wholly spiritual and individual, as lifting us to higher levels of apprehension and enjoyment than are possible in the world of things and rites and ceremonies. Sometimes this yearning for spirituality resorts to such extravagance as to claim that religion is something purely inward, that it needs no outward forms or social institutions. Indeed, we are frequently told that outward form only kills religion, that outward forms are mere trappings, that religion is only what we do with our solitariness.

Here again, as well as with music or poetry or architecture, religion must be seen, touched, heard, in order to be expressed or identified. A religion that has nothing to do with the community, that has nothing to do with the body, with the life of the senses, with outward forms of expression, does not exist except in the imagination. Religion must express itself through communal forms, through books, music, the spoken word, spoken prayers, as well as through buildings and sacrificial action. To claim to be religious and also not to be interested in these things is like saying that one is interested in poetry but in no specific poems; it is like saying that one is interested in government but not in legislatures and ballot boxes. There is no such thing as poetry apart from poems; and there is no such thing as government apart from constitutions or courts or police.

The religion that is purely spiritual is purely non-existent. We often hear it said that the greatest enemy of religion is materialism. This is by no means true. The greatest enemy of religion is sham spirituality, pure spirituality. It is angelism, an indifference to the needs of the body and especially of the body politic. Indeed, it was precisely the false spirituality of the Russian church which bred the needed materialism of the revolutionists. The German churches tried to be purely spiritual; they got fascism as their reward. One is reminded of Gibbon's dictum that the virtues of the clergy are much more dangerous than their vices. Religion must be realized in particular acts in order to insure its continuing life. With reason T. S. Eliot has said, "The spirit killeth, the letter giveth life." In short, angelism can kill religion.

I am not especially concerned here to derive a defense of institutional religion from the medieval angelology. The general principles implicit in the human condition have a far-reaching application to the *whole* of our life. The good life must be realized in particular acts in order to exist at all. The angel is already perfect, being only commanded to maintain appropriate status to avoid falling into the pit; in short, to avoid becoming, like Lucifer—a fallen angel.

The point is that human beings must express themselves through the institutions of the community. There is no such thing as a good person as such. He or she will be good only as a good husband or wife, a good health professional, a good lawyer or legislator, a good citizen. Anyone whose goodness does not take form in the institutions of family, school, church, and state is a person who is good for nothing. Human virtue and happiness require a local, a communal habitation. We are considerably lower than the angels.

The state of the world today helps us to understand why John Calvin asserted that despite our being created a little lower than the angels, we are now but little higher than the devils. If this seems a harsh judgment, we may at least say that anyone who sets out to be an angel by ignoring the fact of having to learn from experience, by ignoring the fact that we are members of a species, by ignoring the fact that we live in a world of things and that only through things can our spirit express itself, will end where Satan wants us to end. As Pascal put it, we are neither angels nor beasts but whoever sets out to be an angel will only end by becoming a beast.

Today we are discovering that we are so much lower than the angels that we cannot escape history. It has a way of catching up with us. We have been living in an era that thought self-interest through some pre-established harmony would create community, but we are now learning that selfish interest on the part of individuals and societies brings only chaos and death in its train. Unless we believe that Demon Chance rules the world, we recognize now that we have just the sort of world we deserve. World history is world judgment.

Yes, that is true, but this fact is only the obverse side of the human condition in the historical dimension. For us, if not for angels, history is also an arena in which divine fulfillment is possible. We are confronted with the possibility not only of judgment but also of fulfillment. This is our greatness as well as our misery. We need to act to create a world community. This will involve struggle, for peace is possible only in the teeth of strife. Peace is possible only through organized power. Civilization is always a combination of love and power. Love without power is obviously impotent. Power without love and justice is tyranny.

Today, when a great democratic revolution is under way, a great counter-revolution is also again on the move. We must not deceive ourselves. We are caught in a struggle, and we can exercise positive choice only if we accept the responsibility of making our will count. Every angel may be an island unto itself, but human beings must cooperate—or perish!

I don't count and you don't count very much as individuals alone, but together we can count if we are now willing jointly to do the humdrum work, the spade work of democracy, the work that can alone bring liberty and justice for all. To do this we must be seized by a love that will not let us go; we must be seized by the primordial love that was expressed when the morning stars sang together at the dawn of creation, the love that alone can recreate the world. If we are not grasped by this love, we shall only contribute to the poverty and insecurity of women, men and children throughout the world, and the wrath of God will be upon us.

An example of what I mean comes from my experience of a man who was working with a group of us from churches and synagogues considering the problem of relief. This man identified himself as a "conservative" and spoke in protest against there being any relief at all.

"I have worked hard," he said. "I have saved my money, and now the government comes and takes my money and gives it to these people who don't want to work."

Nevertheless, the man was persuaded to call personally on the people across the tracks who were on relief. He visited family after family, saw children without proper food or housing, without shoes, saw fathers who could not find work or who were ill, saw emaciated mothers trying to maintain something of human dignity in the midst of poverty and degradation. Gradually, his attitude began to change. Finally, one evening at a meeting of the people in the neighborhood, he heard a young mother on his list tell her story again. She was only 35 years, but she looked as though she were 50; she was poorly clad; she had few teeth left; and she was already hunchbacked from her strenuous life.

Suddenly the former pseudo-conservative jumped to his feet and almost shouted: "Why do you stand for this, you people on relief? I wouldn't take it. I would steal first. I want to know why you don't have the spunk to start a revolution?"

Hyperbole, you say? An emotionalist, you say? Yes, he indulged for a moment in undisciplined thinking, in undisciplined sobbing. But that evening a man was converted. He got mad about our inhumanity to other human beings. Let us hope that he did what all who know they are a little lower than the angels must do. Let us hope that he stayed mad and went on to organize his indignation.

2. Religion's Word Against Religion

When we speak of true religion and false religion, we may, of course, use nice words, polite words, academic words, respectable words; but when the Bible speaks of false religion, it speaks of blasphemy, of hypocrisy, of idolatry. These are rough words, harsh words:

> Depart from me; I never knew you, you who work iniquity.
> Woe unto you, hypocrites! You devour widows' houses, and for a pretense, make long prayers.

> If the light that is in you be darkness, how great is that darkness.

Evidently one of the greatest mistakes we can make is to suppose that all religion is good, or that religion is something sacrosanct, something that should be exempt from criticism, something that can escape from the wrath of God. The prophets of Israel and the prophet of Nazareth knew better. They knew that the Devil is a gentleman, that evil in order to make headway in the world needs the cloak of religion. They even give us to understand that "religion" is the subtlest and most dangerous enemy of God, that "religion" is our human trick for rejecting justice; it is our way of "using" God as an instrument of an ungodly policy.

I once had some conversations with the Nazi Archbishop of Germany, who said that Hitler had been sent by God to fulfill German destiny. I ventured to remind him that the God of the ancient Hebrew prophets had a controversy with the people of Israel, for they thought God had a special destiny for them because of their blood and soil and regardless of their disobedience to the command of justice. The archbishop jumped from his chair and shouted, "How could God be against *us*? God is in *us*."

The Germans met destiny with blood and tears partly because they could not hear the word against religion, the word against their church religion before Hitler came to power, and the word against Nazi German Christian religion after he came to power. It is also worth recalling that the old Russian Orthodox Church brought destruction upon itself just because it did not proclaim or could not hear the word against religion.

Religions such as these became what John Milton might have called a darkness visible. Perhaps it was for this reason that the Archbishop of Canterbury said, "It is a grave mistake to suppose that God is exclusively, or even chiefly, concerned with religion." The first word of prophetic religion is the word against religion. The Old Testament prophets went so far as to declare that the false prophets of their time went awhoring after false gods. Yes, they said that false believers are prostitutes!

The prophet Hosea had an experience which made clear to him what false religion is. He married a woman who became unfaithful to him. She pretended that she was faithful to her husband, but she was essentially a paramour. Brooding over this sad experience, Hosea came to the conclusion that just as his wife was a kept woman, so the false religion of his people was a "kept" religion. It had all the outer signs of respectability; it received the praise that belongs to piety and virtue; it gave an outward appearance of charity, but it was actually a prostitute.

What an astonishing thought! Very seldom are atheists attacked in the Bible. Hosea hurls his charges at the religious people. Evidently irreligion is not the dangerous thing. The dangerous thing is the false imitation. It claims to serve God, but it is really already possessed. Or, to put it another way, it has taken God into its possession and domesticated deity; it has a "kept" God that does their bidding rather than commanding their lives. A "kept" religion, then, has a "kept" God who rules only for the sake of those who do the "keeping" and not for all the children of God. For it the cross is only a double-cross. That is why the people of this age and every age must never be deaf to the painful, prophetic word of religion's word against religion.

3. The War Of The Gods

Each age of humanity has its own illusions. One of the characteristic illusions of recent history has been the assumption that our civilization has progressed beyond the possibility of engaging in a war over religion. The proposition that "people will no longer fight about religion" became part of the modern Credo, the implication being that religion no longer matters enough for us to fight about it. The facts, however, do not support this comforting belief, for religion—even the religion that people will fight about—has a strange way of intruding itself into the most civilized societies. In actuality, our age is now engulfed in one of the bloodiest struggles over religion known to history. Indeed, our period might well be characterized as the New Wars of Religion.

In appearance, the conflicts of our age are more directly concerned with rival economic, racial and political creeds than were the Wars of Religion in the seventeenth century, but in reality they are the age-old religious conflicts. Indeed, it is precisely in these areas of economic, racial and political struggle that one finds today the best evidence for the familiar adage that "people are incurably religious." This aphorism has, of course, been most frequently quoted in support of the idea that we cannot in the long run escape or resist the claims of true religion, and there is some basis for this idea. The Hound of Heaven "on following feet" has again and again prevented people from finding enduring value apart from devotion to the Highest, but the adage has a much broader application than that. It suggests also what many modern people have naively overlooked, namely, that there is such a thing as religion in reverse; there is a certain perverseness in human nature which causes people to be religious in spite of themselves. When we do not give our highest loyalty to God, we end by surrendering our life to the service of an idol. We are so incurably religious that we abhor the vacuum of religious experience—the empty altar. Or to change the figure, if we unseat the Most High from the throne, then inevitably we set up a substitute. A few people here and there do for a time escape the necessity of choosing between the Most High and a substitute,—seemingly they do not feel the need of the lighted altar, but the escape is only temporary. They too are in the end willy nilly drawn into the idolatry of their tribe, for every tribal god that is worshipped by the many finally demands sacrifice (and gets it) from the few who have remained "above the battle." No one is ultimately immune to the contagion of the false religions or exempt from the destruction they bring.

Human history seems to be a history of the recurrent fall of old tribal gods and the rise of new ones. Half-gods are Protean creatures. They disappear only to reappear in new forms. Observing this recurrent tendency in the history of the race, the philosopher David Hume once suggested that the "natural" religion of humanity is polytheism. Certainly there is much in human history, even in modern history, to support this thesis.

What, after all, is polytheism? It is the giving of absolute status and loyalty to limited, finite objects, to deified sticks and stones, to rivers and mountains, to sun and stars, or—if we turn our attention to "civilized" polytheisms—it is the giving of absolute loyalty to such local deities as the state, the race, the economic system. All of these are forms of idol worship, whether primitive or "civilized." But the idols never remain in "place." Polytheism is never static. A war of the gods always ensues, and a hierarchy of the gods usually emerges with one god on the top, but the competition does not end even then. This is the "cunning" of polytheism. Having conquered in its own tribe, having fed on ambition, the "crescent" god of one tribe wants to be the god of other tribes. Therefore, the struggle begins again, the struggle between the primary gods of the different tribes. The different local deities enter into internecine struggle.

Precisely this process has been taking place in our time. Within each of the nations of the modern world a number of gods have been vying for first place, the gods of blood and soil, the gods of the economic systems, and the gods of the State. They may not be given the names of gods. Nevertheless, they gain possession of the inner life of the tribe and provide the dynamic or the "drives" of the common life. These drives constitute modern religions, pushing people into the destructive vortex of the competing polytheisms, the war of the gods. Indeed, this powerful, self-destructive impulse operates as a sort of "civilized" demonic possession impelling the group to race down the Gadarene slope to catastrophe. This is what is happening on the human stage at this moment. The devotion of the different tribes to bourgeois capitalism, to imperialism, to the "superior race" or to the omnipotent state, has brought the old "cunning" of polytheism into play. Each of the creeds that has set up its bloated claims to allegiance has called forth a struggle that is no less savage than that between primitive tribes of the forest. Having attributed highest value to incompatible ultimates, people must fight.

No doubt the greatest god of the modern age is nationalism. A French writer of a generation ago suggested that one can tell what the religion of any group of people is by determining for what they die. If we apply this test, he added, we must conclude that nationalism is the average modern man's religion. It is for nationalism, our other religion, that modern citizens have died by the millions. The American, the British, the French, the German, the Japanese nationalistic prides and ambitions coupled with the inflated claims of imperialism, of monopoly capitalism, of racism, of Fascism, and of Communism, have brought the local deities of the planet and their "possessed" devotees into a life-and-death struggle that threatens to decimate the peoples of the earth. It is true that not all these tribal deities deserve the same rank in the modern pandemonium of the gods. Some of them are more largely compounded of death than others. Some may even have the promise of "new life" within them, but in the light of contemporary history, is not Hume's suggestion essentially correct that the "natural" religion of humanity is polytheism?

To be sure, the polytheistic tendencies of our time have by no means been confined to the political and economic and racial spheres. Essentially the same sort of absolutism is also to be found in certain religious groups. Certain types of Christianity must be included among the polytheisms: for example, those types of Christianity which have given an absolute status to the Bible "from cover to cover" or to a church that claims to possess the infallible truth once and for all delivered. The point that needs stressing is that almost every place we look today we find incurably religious humanity attributing to things of earth the quality of sovereignty that belongs to God alone.

The iron vice in which all these polytheisms are caught is authoritarianism, the claim that a given form of society or a given and exclusive set of principles is above criticism. In all of these polytheisms, people are asked to submit to some sort of Fuehrer. To ask a radical question is to commit blasphemy. To assert that no one group of people has a monopoly on truth or destiny is to be guilty of "cosmopolitanism" and of disloyalty to the "superior race," or of ideological defense of the middle class, or of a lack of patriotism, or of the sin against the Holy Ghost.

In this arena of the war of the gods with its bedlam of power politics, the democratic churches—with their faith in the God of the prophets and of Jesus—have a special mission to perform. It is their mission, and the mission of other groups that have elective affinities with them, to point to a way beyond these polytheisms. How can this happen?

The democratic or congregationalist churches make their final appeal to reason and a critical estimate of the evidence. This is another way of saying that congregationalism recognizes no specific authority as absolute. For the congregationalist, life cannot have enduring value if either church or state, whether a Holy Book or an economic system is given some special privilege whereby it may impose from above the form which the society shall take or the limits of freedom that are to be observed. The setting up of any such external authority is in actuality a presumptuous and even blasphemous attempt on the part of some ruling class or clique (priestly or racial, economic or political) to usurp the place of God. No free people's worship can be given to any people-made God. This does not mean that the democratic or congregationalist churches reject or neglect the Bible or the Christian tradition. It does mean that these churches were among the early fighters for freedom, freedom from hierarchical authority, freedom from "cover to cover" Biblicism, freedom of the church from state control. The congregationalists were also among the early fighters for freedom to worship God according to conscience (and even for freedom not to worship God if one chooses), freedom under the great Taskmaster's eye to form the kind of church and society which conscience and justice and reverence demand.

The freedom of the congregationalists reaches even to the doctrines that articulate the common faith, for they assert the freedom to discuss the doctrines of the faith as against being told what to think. They recognize that the symbols of their faith are themselves earthen vessels and thus subject to criticism and change. They therefore expect that there will always be devout people who will not be able to use the traditional symbols without embarrassment or reservation. Unity does not require uniformity. Hence, the congregationalists refuse to dogmatize about how God shall be defined. Each usually has his or her own opinion but recognizes that she or he may be mistaken and that a neighbor, whose notion of God differs in many details, may be right. Each new insight into Nature which science brings us, each new experience of the human heart, each new discovery of the intellect, each new experiment in the social process, and each new movement in history, may add to the revelation of the Divine.

Thus the congregationalist or democratic churches stand in a prophetic tradition that permits, nay even requires, self-criticism for the sake of its own health and vitality; but they also stand in a creative tradition that asserts that we can fulfill our destiny as human beings only when we rise above the absolutisms of race, state, and church to the worship of a God whom no individual or group can domesticate and impress into their own private service. Freedom is a gift of God, and the freedom that we derive from God cannot manifest itself with deepest meaning or in richest fulfillment unless it is integrally related to the creative power upon which all existence depends, the power that reconciles and overcomes the conflicts of the half-gods and the idolatries, the power that sustains and transforms the world.

The congregationalist churches, therefore, appeal to something beyond and greater than humanity as the basis of their freedom. As a guide and check to this freedom, they also rely upon a love that in some degree inheres in everything that exists: upon a love that is a gift to us, a love that we freely appropriate in the very continuance and enrichment of our existence, a love that takes possession of us and that will not let us go, a love that transforms our vanity, our perverted freedom, our selfishness, into a cooperative growing comradeship between human beings and the God of all love. Faith in this God of love induces a loving spirit among us, and faith in this God of freedom induces among us a spirit of freedom. These are the two foci of congregationalism as an immanent force in human society.

Christianity as understood by the democratic churches is essentially concerned with both the individual and society, but it is not limited to any one society nor wholly subject to any state. It is essentially universal and transcends all national lines both in space and in time. It has to do with the local and temporal and with the universal and eternal. For this reason it is necessarily and radically opposed to every sort of polytheism or idolatry. If the half-gods are to be overcome, that will happen through a free or democratic fellowship of freedom and love among congregationalists themselves, as well as between them and those of "other folds." Indeed, amidst the war of the gods, congregationalists demand that they be an inner fellowship dedicated to a larger human fellowship and companionship with God, the ground of all true fellowship, the author and finisher of all true faith, whose law is love and whose service is perfect freedom.

4. Betraying the World With a Kiss

Jean Paul Sartre's play *No Exit* is a classic expression of existential loss of human fellowship. The scene is hell, which is presented as a French drawing room in Second Empire style. The author depicts the inferno of human isolation, the loneliness and despair, the alienation of three souls: a man and two women. They are all three lost and dead, imprisoned and condemned to the eternal torture of keeping each other company. For them there is No Exit from this torture of loneliness even though they are together. They share no common values which can give them dignity either as individuals or as a group locked in their room in hell. The souls in Dante's Inferno retain human dignity; they seem to be worthy of punishment; but the souls in Sartre's hell have lost even that dignity. The three people struggle for each other's attention but do so without believing they have anything worth giving and without believing the others would really esteem anything worth giving anyway. In the end, the man cannot decide whether his own spiritual leprosy allies him more strongly with one woman or with the other one. Nevertheless, all of them are compelled to remain together for eternity without any other companions. Finally, in desperation the man says, "There is no need for hot pokers in this place. Hell is—other people." That is, hell is other people with whom one may not enter into moral community.

In its emphasis upon alienation, contemporary existentialism finds a place alongside many other criticisms of our society. Sigmund Freud conceived of the discontents of civilization as such as a sickness, a neurosis, a polymorphous separation of person from person. Friedrich Nietzsche viewed the bourgeois society as creating the weakness and mediocrity and loneliness of individualism: "Oh, loneliness," cries Zarathustra in protest, "Oh Thou my Home, loneliness."

Karl Marx depicted the bourgeois society as split in two; it is in a state of alienation through the class struggle. Community, sociality, has lost its sacred character. The middle classes find only irresponsible ownership of private property sacred. Bourgeois thinking thus rests society completely on the individual and dissolves society into the natural automatic law of economics. The individual becomes a mass separated from God. Religious and communal ties have been dissolved in a *laissez-faire* society. In its distress this society appeals to nationalism, our other

162

religion, to create solidarity and to protect itself against allegedly alien ideas.

The sociologist Max Weber describes the same process in similar terms. The development of capitalism and the introduction of an impersonal ethic involved the bringing of calculation into human relations, displacing the old religious relationship. A kind of immoralism is upon us, he says: "The relations between the mortgage creditor and the property which was pledged for debt, or between the endorser and the bill of exchange, would at least be exceedingly difficult if not impossible to moralize."

In literature, Franz Kafka, the novelist, sees people alienated from each other by their striving for prestige and by the guilt arising from the desire for self-justification. They are also alienated from the center and fount of meaning, what he calls the Castle. Thomas Mann, in *The Magic Mountain,* symbolizes the bourgeois society by a sanitorium which is nothing but an island on which the sick have landed for a while in order to await their slow death.

At the turn of the century, a German artistic magazine was initiated in protest against a meaningless bourgeois world. The magazine's title, *The Island,* symbolizes the artists' desire to retire to "a beautiful island existence" where a fragile tower of beauty could be built. In their distance, these artists asserted that the modern mass society is only part of a society. Recalling St. Paul's symbol of a coordinated body, they described contemporary society as only parts of a human being in community with parts of other human beings. Parts of a body or of any object were described and enumerated. "Two legs walk," they say. "A knee walks lonely through this world." These characterizations of people remind one of the poet who compared separated people to the empty spaces in a piece of lattice work called civilization.

Consider the principal message of Søren Kierkegaard. When in his retreat from the outer world he believes his alienation from God is overcome, he finds solidarity only in the moment, in the individual. The individual, even the regenerate individual, is alone, having made the flight of the alone to the alone. We may think that Kierkegaard has been properly condemned as a bourgeois pietist by one of our contemporary theologians. We may feel that he has been properly censured for not having developed a concept of the community or of the church, but we cannot deny the existence of the loneliness, the isolation, the alienation, the despair of which he writes. Those who do not see it and feel it in themselves are also isolated. They live on an island where they cannot see that fascism and communism arose out of a demand for *Gemeinschaft* and comradeship. Those who do not see or feel the isolation may be so isolated that they do not even see what is visible about them: "the people across the tracks." Not only does "education" protect us from seeing such people even when we look at them, but religion itself has a way of protecting us by its deceptive diverting of attention to the ineffable heights. We do not see the destitute family living in an abandoned building which has been taken over by homeless people. The more people are separated from each other, the less they care about each other, and the less they even recognize their own shabbiness.

Whether we consider human beings from a purely sociological or from a theological-ethical standpoint, they can be understood only in relationship. Our creatureliness and our dignity is understood in relation to the creative source in which we participate. Our creatureliness, like our dignity, is rooted in what the poet, Gerard Manley Hopkins, calls the deep down freshness of things. I may be a self, but my self is not ultimate. My relation to the creative and re-creative power of the divine is the essence of my human nature. In this relation arises my fate and my freedom, and in my relation to other selves who likewise are supported and judged, I find my responsibility not only for my own inner life but also in my confrontation of the need of my neighbor. My freedom exists in the context of independence and dependence and interdependence. My separateness is the precondition for both freedom and unfreedom, for both companionship and alienation. My dependence is both freedom and unfreedom. My interdependence with others is both freedom and unfreedom. My separation is necessary for both freedom and unfreedom. My freedom and my responsibility before God and among other human beings require the overcoming of alienation in a love and justice that preserve the independence of the self and other selves. Thus my freedom involved a group freedom as well as an individual freedom, a group unfreedom as well as an individual unfreedom, a group responsibility as well as an individual responsibility. This is the great truth long ago envisaged by the Old Testament prophets. God's covenant is with the group as well as with the individual; guilt and salvation are both individual and social.

Obviously freedom and responsibility require more than the abstract understanding of freedom and responsibility. They require also more than a mere enunciation of the eternal demands of love and justice. Perhaps Jane Addams had this in mind when she said that "we must struggle lest the moral law become a far-off abstraction utterly separated from the active life."

There is a frustrating alienation that ensues if the Christian does not achieve an application of general principles to a particular situation. This frustration reveals the need for middle axioms or middle principles to mediate between universal, abstract ethical principles and a particular structural situation. This is not the sort of frustration that Jane Addams had in mind. It is rather the frustration that comes from failure actually to make decisions and to take responsibility. Therefore, it is to the need for participation in what we might call middle organizations, and to the alienation that results from the neglect of this participation, that I should like to direct your attention.

The most important responsibility any person has is in the fulfillment of her or his vocation in the narrow sense of that word, but the fulfillment of freedom and responsibility requires more than the performance of one's vocational duties. This is especially true in a democratic society where mere obedience to the state violates the very spirit and letter of the democratic process. The Christian or the citizen in a democratic state has the responsibility of helping to shape the social policies. It is just the absence of the possibility of this kind of participation that gives a certain provincialism to the New Testament community. Anyone in the democratic society who is content with striving to do vocational work well is not yet a citizen. As an epitaph in an old Puritan burial ground reads:

> Here lies John MacDonald
> Born a man
> Died a grocer.

Freedom and responsibility in a democratic society require disciplines peculiar to that society. Leaving aside the important question as to the nature of the democratic society as such, and leaving aside also the question as to how moral judgments are formed and transformed, we must confront the question as what the disciplines of freedom are in a democracy.

Freedom is primarily related neither to the individual as such nor to the individual in pursuit of a vocation. The work of culture is not done by any community as a whole, nor yet by individuals, but by smaller organized groups, which are organized to integrate the community. These groups, often called voluntary associations, are especially characteristic of American democracy. The point is that we are never in any exclusive sense members of society at large. Rather, we are members of social groups within every society. One of the most important of these groupings in modern society is the business corporation, but the noncommercial or nonprofit organizations which are formed to shape the policy of the society are equally important. One might say that the club and association have tended to become in the noneconomic life of our society what the corporation is to its economic life. Some of these associations are merely adjuncts of business corporations, or they are associations for the maintenance of vocational standards. The associations that are merely adjuncts of business corporations are usually more concerned with affecting the behavior of nonmembers then they are with affecting the life of their own members. These are the pressure groups. The vocational associations exist mainly for the purpose of affecting the members, but the voluntary associations that give the fullest opportunity for expressing freedom and for assuming responsibility are the groups that aim to work for the common welfare and seek to affect the life of all. They seek the rewards of a more harmonious society or of a better government.

One of the ways in which human alienation is continued and aggravated in the world is through the neglect of these middle groupings. This neglect takes two major forms: the neglect that results from a merely general concern with social responsibility and the neglect that takes the form of concern for only direct person-to-person relations. Both of these forms of neglect are characteristic of certain types of religious people, even of people who praise a Kierkegaard for having discovered "the nodal points of the individual's irrevocable responsibility before God." This inmost sense of responsibility is the navel-string of creation, but the creation of the good society under the great Taskmaster's eye will never be brought about by the Kierkegaards alone. They are irresponsible in so far as the navel-string of their responsibility only leads the Christian to will one thing, a more Christlike spirit in person-to-person relations. This to betray the world with a kiss.

St. Paul's metaphor concerning the body and its parts needs a new exegesis. The parts should be interpreted not only as individuals but also as groups. The New Testament does not directly concern itself with what we have called middle organizations. This fact is understandable if we recall that the voluntary association, like the concept of the professions, is almost entirely a modern idea. The point can be expressed in another way. In earlier and simpler societies the individual usually belonged only to three groups: a community, a church, and a family. Today the individual must work through corporations and through voluntary associations in order to have a workaday vocation and assume responsibility in living with contemporaries. Insofar as Christian ethics does not stress this fact, it creates irrelevance and irresponsibility. It creates a slipping clutch, perhaps a beautifully purring motor but still a slipping clutch. Even people who demand a change in the very structure of society may reflect the bad influence of the church in the direction of irrelevance or irresponsibility if they merely form study groups. Indeed, we should not expect the study of even one hundred best books to contribute to democracy in a responsible way if it does not induce those being educated for freedom to discover group activities as the real centers of responsibility and persuade people to do the hum-drum work of democracy.

It is important to note here that it would be entirely false to suppose that Protestants historically have ignored the middle organizations. Both within the church and outside the church the most significant social changes have been effected by the middle organizations. Actually many of the voluntary associations were brought into being under the influence of Calvinism, pietism, the evangelical awakening, and a host of other Protestant movements. This very fact is a sign of Protestant vitality and a consequence of its radical laicism, its principle of the priesthood of all believers. These voluntary organizations have become the major instruments of modern prophetic religion, whether it is churchly or secular. They have been the means whereby a moral like-mindedness has been created in the citizenry and then been given social expression to the felt demands. They have at once provided fellowship and organized social power for the changing of both church and society.

Here we can see their greatest significance for the Protestant strategy of social change. The Roman Catholic church aims to affect society directly through the established church which uses the secular arm. Operating as a political power, it maintains a world-wide diplomatic corps for directly dealing—on churchly authority—with the state; and, pending restoration of ecclesiastical control over society at large, it establishes Roman Catholic political parties, professional and commercial associations, and even Catholic trade unions.

The Protestant free church strategy calls for no establishment of religion; it calls for no diplomatic corps, no Protestant political party, no Protestant interlocking directorates, no Protestant trade unions. It does not claim to provide *the* official Christian program. Eschewing official blueprints, it calls upon people to take up the priesthood of all believers by cooperating in the shaping of middle principles to make the Christian ethic relevant and by cooperating with the people in the middle organizations which shape our common life. In the social and political arena, this is the Protestant vocation. It is a vocation that calls for participation in the group process that criticizes and moulds the structures of society. This larger vocation can alone keep meaningful the narrower vocations of daily work, for it alone can create and maintain a society in which there will be work for all and in which work will be worthy of the name of a "calling."

The commandment to love one's neighbor calls for a robust, delighted interest in other people, but it calls for more than that. It calls for a robust, delighted interest in the institutions that give *body* to human responsibility and freedom and that overcome human alienation through human fellowship. This is no time to betray the world with a kiss. As a true wayfaring Christian, John Milton, says to us across the centuries:

> "I cannot praise a fugitive and cloistered virtue, unexercised and unbreathed, but never sallies out and sees her adversary, but slinks out of the race, where that immortal garland is to be run for, not without dust and heat.

5. Perspectives on the Pluralistic Society

In the annals of heresy, the certified heretics are generally presented as having been heretical in their theological doctrines, in their deviation from official dogma. In actuality, however, the heretics have been equally significant by reason of their social-institutional views, and specifically by reason of their promotion of voluntary associations. A study of the word *heresy* in the sixteenth century reveals that its fundamental meaning at that time is not to be discerned in the specific theological doctrines they promoted but rather in the root meaning of the word in Greek — free choice. The heretics were heretical because they adopted the *voluntary* principle.

Martin Luther is credited with having said that you must do your own believing and your own dying, but Luther did not believe that the intention of doing one's own believing could in the slightest degree justify the forming of a religious association organization independent of the Establishment. For Luther the religious association within which one was to do personal believing was the association sponsored by the Elector. Religion turned out to be a territorial matter. To be even more specific, historian Jakob Burckhardt asserted that the religion that prevailed in any territory in the sixteenth century was the one that possessed the strongest battalions.

The presupposition of the *Corpus Christianum* was that uniformity of faith is a moral-spiritual prerequisite for maintaining the fabric and integrity of the society at large. Heresy in the sense of the voluntary principle was, therefore, held to be subversive of the stability of society. In that historical context, therefore, heretical groups or sects of the late Middle Ages and of the Reformation period were voluntary organizations. Accordingly Max Weber has asserted that the sect represents the prototype of the modern voluntary organization. To be sure, some of the sects denied authenticity to any other sect or church, but other groups, especially the left-wing mystical groups, rejected this exclusiveness. On the Continent in the sixteenth century, sects were almost entirely liquidated.

Ernst Troeltsch has classified these sects as withdrawing and aggressive, the withdrawing sects removing themselves into isolation from the sinful world, and the aggressive sects attempting to bring about social change within the society. One must wait until the seventeenth and eighteenth centuries in England and North America to encounter a relatively successful assertion of the voluntary principle. Thus we can say that the heretical sects of the Middle Ages and English and American Puritan Nonconformity, in principle, constitute the origin of modern pluralistic society.

We should note here some characteristic features of the left-wing Puritans: voluntary membership in the covenanted or "gathered" community; separation of church and state; the principle of the progressive interpretation of truth (the doctrine of the Holy Spirit); tolerance and the protection of minorities within the covenanted community or in the society at large; the rights of the laity (the principle of the priesthood of all believers or the principle of the consent of the governed), in short, governance by discussion. The collection plate in the service of worship in a gathered congregation may be taken as a symbol of the voluntary congregational independence of the state and of the belief that unbelievers should not be required to lend support. These ideas came into history not without dust and heat. According to a view held widely today among historians, the modern democratic state was born out of an analogy between the doctrine of the voluntary church in the 17th-century conventicles. In important respects John Locke gave secular expression to the ideas of the left-wing Puritans. He defined the church as a voluntary organization.

Ideas such as these emerged not only from religious groups. In the seventeenth century, demands for voluntarism were breaking out all over, in attack upon the political and the economic as well as upon the ecclesiastical Establishment. From similar principles there emerged also a new ethos for secular voluntary associations. It is extremely difficult to sort out the ingredient ideas and strategies. It would be highly instructive if we were to identify the personnel, for we would find that the people who were promoting the voluntary principle in congregational circles were also promoting this principle in political and economic groups. The Levellers may be taken as an example here and the left-wing Whigs of the eighteenth century. Within a fairly short time we see emerging political parties and also the principle of loyal opposition. By the end of the first quarter of the eighteenth century, the Quakers had worked out the principle features and strategies of the modern pressure group in face of the state and of the economic order. In general, we observe here a dispersion of power and responsibility in groups that bring about innovation or resistance to it.

Here we must give critical attention to Max Weber's conception of the Protestant ethic. Weber, like R. H. Tawney later, has shown that in practice the Protestant ethic became one of the supports for the spirit of capitalism. This kind of Protestant piety issued in an individualism that effectively segregated piety from broad social responsibility, especially in the sphere of economics. However as a consequence of centering attention upon economic behavior, Weber overlooked an extremely important feature of the new pluralism emanating from left-wing Puritanism. In the eighteenth and nineteenth centuries, the Protestant groups and secular fellow-travelers spawned or participated in voluntary associations that offered sharp criticism of what Weber calls "the Protestant ethic," and they initiated a wide variety of social reforms. Voluntary associations criticized the state and the church and economic developments. Weber's conception of the Protestant ethic is egregiously lopsided. In his defense, one must say that he repeatedly asserted that in his study, he was concentrating attention upon economic, and not political, behavior. Nevertheless, the average student and scholar has succumbed to misleading clichés about a Protestant ethic devoted to thrift and "the gospel of wealth."

By means of our seven-league-boot tour of modern Western society, we have observed major ingredients of a pluralistic society. Pluralism may be defined in two ways: first, descriptively; and second, normatively. The term is used to describe a social system in which authority is distributed among a number of autonomous, yet interrelated and interdependent, groups, some of them voluntary and others nonvoluntary. As a normative concept, pluralism holds that a system of autonomous groups is morally desirable and is to be preferred to the concentration of authority in any one set of institutions. These groups are classified as nonvoluntary and voluntary, the state and the family being in important respects nonvoluntary. The state, then, is one association among many associations; it is created by the community and given delegated powers by it. In terms of federalist theory, the state as a nonvoluntary association is itself pluralist in the correlation and tension between federal, state, and municipal configurations, and also in the separation of powers between the executive, legislative, judicial, and administrative branches.

Voluntary associations also are often classified as instrumental and expressive, the former aiming in the main to effect public opinion and policy. These associations stand between the state and the family, between the state and the economic order, between the state and the individual; and in a special way, they are intermediary associations. Therefore, the pluralistic society involves an ecology of associations which presupposes a separation of powers not only within the several branches of public government but also between public and private governments. All of this in both theory and practice may be said to have issued from the initial heresy of men and women's decision to extend their choices in the face of a centralized Establishment. Much of this is summarized or presupposed in James Madison's Federalist Paper No. 10.

If we left our account as it stands, we would have an attractive portrait of the pluralistic society. John Bunyan in the seventeenth century composed a charming parable of pluralist ecology. "Christians," he said, "are like the several flowers in the garden that have upon each of them the dew of heaven which, being shaken with the wind, they let fall their dew at each other's roots, whereby they are jointly nourished of each other."

This view of the projected human situation presupposed the providential working of an automatic harmony. The early Protestants assumed that by the inspiration of the Holy Spirit the untethered interpretation of Scripture would issue in divine truth. The Independents of the seventeenth century assumed that an automatic providential harmony would ensue if the Holy Spirit were not prevented from blowing where it listeth. Adam Smith, for his part, apparently believed that we could rely upon a providential Invisible Hand to bring about ecological harmony in a world of free trade and free enterprise.

Several things got in the way of this pattern of equilibrated harmony, bringing it into imbalance. One of these things has been the development of the industrial, commercial corporation, an association that is generally not considered to be a voluntary association because its purpose is the direct economic emolument of the participant. The modern corporation touches every aspect of our lives, and in many ways it is an institutionalized expression of our way of life since we live in a corporate society. Adam Smith could have agreed with this statement, but he did not envisage the appearance of giant corporations or the so-called corporate community.

Various chronologies or morphologies of economic corporate growth have been contrived to graph the emergence of the corporate community, tracing the corporation from the medieval borough or guild to the liberal stage when, through government favor and protection, it became a self-determinative, unaccountable association supported at crucial points by subsidy, to the contemporary corporation issuing from the managerial revolution. This acquisition of crescent perpetuity confirms Chief Justice Marshall's comparison of the corporation to an "immortal being." Like Adam Smith, however, John Marshall did not envisage the arrival of the giant corporation or the transnational corporation. However, Henry Demarest Lloyd in the 1890s asserted that the abbreviation U.S.A. should be read to mean the United Syndicalists of America. The World Council of Churches recognizes the new situation for Christian ethics in the fact that the corporate community is more powerful than the state. Indeed, the American Congress has been described as the clearinghouse of the special interest pressure groups.

Corporation advertising is used to effect postponement of legislation on environmental protection or on application of safety devices or anti-pollution devices on automobiles. Moreover, advertising for the sale of goods is practically coercive at the consumer end of television and radio. The Federal Communications Commission has never seriously considered adopting the requirement that advertising on TV and radio be confined to the first or last ten minutes of the hour, as is the practice in certain European countries. Finally, moreover, both advertising and lobbying are deductible as "ordinary and necessary business expenses."

Ralph Nader has made us aware of the fact that a basic flaw in the present system of corporation power is the dominance of producer over consumer interests. Competition among producers no longer provides sufficient restraints to protect consumers, not to mention the influence of producers on administrative agencies in the government. In short, the principle of the consent of the governed among consumers is largely ineffective in face of corporation power. Indeed, the consent of the governed in the political as well as in the economic sphere is partly an engineered consent. So much has corporate power corrupted the pluralist ecology that certain political scientists have developed an elitist theory of democracy to describe the new situation. Much of this literature is briefly and ably analyzed in Anne Freedman and Constance Smith's book on *Voluntary Associations*.

In any event, I must recognize that the charges I have made regarding corporate power are subject to dispute and to a variety of interpretations. Much can be said for a theory of countervailing powers; also for the notion that enormous corporate power is indispensable in a technological society; and also for the notion that many of the abuses attach to bureaucratization, whether in a capitalist society or a welfare state or in a socialist economy.

No dispute is supportable, however, if we say that our pluralistic society in the twentieth century has not substantially changed the proportion of the population which lives in poverty without proper education or health care. Moreover, our pluralist society has retained large residues of racism; slums and ghettoes are a part of the orders of the day. In face of this situation, we would indulge only in hollow homiletic rhetoric if we should say that as in the sixteenth and seventeenth centuries, we need a new Reformation.

So far as policy oriented voluntary associations are concerned, we must recognize that they are largely a middle class phenomenon. Even then, they represent a small minority movement. Mass political apathy prevails. Devotion to one's own family takes precedence over larger public responsibilities. The situation is analogous to that obtaining in the corporations: the growth of the corporation takes precedence over concern for the public weal.

What shall we say of the churches as voluntary organizations? Apart from the fact that they largely promote privatization of piety, the very principle of voluntarism has issued in fragmentation. James Madison once said that it would be a great danger to democracy if the nation were to have only one church; it would dominate the halls of government. The spirit of congregational polity, regardless of the actual polity, serves to keep people apart, all the more by reason of the ethnic and class character of the churches. Indeed, denominationalism in its turn compounds the isolation of each from the other. Denominationalism in American life has served, in some measure, to keep the prophetic forces from working with each other. The time is ripe for prophetic forces to enter into new coalition not only across denominational boundaries but also in collaboration with secular, nonchurch forces. Even within the churches we may perhaps see some promise in cooperation between liberal Protestants and the left-wing of the evangelicals. Certain forms and degrees of coalition have been promoted by the interdenominational council, but we should consider the possibility and also the symbolic attraction of assisting to bring about cooperation, for example, between the elderly and the youth. It is precisely in segments of society where alienation is acutely felt that urgent demand for emancipation is to be found. Moreover, particularly in smaller cities, policy oriented secular organizations are feeble, if not nonexistent. Would it not be possible for prophetically minded people in the churches to collaborate with and to enhance the strength of these secular organizations? Perhaps concentration of effort on particular policies, instead of on a wide range of issues, is the appropriate strategy, especially with respect to particular policies pertinent for the local community. The point is that we have at present something less than a pluralist society, and from the past we surely have learned that automatic harmony is not available. The God of all history expects all of us who belong to the hidden covenant of justice and peace to find new ways of expressing and eliciting responsibility not only for individual behavior but also for the character of our institutions. Strong beliefs win strong people and make them stronger. It was strong beliefs that initially called forth the heretics who asserted: We venture to *choose.*

6. The Wrath and Love of God

Charles A. Bennett, a Yale University professor, was walking in the country near New Haven. When coming over a little hillock, he observed in the distance a meeting house which seemed by the accident of perspective to have over its roof a large billboard. In a momentary absence of mind, he misread it to say: GORTON'S GOD—NO BONES. Immediately, of course, he realized that he had misread the sign and that it actually announced: GORTON'S COD—NO BONES.

A similar absence of mind might be said to operate in some people's reading or misreading of the character of the physical and moral and spiritual order in which our lives are cast. Perhaps Dr. Bennett's misreading of the billboard was actually conditioned by his own often expressed suspicion that the God of many people is a God with no bones, a flabby, spineless non-entity pushed around and manipulated by a self-indulgent humanity, a God that exudes only a warm, sentimental glow of indiscriminate indulgence.

Precisely because of this it should be rewarding from time to time to reflect on passages in the Bible about the last judgment. These may remind us of the full-blooded vigor and rigor of the message of primitive Christianity. Its God was not a God without bones. The early Christians, like the Jewish prophets before them, believed that we are confronted in existence by an order that has a definite character that makes certain demands upon us, demands that may not be ignored with impunity. Such recognition of the demands made upon us by the very character of existence has again and again been lost. We are prone to center our attention on the assertions in the Gospel which speak of God as love. The word love is always in danger of being cheapened, with the consequence that we try to snuggle up to the Almighty and go to sleep in God's protecting arms. Actually, this cuddling up to the Almighty is a dangerous practice which turns out to be something like cuddling up to a tiger.

We can readily understand why many people have, in religious or secular terms, been moved or tempted to snuggle up to reality as though it requires only softness and cuddling. They have revolted against the religion of fear, the religion of fire and brimstone and everlasting punishment. Integrity of mind is more important than slavish subjection to this kind of fear which deprives human existence of its true meaning and dignity. Down through the ages artists have indulged in a veritable orgy of sadistic imagination in attempting the topography, the personnel, and the tortuous machinery of Hell. They remind us of Jonathan Edwards's sermon on *Sinners in the Hands of an Angry God,* as well as the pious early American Sunday afternoon assignment to children of Michael Wigglesworth's poem of over two hundred stanzas entitled *The Day of Doom.* In response to the pleading of the unbaptized infants before the throne of God at the Last Judgment, God replies that, although they cannot properly be sent to Heaven, He will, in deference to their pleas, assign them to "the easiest room in Hell."

Many of us would agree with Alfred North Whitehead's renunciation of this sort of religion of fear. Nevertheless, we are not without recognition of Ralph Waldo Emerson's assertion that, "The world is full of judgment days." There are certain inescapable coercions in life, and woe betide us if we do not take them into account. I may be active so long as I walk along the roof of a house, but the moment I step off the edge, I become passive; in short, I become a patient.

William James vividly reminds us of this element of judgment in life in his study of habit: "Every smallest stroke of virtue or vice," he says, "leaves its never so little scar." The drunken Rip Van Winkle vows he will reform his habit, but he excuses himself for every fresh dereliction by saying, "I won't count this time."

"Well," says William James, "he may not count it, and a kind Heaven may not count it; but it is being counted none the less. Down among the nerve cells and fibres, the molecules are counting it, registering and storing it up to be used against him when the next temptation comes."

Evidently there is no such thing as successful cheating. The universe not only contains power working for righteousness but power working for catastrophe. No doubt it was the sense of this possibility of catastrophe as the consequence of our acts which made Whitehead say that before we can know God as a God of love, as a Companion, we have to know God as the Enemy. In short, we have to know of the wrath of God before we can understand the love of God. It is, then, at the same time a comforting and a terrifying thing to live in a world of physical and moral and spiritual law. It is part of the educative process whereby, under the Great Taskmaster's eye, we learn with others to live the examined life, the only life worth living. It is a part of the bone structure of a God who is nothing but love.

7. The Creative Thrust of Conflict

There is a famous aphorism that comes from Lord Acton, the British historian: "Power tends to corrupt. Absolute power corrupts absolutely." This dictum has been widely accepted as an axiom of social philosophy. We have seen it vindicated all too often in the twentieth century. Indeed, the corrupting power of this absolutism has cost millions of lives during the past generation alone.

The first half of the dictum, however, has often been misquoted to read, Power corrupts. Lord Acton's formulation is that power *tends* to corrupt. To say that power as such corrupts would be a great error. It would be tantamount to saying that the ideal condition of human nature is powerlessness, impotence.

In speaking of the creative use of controversy, why do I speak of power? Controversy involves the use of power. Obviously, controversy occurs in all spheres of human existence, directly between persons and collectively within and between groups of all sorts and sizes, including churches, communities, and nations. That is a large spectrum to ponder. I shall here be concerned with only a portion of the spectrum, that is, with certain of the larger collectivities within the nation, and with the use of power in these collectivities.

What has power to do with controversy? To answer this question we need a definition of power, but as a preparation for this definition I should like to indicate what power is not, by pointing to its opposite. For this purpose, let me offer a variation on the Lord Acton dictum. Let me put it in reverse. Impotence tends to corrupt. Absolute impotence corrupts absolutely. An illustration of the truth of this dictum will serve better than a catalog of abstractions.

I have had the opportunity at Harvard to participate in an interdisciplinary seminar on population problems. In this faculty seminar, we have been considering various types and problems of population control. For example, we have been studying conditions in Appalachia, conditions that are appalling. They are exhibited more or less typically in an all white community, Granny's Hollow, in eastern Kentucky. Here fifty families are now living on a one mile creek where two families lived four years ago. These people are castoffs of technological unemployment. Lacking competence for work in our urban, industrial society, and lacking also the land that is requisite for a rural economy, they live in isolation and penury. Some of the families live in chicken coops.

These families bathe in, defecate in, and drink from the scrawny creek which at certain seasons is a rushing torrent. The creek is the road, and there is no path. The children always get wet when they go to school. One-third of the people, on the average, have the common cold. The whole community exhibits a high incidence of other diseases. Hypochronic anemia, hepatitis, tuberculosis, eye, ear and tooth diseases are common. One of every three adults in the region has a goiter. The most efficient means of dealing with tooth decay is to get rid of all the teeth at an early age. As a consequence of malnutrition, the children commonly bear large scabs on the torso and the limbs. Worms are a common carriage. The dogs are infested also. Surprisingly, infant mortality is only three times the national average. Many of the people are illiterate. They have practiced inbreeding for over a generation. The consequence is that many of the progeny are of retarded mentality; others are deaf and dumb. A principal escape from the consciousness of squalor they find in moonshine liquor and the snake cult.

Although these people reject the ways of the town and city, they are dominated by a political clique from the outside with either buys their votes or refuses to count them. Medical workers immediately lose the possibility of effective communication if they ignore these political structures. The same restrictions will obtain for the anti-poverty workers. The few people who have successfully escaped from Granny's Hollow will have little to do with their relatives who have remained behind. The residents of the nearby towns also will have nothing to do with them, except to sell them food and tobacco, broken down radios and discarded jalopies. They generally call them "bums, hopeless bums." Do they not trade the cheese from surplus food supplies for cigarettes and liquor?

In their acceptance of their enforced ostracism, the people of Granny's Hollow want to be left alone. They are Americans, and they cherish their own style of life. They want no controversy with outside people who possess power. Their freedom is strictly limited by internal as well as by external forces. They are Americans, but they are slaves to their impotence, to the impotence that corrupts. The system of which we are a part has helped to make them what they are. They belong to our own "underdeveloped country." Our power has been the power that corrupts.

To change their condition will require a special kind of persuasion and philanthropy not yet clear to anyone.

The positive power that engenders high temperature conflict is the power that challenges expansive or dominant social power. This is the power that in our time has overturned most of the colonialisms of the world, the power that has brought forth sixty-three new nations in a single generation. This is nothing new, for it is the power that initially gave rise to the Reformation, especially to the Left Wing of the Reformation. It is the power that brought the middle classes into existence in the face of feudalism. It is the power that has extended the suffrage. To come to our own day, it is the power that has given rise to the civil rights movement. It is the strength that has dispersed power and responsibility.

The civil rights movement is a fine test case for discerning the character of creative controversy. We need to consider salient features of the conflict in relation to the creative use of controversy. The dramatic change that is taking place among us is very much like the previous revolutions just mentioned. It has been initiated by outsiders. The Left Wing of the Reformation, from which we of the congregational polity and of the rational thrust have descended, was instigated by people who were outside and in opposition to the Establishment. They were the deprived, and they rebelled. They were viewed by the Establishment (Protestant and Catholic) as heretics who were threatening and subverting the traditional order of church and state.

The Left Wing of the Reformation wished to choose freely its own religion. Our forebears, in short, were upstarts, rebels against established authority in the name of a new conception of authority. Col. Rainsborough of the Cromwellian Army defended this rebellion by saying, "Every English he hath his own life to live." From this movement, broadly conceived, came modern pluralist democracy. The demand for a democratic constitution, the demand for separation of church and state, the demand for respect of the minority and of a loyal opposition, the demand for the extension of suffrage, the demand for a pluralistic education—all of these innovations—were initiated or carried through by "outsiders."

Dean William Wallace Fenn of Harvard Divinity School, speaking of how the Quakers defied the old New England theocracy, used to say that if trouble was brewing anywhere in the colonies, one could be sure that soon a boat load of Quakers or other Dissenters would be on the way to that place. Who were the Methodists and the Unitarians who initiated the social reforms of the early nineteenth century in England? Outsiders. Who were the people who initiated and carried through the labor movement of the nineteenth century in England? Protestant outsiders, challenging the traditional power of the middle classes. Many of their leaders were renegades from the bourgeois, people who chose to identify with the outsiders. Moreover, who were the people who carried the American labor movement to its high peak in America? Outsiders, in large measure Roman Catholic outsiders, the sons and daughters of recent immigrants. Still earlier, who pushed through the demand for universal suffrage in the USA in the 1890s? Women, up to then outsiders with respect to politics.

When we here praise famous women and men, we give these outsiders a special and high place on the scroll. We add to the list the real old-timers, the members of the earliest Christian churches, outsiders from the lower classes and from several races. They insisted on choosing their own religion and their own way of life, and that in the face of Jerusalem and Rome and Ephesus. The founder from a country town had nowhere to lay his head.

But for all the outsiders, where would we be today? Probably we would live in a more monolithic society where creative controversy would be severely limited. These outsiders have helped to extend the uses of human powers, especially the power to form and to transform.

We are now ready for a definition of power. Many people cringe at the word, perhaps because it suggest muscular power, or the power to dominate. Nonetheless, there is a power that contributes to creative controversy, whether it be the capacity of an individual or a group. In this sense power is the capacity to participate in the shaping of social decision. Its sphere of operation may be in the family or the small group; it may extend to the larger groups of the church or the professions or industry; it may embrace the total community, the government, and the nations. Power in this context is the capacity to participate in creative controversy; in short, to change the profile of participation. As such it is the principal freedom available to us. It is a freedom that requires organization. The history of freedom (and of unfreedom) is largely the history of effective organization. It is not that the individual is insignificant, but rather that if one's contribution is to make an impact upon communal decision, it will require organization. Otherwise, the individual (so far as public affairs are concerned) will remain socially uncreative. Power then, as we understand it here, is the ability to make oneself heard, the capacity to cause others to take one's concerns seriously. It is the capacity to make one's concerns felt as an impact in the communal decision-making process. It is also the capacity to listen. It is the capacity to respond creatively to others, to the needs of others. In all of these dimensions, power engenders conflict, for in crucial matters of public policy one encounters competition for a share in power.

Our central question is, What are the creative uses of sharing in power and also of the effort to gain a share in power? The moment this question is posed we may encounter persons who ask, Why do we need to have controversy? Why not talk about harmony, and how to achieve it? They ask these questions despite the fact that they are the inheritors and beneficiaries of those previous controversies and struggles which I have mentioned.

Let me be boldly unharmonious and say that there is probably no more deceptive enemy of creative controversy than the strategy of "harmony." I shall call it "harmonism." The yearning for harmony forgets that freedom entails the freedom to differ. More than that, it overlooks the fact that at any given moment many people will be profoundly dissatisfied with their lot, profoundly deprived, and will not feel at all like talking about harmony. The demand for harmony all too often means, "Don't disturb the present power structure! Sit down! You are rocking the boat!"

Something must be said, to be sure, in favor of harmony. It must be admitted, indeed we should insist, that controversy cannot be creative unless some consensus, at least in principle, antedates the conflict. If there is absolutely nothing which people in controversy agree upon, then conflict will be so savage it can lead to violent revolution.

At the same time, we must recognize that power is never "in widest commonality spread," and that the growth of democracy depends upon the *extension* of power, that is, of the freedom to participate in making social decisions. It depends upon letting the "outsider" in, indeed of helping the outsider to get in (if only for the sake of the vitality and viability of the society). The authenticity of democracy rests upon its

182

protection of differentiation and upon its allowing everyone an effective voice for the sake of justice. In face of this promise, "harmonism" is oftentimes a device to stifle discussion, and also to prevent a shift in power. Accordingly, the persons or groups demanding change will be called disturbers. They may even be called sick.

I recall an incident of this sort. To a leader in the movement for better race relations, a real estate promoter in Chicago asked the question, "Are you really happy at home? If you were happy in your home, would you be causing all this disturbance in the community? Aren't you a little neurotic?" This sort of argument can, of course, cut two ways, eliciting the question as to whether the accuser is not becoming neurotic about a certain brand of harmony. Those who speak much about such harmony are seldom eager searchers for facts or remedies of correction.

Indeed, there are, in the name of harmony, devices that lead to the suppression or the distortion of information or the attempt to control of information. In *Kohler on Strike: Thirty Years of Conflict,* Walter Uphoff shows vividly what happens when information is distorted: agitators are called communists, and communications are controlled or restricted. Two of the clergy who were on the national church commission (Protestant, Catholic and Jewish) to investigate this protracted strike have told us that in their judgment the principal reason for this long drawn out controversy was that the people in Sheboygan seldom, if ever, heard the two sides of the controversy, let alone becoming personally acquainted with the people on strike. Creative controversy absolutely requires personal acquaintance with the situation of others in the controversy. As Martin Luther King succinctly stated in an axiom: " We hate each other because we fear each other. We fear each each other because we don't know each other, and we don't know each other because we are separated." In Sheboygan, the people in the Protestant churches and in the synagogues knew only the management's view of the conflict. This is an egregiously uncreative use of controversy, which obviously requires that all of the alleged facts shall have a hearing, and also that the biases of the various interested protagonists shall be scrutinized. Harmonism is an uncreative outlook insofar as it does not want to take seriously the emerging concerns that call for a shift in power, a shift in the effective capacity to participate in the shaping of public policy. Human beings have the right to enter into decisions that affect their own destiny.

There is another kind of harmonism which is of special interest to us here. This is the harmonism that, in the name of peace and reconciliation, prefers a settlement of conflict which is premature. In the present situation of Blacks in the United States, there is no likelihood that a significant shift in power can take place without relentless struggle. Many people, when confronted by heated controversy such as the civil rights movement, claim to prefer, in the name of love, a policy of sweet persuasion, sweet and slow. We have observed this sweet but ineffective persuasion both among church people who are involved as well as among those who are on the sidelines (of which the number is legion). In both the North and the South, such people deplored the appearance of Freedom Riders, sit-ins and pray-ins and the demand for upgrading in employment. They are wont to say that "agitation" only makes people hate each other, but in actuality they themselves are far from being makers of peace. They simply cry peace when there is no peace.

The lovers of "harmony" have refused to believe that the situation is grave. Church people of good will once claimed for weeks on end that no churches were being burned, that news of this sort was propaganda. Then when they became convinced that churches had been bombed or burned, they helped to raise money to rebuild them, and possibly also to assuage their sense of guilt. In this way they aimed to exhibit good will, although their own churches remained segregated. When three young men were reported missing, people favoring harmony insisted that no real harm would come to them. When the fact of the murders was confirmed, these people were shocked, and some wept; but we must remember that two of these murdered civil rights volunteers were white. In any event, the display of violence revealed the illusion of harmonism.

This kind of harmonism would not have become vividly and generally known had it not been for persistent agitation, and such persistence of agitation is required. People like to believe that new legislation will solve the problems, legislation supported, of course, by good will and the love of harmony. Actually there is mounting evidence that Black people (not to speak of Puerto Rican, Latin American and Asian-American citizens) are so far from being heartened that they are increasingly disenchanted.

When, then, do developments of this sort tell us about the ideal of so-called harmony and about the nature of creative controversy? They tell us that conflicts regarding serious conflicts of interest should not be viewed merely as a disturbance of harmony but as the occasion for growth into an authentic harmony. The growing edges of any group or of any society are to be found precisely at the point of tension. In the words of Whitehead, "The clash of doctrines is not a disaster; it is an opportunity."

The failures of harmonism also remind us that effective change requires something more than good will and more than good legislation that is haltingly executed and politically subverted. The test of the success of creative conflict is the question whether previously neglected concerns are taken seriously. Creative controversy finds an effective place for more inclusive interests and concerns. In the public domain, it brings new decision; it brings a shift in power. In this whole situation and in the face of the spurious demands for "love and harmony," we find insight in the folk wisdom of the adage, "The meek may inherit the earth, but hits win ball games." Authentic love is not the outcome of weakness or indifference; it is the expression of abundance.

In any sharp controversy, to be sure, there are not only the hits that win ball games. There are also many strikes and foul balls. Here we encounter the most fundamental prerequisite for the creative use of conflict. All of us on all sides of the irrepressible conflicts of our time will be doomed to uncreative and perhaps to violent conflict unless we can, at least in crucial moments, be grasped by the spirit that was in Jesus when he said, "Let whoever is without sin cast the first stone." To the sinner in the dock he said, "Go and sin no more." Forgiveness, acceptance. These are the first prerequisites of creative controversy. They are the antecedents of new beginnings, of constructive innovation, of new creation. However, they mean that we must give up something if the new is to come into being.

Thomas Wolfe, in *You Can't Go Home Again,* has said the right word to enable us to assist the deprived and the dispossessed to move on to new power:

> To lose the earth you know for greater knowing; to lose the life you have lived for greater life; to leave the friends you have loved for greater loving, to find a land more kind than home, more large than earth whereon the pillars of this earth are founded; towards which the conscience of the world is tending: a wind is rising and the rivers flow.

8. By Their Groups Shall Ye Know Them

Several years before the Nazis came to power in Germany I, as a student, was standing on the street in the city of Nuremberg watching a parade. The Horst Wessel was being played by the band, and the parade lasted about four hours. Some of the banners were swastikas, and I thought it would be interesting to see what some of the people watching the parade would say. I asked a couple of "hair on the chest" men standing there what the meaning of the swastika was. They then gave me the Nazi story on anti-Semitism. I began to ask a few questions, and the conversation became rather heated. People standing around us could readily hear what we were arguing about. Suddenly I was seized from behind by two elbows and pulled out of there. I couldn't get loose from this sturdy gentleman. He pushed me through the crowd, down a side street, up a dead end alley.

By the way, up until that time, I had found observation of the Nazis rather interesting in my detached way; but I want to say that on the little march up the dead end alley, I discovered what the meaning of the word "palpitation" is. When we got to the end of that alley, he wheeled me around and shouted at me in German with a few Christian words—I mean theological words used without theological intent. He said in effect, "You blankety blank fool, don't you know that when you are watching a parade in Nazi Germany, you either keep your mouth shut, or you get your head bashed in!"

The palpitation was really going up, and I thought that he was giving me an agenda of what was going to happen. Then he smiled and said, "I saved you from getting sandbagged there. Do you know that? You don't argue with those Nazis in that way. They would flatten you out on the pavement."

I said, "Thank you very much."

He said, "You know, when I was standing there watching you, you damn fool, I said to myself, 'Well I have now been four times in the U.S.A. in the Merchant Marines, and I have been entertained marvelously by Americans, but I never had a chance to pay them back; so I said to myself, I am going to invite him home for Sunday dinner.' You want to come home to dinner with me?"

So I went to dinner with him, an unemployed worker. We climbed three flights in a tenement house, with the bannisters gone and some of the steps out. For a couple of hours during a typical dumpling dinner of an unemployed worker with his small family, I found out something about the economic situation out of which Nazism was drawing.

We have here the contours of a totalitarian society. I say the contours in the sense that there are features that belong to a totalitarian society but which may, in one limited way or another, figure in so-called democratic society. That is, everything is controlled from the center: churches, trade unions, political parties, lodges, schools, commercial and financial corporations. This is the destruction of democracy. No group may exist within the totalitarian society that is not under the control of, under the license of, under the direction of, responsible to the central authority. One group holds a monopoly of power. In this case, Nazism holds the monopoly of civic religion.

The separation of church and state, as an institutional arrangement, is not only a fundamental aspect of the democratic society; historically it was the first important institutionalization of the decentralization of power. The separation of church and state came initially in the seventeenth century in a protest against the establishment that controlled both ecclesiastical and political economic affairs. In that time, the idea of separation of church and state was viewed as subversive. Indeed, a historian of British civilization, Winfield Stratford, indicates his negative attitude toward separation of church and state by describing this part of British history as "Spiritual Bolshevism."

The separation of church and state carried with it the theory that people should be allowed to form associations without the control of the state in order freely to express their own convictions. The first struggle in the history of modern democracy was the struggle for what is called freedom of religious association. We take this for granted as a part of our heritage, overlooking the fact that initially our spiritual ancestors were viewed as "Spiritual Bolsheviks." The word that was used was "Anabaptists."

The separation of church and state did revive an institutional feature that had appeared earlier in Western history with the birth of primitive Christianity. Two very interesting similarities should be pointed out here between early Christianity and the Protestant sect who first fought for freedom of religious association. That is, primitive Christianity asserted that religion is not to be bound up with the nation or with the race.

Religion will have its own free association not under the control of, and not licensed by, Caesar. Therefore, it is asserted by contemporary historians that one of the great innovations in the history of the West was the innovation provided by primitive Christianity in its assertion that people have the right to form a church that is not controlled by, not formed by, and does not directly serve Caesar. Thus, "Render unto God that which is God and unto Caesar that which is Caesar's" was not merely a religio-ethical maxim; it was an idea that required a special form of social organization; namely, the church. In primitive Christianity, you see the separation between religion and government, religion and nation, religion and state. Secondly, you see a separation between religion and kinship. More of the ethnic orientation of primitive Judaism was now rejected, and thus you find, in the primitive Christian church, people leaving the family in order to join the small religious association of the primitive church. That church also brought in people of various races; indeed, it gave both slaves and women positions of authority in the church. These elements reappeared in the seventeenth century, with anticipation from the fifteenth and sixteenth centuries, but they found social institutional implementation especially in the seventeenth century.

At this point I want to remind you that one of the most influential books in the history of Anglo-American political theory was written in opposition to this new trend in the English religion; namely, Thomas Hobbes, *Leviathan. That* work was written to show that if you permit freedom of association, including freedom of religious association, you open the avenue to chaos and social dissolution. Hobbes argued, as did the Catholics, that you cannot have a stable society unless you have a united religion and that religion is also under the control of the state. Therefore, there may be no free associations in the state, for any such free association will mean that the unity and power of the sovereign is thereby jeopardized.

We take for granted the opposition to this view, but in that time one of the most learned people in a variety of disciplines—physics, political theory, and theology—Thomas Hobbes, gave the argument for unity as against freedom of association. He did this so powerfully that you can say that he is the most significant political theorist in Anglo-American tradition. Why? Because every fundamental attempt to spell out the theory of democracy begins with or takes into account how one is going to answer Thomas Hobbes. It is remarkable for someone to have written such a powerful statement of totalitarianism that again and again democratic theorists feel that they have to answer Hobbes, who rejected precisely the thing that began in the ecclesiastical area here and later went into the political arena; he rejected the whole theory of separation of powers. There cannot be a stable society if there is a separation of powers; all powers must be united in the sovereign.

There are many repressive people in democratic American society who talk as though they really agreed more with the spirit of the *Leviathan* of Thomas Hobbes than with the spirit of *The Federalist Papers,* which insist that there must be differentiation and freedom to express differentiation and freedom to form associations to express separation of powers. The theory of separation of powers, as a consequence of this early Protestant movement, worked in two ways: first, in the development of free associations within the commonwealth; secondly, in the theory of separation of powers within the government itself. The idea of the separation of powers actually was spelled out institutionally under the rubric of the New Testament axiom: "Render unto Caesar that which is Caesar's and unto God that which is God's." One not only has the attitude expressed; one organizes society in such a way that one may render to God that which is God's where it is different from that which is Caesar's and where it may even dissent from what Caesar demands.

Actually, Thomas Hobbes suffered a traumatic shock in the face of the swarming sect who in the name of God were claiming that you didn't have to belong to the established church; and that you didn't have to pay taxes to support the established church. They insisted that they should not be coerced into paying taxes for a church in which they disbelieved, and that they could have a church of their own.

Incidentally, the taking of the collection as a part of the Protestant liturgy was in those days of the seventeenth century a symbol of the fact: "Our church is not supported by the state. Our church does not require everybody to pay taxes in order to go to it. Our church is supported and paid for by its own members. We run our own show." It was a revolutionary idea that, "We pay our own bills, and we don't ask other people to pay for religion who don't happen to believe in it." The very act of taking a public collection is a symbol of an institutional change; namely, freedom of religious association in face of the Establishment. Now it is asserted also that it is the right and responsibility of every member of the local church to participate in the determination of the policy of that church. Indeed, church members took this attitude so strongly that they developed a kind of anti-clerical attitude as against the parson and they said, "The church belongs to the laity, and the ministry is only gathered out of the laity to give special function."

Moreover, in the seventeenth century among our spiritual ancestors, there developed the idea that the authentic church must be a church that protects the minority within it. There were formulations such as, "If the Holy Spirit is to speak to us, it is more likely that God will speak to us through dissent and through the minority than through the majority who are in control." So they developed the idea that it is the obligation of the true church not only to listen to, but even to protect, the minority view. You have here a fairly elaborate theory of dispersion of power; that is, scattering of power.

What is power? Power, understood politically and sociologically, is the capacity to participate in making social decisions. The principle of separation of church and state, the principle of freedom of expression, the principle of the autonomy of the local group, the principle that every member has the right and obligation to participate, and the principle of protection of minorities; all of these were the stirring up of a theory of power. Political democracy as we know it was born in the seventeenth century in the small church that Mr. Winfield in his *History of British Civilization* called "Spiritual Bolsheviks." Modern democracy was not born through the Renaissance or through the reading of ancient Greek and Roman classics. As A. D. Lindsay of Balliol College at Oxford puts it, "Modern democracy was born by the principle of analogy whereby the theory of social organization developed by the churches was taken over as a part of the state."

Within the sanctuary people said, "If God requires this kind of free church of us, he requires also a state in which these things can obtain." Therefore, they began to ask for a written constitution, extension of suffrage, regular elections, reduction of privileges coming from the ownership of property. Therefore, we can say that freedom of religious association became a conception of a free democratic state. It then became a conception of freedom in the field of education; and it had a tremendous development in the eighteenth century in the Protestant academies where people could go to school who wouldn't sign the thirty-nine articles which they had to sign in order to get into an academy of the Establishment. Thus also, more and more associations were formed in order to bring onto the public scene new concerns, new demands for rights, or attacks upon forms of injustice. So we have the development of the professional associations, the development of cooperatives, the development of missionary societies, and the development of the anti-slavery movement. We finally have the development of the pressure groups, the basic techniques of which were already invented before the year 1725 by the Quakers, who decisively affected public legislation in the first quarter of the eighteenth century.

We have to say that today the movement in the direction of civil rights represents another application of the principle of freedom of association in order to achieve some kind of consensus in regard to public policy and in order to affect public policy. The general presupposition is that the democratic society, in contrast with the totalitarian society, is the multi-group society, and the vitality of democratic society depends upon the participation of citizens in the multi-group, where they have the opportunity to scrutinize propaganda, to get new information, to achieve a critical attitude, to learn the skill of selecting a good leader, to provide the arena within which leadership itself shall get its training. All of this is tied up with the theory of the multi-group society as democratic in contrast with the Hobbesian totalitarian society where everything is under the absolute control of the Establishment.

Finally, we have to say that in Protestant terms in the history of the multi-group society, a dual concept of vocation has developed. On the one side, every Christian has the obligation to do a good job in a particular vocation. Secondly, every Christian has the obligation also to participate in those processes that may bring criticism through processes that attempt to transform social institutions in the direction of justice and mercy. The litmus test there is how much time, how much energy, does the individual Christian devote to participation in organizations for the public welfare and for the transformation of society in the direction of justice, mercy, and love?

By their groups shall ye know them.

9. In The Fullness of Time

The story is told of a New England town which had grown to such an extent that the old parish church, formerly on the Common, now found itself at the intersection of the main streets of a a thriving little city. Since the members of the parish for the most part lived in suburbs inconveniently distant from the church, they decided to sell the old property and rebuild the church in a suburb. The church was controlled by the old arrangement of parish and church groups, hence the decision of the church members had to be approved at a town meeting. In the course of the discussion at the town meeting, an elderly man who was never known to have stepped inside a church arose and made an earnest plea, without giving reasons, a plea that the old church be left standing where it had always been. The church members and the townspeople were equally surprised at his interest in the church and at his desire to oppose the members in their plan to dispose of the old building. Finally, one of the members arose and said that everyone now realized he wished the church to remain where it was but that no one could understand what his reason was. "Why do you who have never shown any interest in the church wish it to stay where it is?"

The venerable citizen replied, "Well, all I can say is that there is a lot of sentiment tied up in that old church on the Common."

When I first heard of this incident, I was unable to discern more than sentimentality in the objection, and perhaps it was only that, yet there may have been something more. The elder was probably saying that something of himself, something of his own life, would be taken away with that old landmark. It was one of the ways in which he established his own identity, a way of life in which he was able to assure himself of the continuity of his own life. At all events, he was suggesting the way in which every human being achieves self-identity, that is, finding oneself.

If we attempt to trace our own individual history and development, we are forced to do so in terms of certain outstanding relationships in time and space. We think of the date and place of our birth. We recall the day when we started to school wearing the little velvet suit with the brass buttons, or the day when we first had a bicycle of our own. We remember the teacher who first communicated enthusiasm to us. We think of the church in which we worshiped as a child, or of the college to which we still feel our old loyalty. All of these times and places are a part of us; without them we should not be what we are. They are, as Emily Dickinson said, "a single hound" pursuing us, the single hound of our own identity.

In his book on Wordsworth, Willard L. Sperry comes to the striking conclusion that the poet's primary interest was not really nature. Wordsworth was in search of himself; he wished to establish his own identity. His experiences as a farmed-out child at school, the harrowing memories of the French Revolution and of his conflicts with the Godwin circle had left him disintegrated, a discordant personality. He wished to find something stable by means of which to get his bearing. He could not find himself in the dark cave of subjectivity. He had to search for the guarantee of the integrity of his life by reference to some shrine of constancy in the world outside. The unstable causes with which he had been identified provided no constant fact by which he might reaffirm the unimpaired integrity of his own life. Just as the old New Englander turned to the church on the Common, so Wordsworth turned "to the permanent forms of nature." This is the deeper motivation of his love for nature. The dance of the daffodils, the rainbow in the sky, the primrose by the river's brim, were all more than objects of nature for him.

> My heart leaps up when I behold
> A rainbow in the sky:
> So was it when my life began;
> So is it now I am a man;
> And I could wish my days to be
> Bound each to each by natural piety.

The poem is not about a rainbow. It shows rather the way in which one man found something stable with reference to which he could determine his location. The poem is a study of the soul's identity. It might bear as its title Emily Dickinson's phrase, "The Single Hound." Natural piety for Wordsworth is not simply the love of nature; it is rather the reassurance that life has continuity, coherence, unity. The rainbow came to his rescue when he doubted whether he was William Wordsworth. Indeed, our self-realization is accomplished only as we enter into significant and stabilizing relationships. We come to be, and we come to know ourselves, only as we are consciously related to nature, to human institutions, and to other human beings.

All of this, you will rightly say, is quite obvious. What is not so obvious, however, is that this achievement of self-identity does not take place without effort. In a very real sense, our personal identity is something which we must create; it is not something that is self-existent. Natural piety is achieved by selecting from one's own past those features which give it meaning or integration.

In the novels of Marcel Proust, we find a vivid awareness of this necessity to create our sense of identity from the remembrance of things past. Over and over again in the writings of Proust, we find the author singling out some apparently trivial, though really significant, incident of his past which relates to an experience of the moment, an incident which, in the alembic of his creative imagination, serves to establish his identity in his own mind. It is by this method of envisaging his identity by relating it to characteristic events in his past that he comes to know himself. Even his taste of a madeleine cake dipped in herb tea brings back the memory of his mother and, as he says, the memory "of all the flowers in our garden and in M. Swann's park, and the water-lilies on the Vivonne and good folk in the village and their little dwellings and the parish church and the whole of Combray and of its surroundings, taking their proper shape and growing solid, sprang into being, town and gardens alike, from my cup of tea."

The whole series of sixteen novels which Proust entitled *Remembrance of Things Past* represents the author's attempt to establish his own identity by a creative artistic endeavor. We do not find ourselves by simply having been in relations; we must ourselves create our past in the sense that we must by an act of mind lift our experience into a pattern of meaning. By the way, Dr. Richard Cabot used to define an idiot as a person without a sense of the past.

We may find in Wordsworth a deeper wisdom than is customarily attributed to him as the poet of nature. Wordsworth, wandering lonely as a cloud, saw the daffodils beside the lake. At the time this experience seemed to be its own end, self-explanatory, self-sufficient. He says he gazed and gazed but little thought what wealth the show had brought to him; but later reflection on the pensive couch revealed the true significance of the experience. The remembered emotion was more significant than the emotion first felt. Indeed, Wordsworth is well known as the poet who defined poetry as emotion recollected in tranquility. The daffodils demanded something more than perception; they demanded assimilation.

George Tyrrell, the Jesuit priest and philosopher who was excommunicated for his role in the Modernist movement seeking to relate Catholicism to scientific thought, says on the very first page of his autobiography that "our experience is given to us to be the food of our character and spiritual life; but, in point of fact, we spend our lives in storing up food, and never have leisure to lie down quietly with the cows in the field and ruminate bit by bit what we have swallowed so hastily."

There would seem to be a sort of acquisitive instinct with regard to human experience. We incline always to be in search of new experience to devour when in reality we should be digesting our past experience. The memory has work to do; it is not a mere pocket for repellent, undifferentiated particles out of the past. When it is properly creative tending towards the true fulness of time, it is a living instructor with a prophetic sense of the values which it guards. Carlyle seems to have had some such idea in mind when he said of Tennyson: "Alfred is always carrying a bit of chaos around in his pocket turning it into cosmos."

Here then is what we might characterize as the religious use of memory. It is the means by which we approach the fulness of time. Perhaps the reason for much of our irreligion is simply idiocy, as Dr. Cabot defined it, the tendency of people to live in the experience of the moment, the tendency to forget their own best moments and those of the race, the significant relationships established in the past. Our days are not bound each to each by the natural piety which is the child of remembrance.

At all events, I am persuaded that there is more than metaphysical or logical truth here. We are very near the heart of religion. What I have been saying has very much to do with the experience of conversion. Not, of course, the religious experience which Jonathan Edwards described as the "thunder claps and visible upsets of grace," but rather the Christian nurture, the gradual and progressive turning towards the light in the fulness of time.

St. Paul used the phrase "the fulness of time" to describe the point in history when Jesus Christ came. Jesus was a member of a race possessing a creative memory, a race which had not failed to roast that which it had taken in hunting. Israel was the only nation in that part of the world at that time which could boast a continuous religious tradition of more than a thousand years.

Here we have exemplified what may be called a natural law in the spiritual world, a law which applies to individuals as well as to entire cultures: *the conversion of a people or of an individual can occur only in the fulness of time.* Hence we need not only to discover our identity by reference to constant features in the objective world and by the creative work of memory giving patterns of meaning to our relationships. We need also to strike root into a definite plot of soil. We need somehow to find our place in a continuing and promising tradition with its sacred books, its communion of saints and its discipline. This is just what academic life for most students seems to prevent. We get ourselves into a spectator attitude. We get into the habit of classifying religious movements and ideas according to historical, philosophical, theological, or psychological terminology. We can perhaps name the many seeds, the potential rootings that are blown our way by the winds of doctrine, but we do not actually strike root into the soil ourselves. This is the reason the university is not wholly adequate for our nourishment. We need the church's community of memory and hope through the sharing of which we may in the fulness of time first sense our need for conversion and then grow in the grace and knowledge of Christ.

In the church we may find satisfied the three needs we have mentioned: (1) significant relationships, (2) a pattern of prophetic meaning for our past, (3) the soil of a continuing community. In the church, we accept the truth: By their fruits shall ye know them; but we also accept the truth: By their roots shall ye know them. Where there are no roots, there will be no fruit.

10. Originality

The drifting of the individual with the tide of the group has always been accompanied by the struggle of each against all. Human nature has followed and revolted against conventions ever since people became gregarious. The types radical and conservative are perennial, and both seem to make for advance. In general, we assume that the great changes in the world have taken place because of the reformers and revolters. We have heard so much about the dependence of the world's progress upon revolt that we, at least theoretically, look with some interest and even favor upon the insurgents, though their interests may conflict with our own. We may feel that the revolter is a painful necessity.

It is easy to find the reason for this admiration of the nonconformist. We are proud to be the inheritors of a great tradition of individualism that comes down to us from the early days of colonial America. We also look back to Thoreau, Emerson and Hawthorne as great prophets, and feel a certain kinship with them and their ideals. Individualism is one of the distinctive characteristics of the American. We strive for originality. This is not a purely local ideal, of course, but our tradition is one that has stressed it as a philosophy of life.

Emerson wrote in his Journal: "Societies, parties are only incipient stages, tadpole states of man, as caterpillars are social, but the butterfly not. The true and finished man is ever alone.... Alone is wisdom. Alone is heaven." For Emerson imitation is suicide. What another announces I must find true in me, or wholly reject. I can accept nothing else. The only right is what is after my own constitution; the only wrong is what is against it. So is everything that tends to limit us—creeds, parties, accepted ideals, teachers, books, and our own past even.

In actual practice, Thoreau was a more thorough going individualist then Emerson. For instance, he refused to pay even his poll tax. He was put in jail once on this account, for one night. As he stood considering the walls of solid stone, two or three feet thick, and the iron grating which strained the light, he said: "I could not help being struck with the foolishness of that institution which treated me as if I were mere flesh and blood and bones, to be locked up. I wondered that it should have concluded at length that this was the best use it could put me to, and had never thought to avail itself of my services in some way. I saw that

197

if there was a wall of stone between me and my townsmen, there was a still more difficult one to climb or break through before they could get to be as free as I was. I did not for a moment feel confined, and the walls seemed a great waste of stone and mortar. I felt as if I alone of all my townsmen had paid my tax. They plainly did not know how to treat me, but behaved like persons underbred. In every threat and in every compliment there was a blunder; for they thought that my chief desire was to stand on the other side of that stone wall. I could not but smile to see how industriously they locked the door on my meditation, which followed them out again without let or hindrance, and *they* were really all that was dangerous. As they could not reach me, they had resolved to punish my body; just as boys, if they cannot come at some person against whom they have a spite, will abuse his dog. I saw that the State was half-witted, that it was timid as a lone woman with her silver spoons, and that it did not know its friends from its foes; and I lost all my remaining respect for it, and pitied it."

Undoubtedly this old ideal of individualism has had something to do with our present straining for originality. Not only in the arts, but also in personal and social relations, the cry is made continuously, "Be original," "Be original."

What does it mean to be original?

Probably the first thought that comes to our minds is that it means to be different. It is something unusual, something strange, something rare, unfamiliar, unique. We are always fascinated by tales of new lands, new peoples, the unparalleled, the unprecedented. "What is news?" is our daily inquiry, and whoever can answer it will get our ear. This yearning for the exotic is not a new thing by any means. In fact, it is very characteristic of much of the thinking of the last century with respect to originality. Jean Jacques Rousseau, the French Romanticist, struck the note that has been heard repeatedly down to the present day. In almost the opening sentence of his *Confessions,* he said "If I am not better than others, at least I am different."

It was only a few years until Byron became the idol of Europe, the leader of the new originality cult. Numerous followers of the cult imposed upon themselves a painful discipline in order to appear abnormal. We are told that some of them even succeeded, after a trying ordeal, in giving themselves consumption. This failure to discriminate between the odd and the original has persisted. I remember hearing a disillusioned admirer of Carl Sandburg saying, "Why, he looks just like an ordinary business man."

The ideal of originality received much of its impetus in the last century from such writers as Emerson, Mill, and Carlyle. "Whoso would be a man must be a non-conformist. What have I to do with the sacredness of traditions, if I live wholly from within? No law can be sacred to me but that of my own nature. I hope in these days we have heard the last of conformity and consistency." Such was Emerson's Declaration of Independence, and as such, one cannot deny that it had great value; but we should remember that Emerson did not think that this policy of non-conformity was the whole story. He himself said, "It is the fault of our rhetoric that we cannot strongly state one fact without seeming to belie some other." It was simply, as he said, that one cannot spend the whole day in explanation. The drastic quality of such counsel for independence called for some modification, and Emerson suggests it in the same essay, *Self-Reliance,* when he says that there is nevertheless a law that abides. "If anyone imagines this law is lax, let him keep its commandments for one day." Oliver Wendell Holmes referred to this sentence as Emerson's way of guarding his proclamation of self-reliance as our guide.

If originality is not simply being different, if it is not mere novelty nor pronouncement of independence or non-conformity, what is it?

We have heard many times that human nature is old and unchanging. There is little that is new about religious experience, or love, or friendship, war, danger or death. These are at the core of human experience. Nevertheless, we can compare our age with any age in the past and find ourselves infinitely superior in inventions, in material civilization, in accumulated knowledge; but compare any modern thinker with Aristotle or any modern mystic with Augustine, and the result is totally different. It is not that we have fallen below the standards of those ages, but we are not definitely above them.

Nevertheless, when someone comes who shows us again what life can be, we hail him or her as great, as original. Originality is excellence, the excellence of the oldest experiences. Originality is a playing upon the old themes—a living of life at its center. Examples of this originality which consists in the remolding of the old are legion in both the arts and in the history of humanity. The story of Romeo and Juliet was told many times before the seventeenth century when Shakespeare transformed it into an immortal drama. There were many attempts to portray the American Indian before Cooper; nevertheless, *The Last of the Mohicans* found its place in the affections of people near and far.

One of the most persistent attempts in the history of music to remold the old to perfection is found in the work of Johannes Brahms. Probably no young composer ever received such hearty welcome into the musical world as did young Brahms at the age of 20. Schumann, one of the leaders in the musical world at the time, proclaimed the advent of a "genius in whom the spirit of the age should find its consummation and its fulfillment; a master by whose teaching the broken phrases would grow articulate, and the vague aspirations gather into form and substance." At last a leader had arisen who should direct the art into new paths and carry it a stage nearer to its appointed place. Brahms now found himself suddenly famous. He was discussed everywhere. His pieces were readily accepted by publishers, and his new compositions were awaited with great interest. He was expected to go on producing; he was almost under obligation to justify his impressive introduction. When we consider the temptation it must have been to him to continue these easy triumphs, when we imagine the inward enthusiasm of creation which must have fired him, we are ready to appreciate the next event in the drama. That event was withdrawal from the musical world and the initiation of a long course of the severest study. Thus in spite of world-wide recognition, Brahms, when a little over 21, imposed upon himself some five years of arduous training and self-discipline. He commanded himself to forego for a while the eloquent but ill-controlled expression hitherto his, in order to acquire his broad firm style, which we love today. Brahms was not so much interested in striking out new paths as he was in knowing and using anew the old forms to perfection.

Let us consider the founder of our religion, Jesus. We often think of him as a person who brought much that is new into the world. One of the most astounding truths which modern scholarship discovered is that practically all of the teaching of Jesus can be found in the literature of Judaism of the preceding two centuries. Arthur Cushman McGiffert, the historian of Christian thought who was President of Union Theological Seminary, concluded: "Summing it all up, we may say that Jesus' idea of God was wholly Jewish. At no point, so far as we can judge from the

Synoptic Gospels, did he go beyond his people's thought about God. His uniqueness, so far as his teaching goes, lay not in the novelty of it but in the insight and unerring instinct with which he made his own the best in the thought of his countrymen. His piety seems to have been nourished particularly on Deuteronomy, the Psalms, and Isaiah; and it is the ideas of God found in those writings that are chiefly reflected in his words."

However, Jesus stamped his personality upon those teachings so securely that, in spite of innumerable theological makeshifts, his immutable spirit has survived. It cannot be said that his great value for us consisted in giving us something new, but he was original in the highest sense of that word. It is because of him that we know the highest meaning of love and courage and fellowship with God.

A sequence of such original people interpreting life is like a succession of virtuosi playing the music of Mozart and Beethoven. Their renderings will be different, but the music is the same, and we know it by heart. The player who calls our attention to the most beauty in it will be original and unique in the only way that life or art permits. Life is music already composed. It has been there a long time, and it had already become ancient history when the first heroes began to play it. In the concert hall, the amateurs listen spellbound when the master plays to perfection a piece with which they have struggled. This is more to them than the loveliest of new sonatas, for it is their own world in a new light. It is because the subject is not new that the audience can decide how well it is portrayed.

The great and original people of history have brought upon the stage the old procession of sorrows, passions, and delights. They loved life for its own sake and sought to live life at its best. Consider Dante's expression at the end of *The New Life:* "A wonderful vision appeared to me, in which I saw things which made me resolve to speak no more of this blessed one (Beatrice) until I could more worthily treat of her. To attain this I study to the utmost of my power, as she truly knows. If it shall please God through whom all things live that my life be prolonged for some years, I hope to say of her what was never said of any women." Dante did not set out to write a new kind of book, for women had been praised before, as he implied, and there had been poems of vision and pilgrimages through hell. His hope was to excel. Originality is not so much the creation of something wholly new but the revival of something old. We are most truly individual when we build upon what is common to us and to our kind. Our purpose is not that we should express ourselves but that life should be expressed through us. We must lose ourselves in a greater, higher life. That is what religion means.

11. A Sense of Cosmic Reality

One of the strangest aspects of human nature is the puzzling way in which friendship often expresses itself. It has often been said that the test of the true friend is that she or he knows when not to talk. When an acquaintance of mine returned from a period of years of missionary work among the Indians of the Southwest, he related that one of his most difficult problems was learning how to call upon his Indian parishioners. When he began his work, he set out on horseback to call upon the Indians in his territory. After several days of unsuccessful amiability, he determined to seek advice of a nearby mission worker. After having stated his problem, he was told by this veteran in the work that he must learn not to talk so much. He started out on his work again and soon discovered that the most satisfying kind of parish call was that in which he rode up to an Indian home, nodded his greeting, dismounted from his horse, and took his seat on the ground by the side of his parishioners. He would remain there silently for about twenty minutes, then nod his salutation, exchange smiles, mount his horse again, and call it a parish visit. In this way, he insists, he soon became intimately acquainted with the members of his flock.

There are different ways in which we sometimes are silently aware of a special sacred presence. A poem of William Wordsworth makes that presence explicit:

> We have felt
> A presence that disturbs us with the joy
> Of elevated thoughts; a sense sublime
> Of something far more deeply interfused,
> Whose dwelling is the light of setting suns,
> And the round ocean and the living air,
> And the blue sky, and in the mind of man:
> A motion and a spirit that impels
> All thinking things, all objects of all thought,
> And rolls through all things.

For others of us, this awareness is only implicit, but whatever our own personal religious convictions may be, whenever we attend public worship where there is the absence of an object of worship, we are left in some vague way unsatisfied. It is only the reality of the more-than-human, the intense realization of the presence of a Cosmic spirit that makes possible sincerity and spontaneous devotion in our worship. It is because of the awareness of this spiritual reality of presence that we would object to the reduction of a service of worship to the hearing of a sermon. Indeed, it may seem to some of us that certain churches lay too much emphasis on the sermon.

A contributor to the *Atlantic Monthly* asserts in half-earnest that: "Nothing would be so beneficial as to have our pulpits silenced for a year. The other phases of worship would be restored: Prayer, praise, and enlightened faith. Some of them are entirely gone from the churches. The people no longer pray but listen to a minister as he prays. Worship has become a passive matter. The congregation has become an audience, a body of listeners."

Worship that has reality points beyond itself to God. The real worshipers attend church not merely for the sake of moral encouragement or uplift but because they seek to worship God in spirit and in truth. They do not look upon the anthems and hymns as being sung solely for the pleasure of the congregation. The office of song is to praise God. The most worshipful hymns and anthems are not those which direct our attention inward to an introspective prying into our human condition but rather to those which direct our attention to the glory of God.

The leading form of worship, prayer, depends absolutely upon the worshipers' sense of the objective reality of the Deity to whom prayer is directed. No true worshipers have any thought when they pray of the subjective effect prayer may have upon them. A Boston wit once gave an excellent description of sham worship when he summed up a prayer of an eminent clergyman as "the most eloquent prayer ever addressed to a Boston audience."

Too often evidence of confusion of mind is apparent in churches that have a vested choir seated in the chancel. I recall attending a very important function at one of these churches. The service proceeded in a true spirit of worship until the offertory, and then the choir arose to sing an anthem which included a soprano solo. The chorister who was to sing the solo stepped forward to the center of the chancel and faced the congregation. The rest of the choir remained in place and sang the anthem as it were to God, the object of worship. The soloist sang as if her prayer were to the praise of the congregation. It is this confused attitude that the music of the church is concert music that most effectively destroys the true sense of worship.

James Bissett Pratt, the Williams College professor who wrote *Religious Consciousness* comments on worship as an awareness of a Cosmic Reality and of our relation to it. He says: "For an increasingly large number of people in our days the only form of religious service left is an occasional funeral. With the rarest of exceptions, the funeral is always a religious ceremony, and though the religious value of the funeral is seldom recognized, or at least seldom mentioned, it is very considerable. For in the presence of Death we find ourselves face to face with the dreadful and silent forces which lie beyond our control—the Cosmic Reality, our conscious relation to which *is* religion. Here we stand on the very edge of the mystery. The curtain for a moment is partly drawn, and we get a glimpse of the cosmic process. We return to our little tasks, to be sure, all the more mystified, but with at least a renewed sense of the reality of the mystery. It takes something like Death to startle us out of our complacent scientific and practical attitude, and to reveal to us the vista of cosmic mystery which (in cruder forms) was ever present to our less scientific forbears. It is this sense of the Unknown, this realization of our own dependence, this intimation of the Power not to be exhausted by the study of science, this questioning of the Why, the Whence, and the Whither, this placing of ourselves for once in a cosmic setting that the funeral brings, and to this it owes its uniquely religious value."

Worship gives us a union of awe and gratitude, which is reverence, as well as a time for consecration and communion. The feeling of reverence every thoughtful person must experience in the presence of the cosmic forces and in reflecting upon them. Worship, therefore, is not something to be outgrown. Its forms change with the changing symbols by which the human imagination decks out the determiner of its destiny, but the thing itself is as eternal as our finitude.

Perhaps one of the most familiar pictures in Christendom is that of the Angelus by Millet. Here the painter has depicted the peasant and his wife, who on hearing the ringing of the Angelus for matins, have paused in their work in the fields and have bowed their heads in quiet and peaceful reverence. It has often been said that the painter has given us in this picture a sense of a third presence, the reality before whose inscrutable and eternal power the peasants bow in thanksgiving. It is the presence of that most real mystery and Creator that can give to our worship that sincerity and spontaneous joy which alone can satisfy our deepest yearning.

12. Music: The Language of Hope

The talk about music can be a futile effort, especially for me. I confess that when I was taking lessons on the violin some years ago, I went to my teacher's home for the weekly lesson, and I played for him a movement from a Handel violin sonata. When I finished, and before the teacher could say anything, I admitted that I had played the movement badly, adding that I was frustrated and disappointed, for I had practiced three hours every day. My teacher was a member of the Chicago Symphony Orchestra, a much better teacher than I deserved, and he was a hard master. When I said that I had practiced vigorously that week, he replied, "Mr. Adams, it is not the amount of time you spend in practice that counts. What counts is the intelligence you apply to that bow."

So much, then, for my competence as a musician. Nevertheless, I kept at it on the ground that some things are so precious that they are worth doing badly.

Shakespeare is severe in his judgment of people who have no music in their souls. In *The Merchant of Venice,* he has Lorenzo say to Jessica, his beloved:

> The man that hath no music in himself,
> Nor is not moved with concord of sweet sounds,
> Is not fit for treasons, stratagems, and spoils;
> The motions of his spirit are dull as night,
> And his affections dark as Erebus.
> Let no such man be trusted.

What good is music, then? Does it improve the character of the music lover? William James once wrote that if, after attending a symphony concert, you are not kinder to your grandmother on returning home, the concert has been wasted on you. I doubt that we can accept this Sunday School moralizing. The question is not an easy one to answer. Perhaps the answer cannot be put into words. There is a tale or legend about Beethoven, who had played one of his compositions to an acquaintance. On his finishing the piece on the piano, the listener asked, But what does it mean? Beethoven replied with not a word. Instead, he sat down at the piano and played the piece again.

I suppose that if we try to answer the question, What good is music? we should say at the outset that it is an end in itself, a terminal value. I recall overhearing an argument at Columbia University. A pragmatist philosopher in the spirit of William James was asserting that music helps us to adjust to the environment. The other person in the argument then said, "Tell me, please, what does the music of Mozart suggest to you?"

The reply came, "I suppose music has a certain therapeutic value."

"I see," said the other fellow, "you class Mozart along with pills!"

I have the notion that the answer to our question lies somewhere in between the view that music is simply an end in itself and the view that it creates good character or possesses therapeutic value in some immediately practical way. We have to remember that there is a lot of bad music that can habituate one to bad taste. But more than that, music, even good music, can accompany a wide variety of actions. There are work songs, army songs, love songs, prison songs, hymn tunes. In all of these activities, we see the illustration of the maxim of the art critic who said, Art has a heart full of service. Music can be brought into the service of non-aesthetic ends, good or bad.

Music can be in the service of anything and everything, that is, music with words; but what about music without words? Let us consider what great music without words *does* and what great great music without words *serves*. Authentic music without words is able to say what cannot be put into words. In any time or place, this is an extremely significant enterprise, one that painting and sculpture and architecture share with music. Perhaps Beethoven simply played the piece again, in effect saying, "Listen, my friend."

In a time when the old myths of religion are crumbling, when traditional formulations of religious faith are frayed or fraying, music without words can express the substance of life's meaning, the substance of joy, of tragedy, of comedy, of play, of lament and re-affirmation; in short, the meaning of life itself.

In large measure, we may answer the question, What is music worth?, by saying,

it depends not only on the music but also on the listener. When listeners are looking for or wanting to affirm the meaning of life, they may well be able to enjoy Beethoven's *Missa Solemnis* or Bach's *Mass in B Minor,* even though the religious words themselves appear to be meaningless.

There are two ways in which this affirmation of the meaning of life is expressed in music, whether with or without words. The first of these ways can be illustrated by an incident reported by an eminent literary critic. In an essay entitled, *How to Tell a Good Book from a Bad,* H. W. Garrod, formerly professor of poetry at Oxford, sets forth the view that great art expresses the fundamental emotions of life, at the same time ordering these emotions and stabilizing the soul. Mr. Garrod tells about reading a popular novel in a railway carriage in England. As he read the novel, he began to weep, and the further he read the more he wept. Finally, a benign clergyman in the same compartment, pitying the poor man, moved over to his side of the compartment to sit beside him and asked, "Is there anything I can do to help you in your distress?"

Mr. Garrod gave an inspired reply, "I fear I am beyond the aid of prayer. I am weeping because this is such a bad book."

Instead of giving stability, the novel was unhinging him, dissolving his center.

Great music gives intensified expression to insight too deep for tears, and it does this by lending order and dynamics to sound. It is the genius of the performer of music that he can present a work of music with the ease and mastery that give dynamic order to human experience, at the same time giving the impression of spontaneity. A second thing to be noted here is that the dynamic order gives the listener the experience of perfection of style. Our lives are filled with frustration, disappointment, awareness of the miscarriage of justice or the absence of friendship and love. The artist provides the listener with the opportunity of contemplating perfection, of experiencing unity in variety, of enjoying fulfillment. Music is the language of hope, affirming hope against hopelessness. Music is the language of new resolve in the face of the seven evil angels having vials of seven last plagues filled with wrath. Music as the language of hope joins the chorus of humanity, striving for community while singing, "Great and marvelous are Your works, O God Almighty."

13. Art, Religion, and Utopia

The Peaceable Kingdom, the choral work by Randall Thompson, was dedicated to the late G. Wallace Woodworth and to the Harvard Glee Club and the Radcliffe Choral Society. The title page of the composition reads: "To the Memory of Edward Hicks, 1780-1849, the preaching Quaker of Pennsylvania," with texts from the Prophet Isaiah. The title of the work refers to a series of primitive paintings by this Quaker sign painter and coach builder, paintings that depict the hoped for kingdom of peace envisaged by Isaiah.

Before turning to this theme, I want to be permitted to inject something personal here. Wallace Woodworth and I occupied rooms next to each other in a Harvard dormitory when we were graduate students. Next to Wallace's room was the room of Virgil Thompson, later to become a distinguished composer and critic. In those days, Wallace Woodworth was conductor of the Harvard Glee Club and the Radcliffe Choral Society, and before that Dr. Archibald Davison was conductor of these societies. Mrs. Adams and I were members during those years. Professor Elliott Forbes of the Harvard Music Department after the death of Wallace Woodworth has reminded me that Wallace Woodworth published in the Program Notes of the Boston Symphony Orchestra an article about the first performance of Randall Thompson's *The Peaceable Kingdom,* saying that "Thompson is the first among our native composers of choral music."

One year after Wallace Woodworth published his article for the Boston Symphony Orchestra, Professor Elliott Forbes published an article on Randall Thompson in which he says of this composition, *The Peaceable Kingdom,* that it is the most inspired work of this composer. Then he proceeds to analyze the music of each of the choruses. He points out that Randall Thompson took a great deal of time selecting the passages from Isaiah, choosing them in such a way as to bring into sharp contrast the rewards of the righteous and the rewards of the wicked. Dr. Forbes tells us that the type of scale used for the righteous is different from that used for the wicked. When concerned with the wicked, the harmony tends toward the modal (medieval or Renaissance); and when concerned with the righteous, it tends toward the major of the diatonic scale. On the whole, however, the style is conservative and in the diatonic.

Modern dissonantal music is reserved for the third chorus, "The Noise of a Multitude in the Mountains." In this chorus, there is a lack of real melody, the voices rising to and remaining on a certain plateau. A distinctive feature of this whole work is the composer's simplicity and clarity of style following the rhythms of normal speech.

What shall we say of the title, *The Peaceable Kingdom,* and of that quaint Quaker painter. Edward Hicks lived from 1780 to 1849. He was a man without much formal education, a man who took a skeptical attitude toward higher education, seeing it as a threat to the simple ways of authentic Quaker existence. After some years of his youth which he spent in a lackadaisical fashion in the taverns, he was converted to Quakerism. Of special interest is the fact that Edward Hicks was the cousin of Elias Hicks, the founder of the liberal branch of Quakerism, which at that time struggled against the so-called orthodox Quakers. In his view, these orthodox Quakers emphasized the letter of Scripture rather than the spirit and the Inner Light, and they emphasized certain doctrines of traditional Christianity. The Hicksites were accused of denying the virgin birth of Jesus and the doctrine of the divinity of Christ. Some of them were called Unitarian Quakers. Indeed, in 1817, Elias Hicks succeeded in preventing the Baltimore Meeting of Friends from adopting a set creed. Only two years later, in 1819, William Ellery Channing delivered in Baltimore the beacon light sermon entitled *Unitarian Christianity,* which launched the Unitarian movement in a more of less formal fashion. The struggle of Elias and Edward Hicks against the orthodox Friends generated a great deal of heat and acrimony. At times one gets the impression that the passages from Isaiah about the wicked were applied by Edward to these orthodox Friends. Edward's conception of wickedness brought him near the major conflicts of the time. He, like his cousin, was a vigorous opponent of violence and war; he was opposed to slavery and was an abolitionist. In religion, he was something of a rationalist like the Unitarians, and he vigorously opposed the emotional methods and manipulations of the revivalists. He opposed a professional ministry, what he and the Quakers called a hireling priestcraft, and he served for years as a lay preacher, never accepting any pay. He opposed usury and excoriated usurous bankers and farmers. He put on a battle against phrenology, thinking it was a fraud. He opposed instrumental music in the church, and perhaps it is fitting that Randall Thompson's composition should be a capella.

Edward Hicks also opposed professional training for the artist as well as for the preacher. He was a sign painter, and on the side he pursued the hobby of painting landscapes and animals and farm scenes. He became the foremost American primitive painter in the 19th century.

His favorite theme was the pictorial depiction of the Peaceable Kingdom, relying upon the texts from Isaiah which Randall Thompson has used for this composition, texts in which, according to Isaiah, the lion would lie down with the lamb at the end of time when peace and harmony among people and animals would be realized. Edward Hicks painted about 100 paintings of this theme. About 50 of them are said to be still extant. These pictures make Edward Hicks the foremost utopian painter of the 19th century, a century in which there were hundreds of utopian movements and communities.

That word "utopia" has deteriorated in the course of time. In its original Greek meaning, it refers to "no place" or "nowhere," the perfect ideal. According to another interpretation, the word refers to "a beautiful place." In general we may say that the utopian literature intends to portray human nature and human society in their purified form, in the mode that overcomes the evils of human society. Therefore, utopian literature has been a major form of expression in the history of culture, both Occidental and Oriental. In the West, it stems from the Old Testament prophets to kingdom of God conceptions in early Christianity, through Greek and Roman literature to Sir Thomas More, Francis Bacon, Thomas Campanella, the Diggers of the 17th century, and Edward Bellamy and hundreds of books and tracts in 19th century America.

Ernst Bloch, an anti-Nazi exile from Germany came to Cambridge, Massachusetts. At Harvard he wrote the most compendious history of utopian literature which we have, tracing utopian literature from ancient Israel and Greece and Rome down through the centuries. He viewed it as the principal literature of social criticism and of openness to the future, seeing Karl Marx as a principal stem from this stock.

Some of this literature is highly speculative. Some of it is concretely practical, looking towards the establishment of absolute equality among people, or toward the emancipation of slaves, workers, Indians, or women. Edward Hicks, following in the line of the Quaker William Penn, the founder of Pennsylvania, was especially concerned with the plight of slaves and Indians and with emancipation from war. Many of his paintings include William Penn and George Fox and other Quakers making their treaty with the Indians, along with the animals and children playing among them. These paintings depict what might be called the fulness of being, the potentialities of all creation.

Edward Hicks possessed an elaborate theory of the evils, the foibles, the frustrations, and the pervasions of human nature. He singled out four animals as the manifestations and symbols of the major evils of humankind: the wolf, the leopard, the bear, and the lion. In his writings, he epitomizes these evils which he finds not only in humanity but in himself: greed, deception, cruelty, violence, irresponsibility. The evils referred to by Isaiah also play a heavy role in the texts selected by Randall Thompson. These passages are not viewed as indicating the vindictiveness of God but rather as presenting the self-destructive consequences of greed and selfishness, cruelty and violence.

What, then, is the significance of this theme, *The Peaceable Kingdom*. In the first place, it engenders hope, reminding us always that in our personal existence and our societal existence there is always the possibility of new beginnings; that there are potentialities in human beings not yet realized but possible of realization. Such a work of art offers social criticism touching the imagination and the heart. At the same time, it gives us the experience of contemplating perfection, giving us a vision of fulfillment. So it is that the *Peaceable Kingdom*, in utopian literature and also in visual art, gives us a foretaste of the kingdom of God and a communal experience of the beauty of holiness.

14. Archibald Thompson Davison

For a generation Archibald Davison was professor of music as well as organist and choirmaster at Harvard University; besides this, he was the conductor, and indeed the creator, of the Harvard Glee Club as it has become known. Many a student of his and many a member of the Harvard Glee Club gained from him an orientation that became fundamental for the rest of their lives. I count myself among those grateful students.

Most of us students in Harvard Divinity School in the old days took his course on Church Music, which he gave from the piano bench. My roommate and I, members of the Harvard Glee Club, attended rehearsal three evenings a week, from 7 to 8 o'clock. There we came to know, under Dr. Davison's direction, the classics of choral music. Our long periods of rehearsal were punctuated by the Glee Club concerts in Symphony Hall with the Boston Symphony Orchestra under the baton of Serge Koussevitsky. At the rehearsals immediately preceding the concerts, Dr. Koussevitsky took charge, and these rehearsals were concluded by the great dress rehearsals with the orchestra in Symphony Hall. Through this discipline, I came to understand the meaning of the phrase attached to the name of Johann Sebastian Bach, the Fifth Evangelist.

Let me add here that after I assumed pastorates in nearby parishes, Dr. Davison enabled me and the respective music committees in those parishes radically to transform the choral music of those churches. Indeed, Dr. Davison was a major figure in the reformation of Protestant music in America. His book, *Protestant Church Music in America,* was a culmination of his effort.

It used to be said of President Charles W. Eliot that, under his aegis, Harvard was transformed from a small town college to a university. Dr. Davison performed an analogous function; he was the maieutic mentor who assisted American Protestant church music to come of age. He did not accomplish this feat with the heat of battle. If you have ever looked into his book, you will recall the acid comments on the moralism of American Protestant preaching and on the triviality of Protestant church music of that time. Here Dr. Davison, like Sampson of old, wielded the jawbone of an ass as he smote the Philistines, us Protestant Philistines. Dr. Davison not only convinced us that the man of taste and of genuine piety should be, and also was, offended by the jaunty barber shop music that one could hear in the churches. He also castigated the impoverishment of imagination and the subjectivity of the characteristic music. For Dr. Davison, the reformation demanded in church music was part and parcel of a reformation demanded in preaching, a reformation that would overcome the anthropocentricism of Protestant preaching and music, a reformation that would transform the taste of the people seduced by spurious claims made in the name of the democratic average. Listen to a characteristic sample:

> The average American would as readily admit being deeply moved by beauty as he would wear a monocle and don a silk hat. Now this 'kalaphobia," if we may invent a term, works untold harm to church music which is immediately intelligible to everyone. To use anything else implies an affectation which is undemocratic. To such an extent, indeed, have we democratized our services that, although we admit the almightiness of God, we behave as though God would prefer to be treated like one of us. Whatever may be the merit of such an attitude, it may be stated in behalf of a high standard of church music that no great art has ever issued from any concept of God as the Supreme Benign Rotarian.

Dr. Davison made no claim to being a theologian, but he felt that his deficiencies here were in large part owing to the quality of the preaching he heard in the Harvard Chapel through the many years of his incumbency as organist and choirmaster. He says that for twenty-five years, summers excepted, he listened to an average of five sermons each week; and for a period of years, he said, he consumed between Sundays not less than twelve sermons a week. He was always struck by the discrepancy between the theology contained in the sermon and that belonging to the anthems and the hymns. Something of his theological outlook is indicated by his statement that on the theme of the salvation of the world though the death of Jesus Christ, "It is no exaggeration to say that probably not less than eighty percent of the greatest church music centers about this theme upon which, incidentally, I have not heard a sermon preached in years."

He said that, regardless of questions of dogma, any general review of the last quarter century's preaching cannot fail to reveal that in spite of some preaching of sustained power, much sermonizing has increasingly lost that quality which is one of the richest endowments of great church music, namely, *affirmation.* On this theme, he could be eloquent, and on its absence in preaching and in church music, he could be furiously indignant. However, the quality of affirmation was not the only standard he delineated. He emphasized also the qualities of repentance and humility.

I recall his once saying that a test of one type of church music is that it expresses a sense of the cross, an aloofness to secularity. Christianity for him was compounded of mystery and of renunciation, as well as of affirmation. In his own words, "Music, like religion, is fundamentally a mystery."

15. Why Sing?

The Spanish philosopher, Ortega y Gasset, captures a memory of his childhood: a triumphant act that the circus clowns of his youth used to perform. He says:

> A clown would stroll in with his livid, floured face, seat himself on the railing, and produce from his bulky pocket a flute which he began to play. At once the ringmaster appeared and intimated to him that here one could not play. The clown, unperturbed, stalked over to another place and started again. Now the ringmaster walked up angrily and snatched his melodious toy from him. The clown remained unshaken in the face of such misfortune. He waited until the ringmaster was gone and plunging his hand into his fathomless pocket produced another flute, and from it another melody. Alas, inexorably, here came the ringmaster again, and he again despoiled him of his flute. Now the clown's pocket changed into an inexhaustible magic box from which proceeded, one after another, new musical instruments of all kinds, clear and gay or sweet and melancholy. The music overruled the veto of destiny and filled the entire space, imparting to all of us, with its impetuous, invincible bounty, a feeling of exultation, as though a torrent of strange energies had sprung from the dauntless melody the clown blew on his flute as he sat on the railing of the circus.

What an apt parable of the dauntless melody of existence itself. Is it because the universe is at heart a song that human beings are inveterate singers? Let us be borne down with toil, and we will chant an accompanying song of work. Let us lament our loneliness, our despair, and even then will we sing. All sorts and conditions of people in all the experiences of joy and sorrow, work and play, solitude and society, somehow persist in singing with Emerson:

> Let me go whe'er I will
> I hear a sky-born music still.

Why do we sing? Some people will answer that all experience, especially all intense experience, demands the impassioned utterance of rhythm. They will perhaps suggest that this rhythm issues forth in harmony or in contrast with the rhythm of the heartbeat or with the rhythm of breathing. Some will say we sing in order to have company; others say that we are merely chattering simians; yet others will say that we must give expression to our excess energy. A song may revive some memory of a cherished experience. Think of the flood of remembrance that D. H. Lawrence releases when he says:

> Softly in the dusk a woman is singing to me
> Taking me back down the vista of years, till I see
> A child sitting under the piano, in the boom of
> tingling strings,
> And pressing the small, poised feet of a mother who
> smiles as she sings.

We are told that people sing in order to bring their experience under control. To be able to sing of one's grief, for example, is to view it in perspective, to assimilate it into the whole of one's experience. To sing rightly is at once to give beauty of utterance and to stabilize one's inner life; it is to give form to experience and yet to allow the exuberance of hope to burst through the form. These answers to the question, Why sing?, are provocative but somehow inadequate for the religious consciousness because the depth dimension is lacking.

Something deeper is hinted at by the poet who composed the book of Job. The creation of the world, the divine creativity, is music; it is song. *The morning stars sang together, and all the children of God shouted for joy.* Indeed, the history of the literature of religion includes as its most widely shared ingredient the history of the hymn. Think of the hymns of the Israelites, the hymns of the Christians, the hymns of the Rig Veda, the Song of the Blessed One, the Mahabharata. We sinners seeking redemption are inveterate singers.

Some religions have interpreted the universe as a dance, or as a song and a dance. For the Greeks, song and dance were an imitation of the life of the God who is the creative power of the universe. In the dance, the dancer personified the God being celebrated. The dancer, in moments of ecstasy, became one with the god and partook of the divine life being celebrated. The human song and dance were a striving to participate in the cosmic song and dance. Similarly, the poet Shelley speaks of our attempt to be one with "the ideal perfection and energy which everyone feels to be the eternal type of all that we love, admire, and would become." The cosmic song and dance are a form of communion with the being of God, a standing outside of the prison of one's ordinary identity and experience, a participation in the serious but spontaneously playful drama of love and strife, death and rebirth.

In India we find a similar idea of the character of life as song and as cosmic dance. The cosmic process has often been called the Dance of Shiva, the God of many arms. At every moment, the dancer, whether divine or human, is giving expression to a cosmic meaning or purpose or will. God is the cosmic artist who is ever fulfilling the inner urge of love of life and beauty, dancing to the fullness of joy.

The Christian, in singing, does more than express emotion. Like the singers of other traditions, there are songs of praise, confession, recollection, dedication, and fellowship. Hymns become forms of communion between people and God, providing a bridge that leads to the victory of the creative and recreative powers of the divine, thereby enabling us to find a new flute and a new melody such as the song the stars sang together on the morning of creation.

Why do we sing? Carlyle has told us: "All Deep things are song. It seems somehow the very central essence of us is Song; as if all the rest were but wrappings and hulls. The primal element of us and of all things, the heart of creation, is music."

16. Crosses

A Maundy Thursday Address Preceding A Communion Service

D. H. Lawrence tells us that on a walking tour which he made through the Austrian Tyrol, he saw little crucifixes dotting the landscape in that part of the world. With his usual acuteness, he describes the various interpretations of the crucifixion represented in this peasant form of art. He said that some of the faces represent Jesus as a defiant young man offering resistance to the end; others represent him as a self-pitying, whining figure; still others depict him as in a stupor dully enduring the pain; others show him in a forgiving attitude.

The principal interpretations of the crucifixion as a human experience would certainly have to include one that D. H. Lawrence has omitted. This interpretation might be characterized as the cross smothered in flowers, the view suggested by the ecclesiastical manipulation of religious symbols in the interest of a pretty sentimentalism. This interpretation eliminates all evidence of pain and suffering, sin and evil.

All of the great symbols of the Christian faith have been represented with this same variety of subjective interpretation. The communion service has not been exempt from these perversions. The Lord's supper is sometimes viewed simply as a beautiful ceremony calling to its aid a profusion of light and color. At other times, it is seen as a liturgical act which by some magical potency transmits supernatural grace; and at still other times, it is looked upon as a sacred performance which draws the communicant away from the harrowing experiences of the common life to a restful retreat in the communion of saints.

If the cross is to be seen in its significance, it must be taken up from the lilies and confronted in its stark and rugged reality; and the communion service must be drawn up out of the light and color which only titilate the senses, and seen in the full richness of significance that it carried on that night of the last supper.

One of the ways in which the communion service can be envisaged in its true perspective is to recall that the last supper was not a ceremony in a church at which priests officiated for the assembled worshipers. Indeed, there were no priests present. Neither Jesus nor his disciples looked upon themselves as priests or clergy. They were, as a matter of fact, laymen who were rapidly approaching a fateful destiny at the hands of the clergy. Such a reflection as this is not suggested for the purpose of depreciating the clergy of Jesus' time or ours. Rather it is mentioned in order to remind us that the Christian religion was founded by lay people. As a matter of fact, we may go further and say that the vitality of the Christian religion, and especially of Protestantism, has depended largely upon its laymen and its laywomen. Protestantism has given clear and definite expression to this thought by its doctrine of the priesthood of all believers. That is, in the eyes of God, there is no deeply religious distinction between the clergy and the laity. All laymen and laywomen are priests; all priests are laymen and laywomen. What makes a priest a believer is the same thing which makes a lay person a priest: personal decision. No set of sacred doctrines or of sacred liturgical acts, properly transmitted or performed by the clergy, no act of ordination by the bishop or congregation can relieve the individual clergy person or lay person from responsibility for decision. Not even the Bible can liberate anyone from this responsibility. Individual decision, even concerning the Bible, is inescapable. Hence, the genuineness of this service depends entirely upon the kind of decision and the quality of life which we ourselves actually illustrate. Neither the beauty of the service, nor the hallowed memories which the service calls to mind can actually justify our participation. The circumstances surrounding the first communion service bring this very truth into bold relief. It is an experience which, through personal decision, bound a group of lay people to each other and to their Master.

In the second place, the Last Supper was not held in the temple; it was held in an upper room. It was a meal shared in common in the course of the ordinary and customary activities of the daily round. It was not a sacred act withdrawn from the secular realm. It was, to be sure, a holy act, an act that gave an eternal meaning to those moments when the disciples were alone with the Master. The holiness of this fellowship derived from the common life which these disciples had been sharing every day. The same thing must be said about our communion service. We are participating in this ceremony in a church, but it is not for that reason holy. It is holy only insofar as it points beyond itself, beyond to God on the one side, and beyond to our every day living on the other side. Here again we are appealing to a time honored Protestant principle. Just as we deny any fundamental religious distinction between the laity and the clergy, so also do we repudiate on principle a cleavage of the sacred from the profane sphere. To Protestantism, God alone is holy, and no church, no doctrine, no saint, no institution, and no rite is holy in itself. Everyone and everything and every group is profane in itself and is sacred only insofar as it becomes a symbol of the divine holiness. Just as our participation in this service presupposes that each of us has made a personal decision in favor of the gospel of love which is at the heart of service, so also our presence here presupposes that we are willing to being within the area of that gospel of love in all of our common life: our dependence upon nature, our dependence upon each other, even our ways of earning our daily bread. Our presence here means, then, that we believe that all of our life is sacred as well as secular. The very symbols which surround the nave and chancel of this church remind us of the sacredness of our work and our play, of sun, moon, and stars, of family, state, and church. The mirror of marble behind the altar, on which stands the communion cup, reminds us that we do not leave the world of the secular and the profane when we enter into the holy of holies. Rather we bring all of life to the altar in praise and in thanksgiving, in penitence and in consecration before the divine judgment which knows the secrets of all hearts.

But this service of communion should remind us of more than just the priesthood of all believers and of the inseparable bond between the sacred and the secular. When we recall that tomorrow is Good Friday, the day of the crucifixion, we are brought away from the unreality of surface beauty and into collision with reality with a terrific jolt. This service is not merely an occasion for a communion with God and with each other, re-presenting for us the ideal of love which binds us together. It is also a reminder of the terrible reality of evil. Jesus and many others before and since have been the innocent victims of so-called good people. Indeed, the tragedy of Good Friday was not really the tragedy of Jesus; it was the tragedy of the world. He came unto his own, and his own received him not. This real tragedy of Good Friday, this oft-repeated tragedy, was clearly thought of in this way by Jesus. The women of Jerusalem wept for him, but Jesus did not regard his own life as pitiful. "Daughters of Jerusalem, weep not for me. Weep for yourselves and for your children."

The crucifixion of Jesus was not a judgment upon him, but a judgment upon the world in which we live. The cross is not merely a tree on Golgatha or an ecclesiastical ornament on the altar; it is a persistent and perennial reality. Therefore, the communion service is not merely a sharing of ideals and purposes; it is also in the breaking of the bread and in the pouring of the cup, an unflinching realistic reminder of the evil which we ourselves have brought into the world, the evil which each of us bears within. We must not, then, in this communion service neglect its foreboding of the evil which we share and which goes on crucifying Christ in every age and in every heart. Truly, one might go so far as to say that we may test the genuineness of our awareness of the sacred and divine element in life by asking whether we possess a corresponding awareness of the Satanic element in our lives. The reality and the realism of one's belief in God can be vindicated only by the reality and realism of one's belief in Satan. Wherever the presence of the divine is deeply felt, there too will be felt the presence of the devil.

It is precisely a vague awareness of this truth that makes us reluctant to talk about the cross in our ordinary conversation. It is this awareness of the mediocrity and guilt of our existence, this awareness of the share which we have through sins of both omission and commission in our jerry-built civilization; it is this awareness which restrains us from glib talk about the the cross. What troubles us is the comfort of our lives, their ease, their security, their remoteness from the cross, their indifference to the privations and sufferings of the innocent. How can we be terribly at ease in Zion, then, as we worship here together in the presence of that spirit before whom all hearts are open, all desires known, and from whom no secrets are hid? We cannot, and that is why I say that the communion service is more than a sharing of our ideals and more than a memorial to ancient virtue; it is also an uncovering of the sinful reality which made the crucifixion possible in the first place and which gives point to our remembering it at all.

The communion service does more than remind us of the omnipresence of evil. It is also the source of a great and confident hope, a hope based on the conviction that if we can but to learn to weep for ourselves, if we can repent, we can also find the victory that overcomes the world. This man of Galilee who says to us, "Weep not for me; weep for yourselves," wished to save us from tears wept for him and also from tears wept in self-pity for ourselves. Through his evangel, his good news concerning the love that suffers and forgives, our tears of self-pity are transmuted into tears of repentance. Repentance does not accuse the wicked world around us and within us of the fate which left us to set it right. It accuses self and in humility of spirit begins the work of quiet and gracious reconciliation. Here we find the promise of possible meaning and beauty. Penitence and re-birth make us truly realistic about ourselves, our city, our nation; and the word realistic need not signify merely an awareness of evil but also the possibility of good. It discloses not only the real and the possible baseness of human nature, but also our possible grandeur, which is for all time symbolized and memorialized in the character of the Galilean.

Where two or three are gathered together in my name, there am I in the midst of them.

17. The Crucifixion
A Good Friday Address

"I cannot call him to mind," said Pontius Pilate. The crucifixion of Jesus, apparently, was only a part of one uneventful day's work for the Roman. How could he be expected to remember? Yet there were many things which he could remember.

The very celebration of the service of Good Friday all over the world is evidence that there are still many who can call Jesus of Nazareth to mind with some definiteness. It is a reminder to us that for the abundant life, our memories have their work to do; that memory should not be something accidental in its working, but deliberate.

An old saying is that the Bourbons never forgot anything and never learned anything. I suppose this means that they remembered the wrong things, namely, their grudges, and forgot the wrong things, their subjects. At all events, we can say that the first sign of a civilization is a discriminating remembrance of things past, a community of memory. Indeed, it is from the community of memory that most of the significant movements of thought and action emerge. Matthew Arnold, when asked how he judged the quality of contemporary poetry, replied that he carried in his memory some touchstones out of the past, a few lines from Dante, a few from Shakespeare, a few from Homer, a few from Byron and Wordsworth. He used these lines as touchstones for testing other poets. In order that there may be even significant revolt, he suggests, there must be a memory of what has been of significance in the past.

The memory of a community, or of a person, is an extremely important aspect of its spiritual life. It is only through a disciplined memory of the past that one can judge properly of the present and play one's own part rightly. Nevertheless, our memories are often very short. Henri Bergson once suggested that it is much easier to explain memory in terms of human psychology than it is to explain forgetfulness. Why do we forget? he asks. That is the more difficult question.

Consider with me just one aspect of our forgetfulness. If we should attempt to answer this question as to why people tend to forget what most needs remembering, we might make a long list of tentative answers. We might say that we forget because we are under the strain of settling

225

our own new problems, or because of sheer egoism, moral solipsism, or because of the attraction of apparent novelties around us, or because we carry to an extreme the virtue of thinking about the future. Much might be said concerning these reasons and similar ones; but I wish to speak of only one reason, one not yet mentioned. For want of a better phrase to describe this cause of our loss of memory, I shall call it "pure spirituality," the erroneous supposition that human beings are capable of discovering or understanding the truth without the mediation of the senses or of events that have happened.

At its best, this cause of forgetfulness is a virtue; it is the recognition that significant living and meaningful choices in our behavior, depend upon the possession of some general principles of conduct. Short of its best, this virtue becomes only an interest in ideas rather than in ideas realized by persons and in events.

If we think of the Christian movement in history which Jesus inaugurated, we must realize that although the early Christians were bound together by some abstract ideas, the birth of Christianity was not simply due to the promulgation of certain inspiring ideas. It was due to an event, something that had happened which *illustrated* abstract ideas. Williston Walker, the church historian, raises the question, Why did Christianity win out over the other religions of the first century? He answers the question by saying that it was because the Christians did not have simply a philosophy of life or a mythology. Christianity began with a person, with someone who had actually lived and suffered, met temptation, persecution, and disappointment, yet triumphed over them.

Another church historian, Arthur Cushman McGiffert, Sr., claimed that the Christians were so preoccupied with Christ, whom they looked upon as a god incarnate, that they had some difficulty in relating the founder of their religion to the creator God whom they had inherited from Judaism. I presume it is this same idea which Goethe had in mind in having his Faust affirm: In the beginning was the deed.

At all events, the early Christians insisted upon the fact of the historical reality of their founder. Indeed, one of the first enemies of the Christian movement was that form of Gnosticism which wished to interpret the life or death of Christ as unreal, as an illusion. It is probably for this very reason that the phrase, "Suffered under Pontius Pilate," appears in the Apostles' Creed.

A similar issue was the center of the controversy between William Ellery Channing and certain of the transcendentalists. Channing wished to retain Christ as the focal point of the Christian life. On the other hand, Ralph Waldo Emerson, in the Divinity School Address, declared that the Christians had too much exalted the person of Christ. It is possible that Emerson was here reacting against an exaggerated Christocentrism in his youth; but when we read his *Representative Men,* which was not called representative *ideas,* we see that despite his belief that the ideas of love, justice, and temperance are latent in every mind, he extols the heroes of the race. He says, "Be not a philosopher, but a Platonist; not a soul, but a Christian." Emerson also said earlier, "The interest created by Jesus is of a personal kind. The infinite field of moral truth is but a wearisome and barren immensity till it is peopled with examples."

When we commemorate the life and death of Jesus today, there should be an implicit recognition of the importance of persons, as well as of ideas and principles. This church is not simply a monument to ideas or ideals. It is a monument to facts, to something which has happened. It is a monument not only to the fact of the life and death of Jesus but to other facts as well. We think of particular people associated with the church over the years, people who are not simply ideas or ideals for us of what we wish to be. They have been and are facts. Our church is not devoted to "pure spirituality." It is a community of persons, and it has been this from the beginning when William Wallace Fenn served as the first minister of this church. He used to say that a universe with just one person praying in it is a very different sort of universe from one without that person. We might also say that a universe with the strange man of Galilee hanging on a cross is very different than the universe would be without the Crucified One. Indeed, it is such a one who makes us realize the kind of universe we are in. In the mind of a great Roman official, the crucifixion of Jesus may have been an incident so inconsequential as not to be worthy of memory, but our presence here proves that we refuse to forget the sacred fact of the agony of the crucifixion.

18. The Bridge of Confidence
An Easter Address

One of the more vivid recollections of my youth concerns a long railway trestle which spanned a deep gorge near my boyhood home. It was generally agreed by the boys of the town that the sign of manliness and bravery was to be able to walk that long railway trestle which had no plank walk, but rather only railway ties. It was always a major event in the life of the youth of the town when still another boy could announce, with proper credentials and dependable witnesses, that he had crossed the trestle. Just because our parents knew that all the youngsters were under a perpetual dare, they warned us repeatedly of the extreme danger. What if we should get to the middle and become dizzy and be unable to continue the crossing or be unable to return? What if an unexpected freight train should happen to cross the bridge when a boy was on the way across. If these warnings were not enough, the boys got some sense of the height of the trestle by looking up to it from the valley below. Then, too, there was the fearful sign at each end of the bridge: NO THOROUGHFARE. PEDESTRIANS CROSS AT THEIR OWN RISK.

The feelings that a small boy felt in looking across that trestle are somewhat similar to the attitude that everyone feels at times with regard to the valley of the shadow of death. Is there a bridge that leads from this life to the other side? Is there another side?

For us modern people, the view of the bridge has considerably altered from what is was for the medieval or ancient populace. Our predecessors inhabited a much smaller world than ours. The ancient Ptolemaic universe was a convenient and manageable scheme of things, with the earth at the center of a neat little cosmos with existed primarily as exterior decoration for our *terra ferma,* which was created on March 4, 4004 B.C. Science has revealed to us an utterly different universe, vastly larger and vastly older. We are just now told it is seventy-six light years to the Pole Star, which like all the other stars, is another sun like our own, only larger, and possibly the center of another system of planets. If we imagine our globe to be 16 inches around the equator, i.e., four inches in diameter, our sun is a mile away and is larger than this church. If we adopt the scale of one in ten thousand million, the earth and the sun would be invisibly small: the orbit of Neptune would be the size of a pin head; the nearest star to the earth would be four yards away; the Milky Way would be a good day's walk away. This new universe is vastly older, as well as larger.

The earth no longer occupies the center of the stage but seems to be a second-class planet following a second class sun somewhere out in the suburbs of the universe. Is it any wonder that Blaise Pascal, the seventeenth century mathematician and natural philosopher credited with substantial scientific research, exclaimed: "The eternal silence of these infinite spaces frightens me. The whole visible world is only an imperceptible atom in the ample bosom of nature. No idea approaches it. It is an infinite sphere, the center of which is everywhere, the circumference nowhere. Mankind may regard itself as lost in this remote corner of nature."

Moreover, we find that the solid earth is an illusion since everything is in motion. Indeed, we are poised between two infinities, the infinitely great and the infinitely small. Within this setting occurs the human comedy. Is it any wonder that the most noted modern poet should say:

> Tomorrow and tomorrow and tomorrow,
> Creeps in this petty pace from day to day
> To the last syllable of recorded time,
> And all our yesterdays have lighted fools
> The way to dusty death.
> Life's but a walking shadow, a poor player
> That struts and frets his hour upon the stage
> And then is heard no more.

Is it any wonder that we are told that religion, and especially belief in immortality, is only trivial and irrelevant wishful thinking, illusion, colossal human egotism?

Is there no bridge by which we can traverse the valley of death to the ground of all being? Is there nothing on which we can depend?

As the spectroscope reveals, throughout the known universe there seems to be a unity of matter and a marvelous correlation of forces. We seem to be living in a universe which is not mere anarchy or blind confusion. It summons our reason and intelligence to understand it with our groping minds. Still, you may ask: What support is there in this worldview for religion, and especially for immortality?

Religion implies that there is something of utmost significance in our very appearance in the universal process. It urges us to recognize the fact that there have been a Socrates, a Shakespeare, a Confucius, a Buddha, a Christ. I do not propose to offer any arguments for immortality. Indeed, when anyone begins arguing for or against immortality, the affect on me is usually pretty cold. I would only remind you that there are some good evidences to show that there is meaning and purpose in that corner of the universe that we know. The fact that we are children of the universe and heirs to all its glories is trustworthy.

What then about the bridge which leads across the valley of the shadow of death? We may answer that what is yet unknown will probably bear the same quality as the known. The bridge to the unknown is a bridge in which we may have some confidence. The possibilities of the universe are not exhausted. Thornton Wilder gave expression to this conviction with these words:

> We ourselves shall be loved for a while and forgotten. But the love will be enough; all those impulses of love return to the love that made them. Even memory is not necessary for love. There is a land of the living and a land of the dead, and the bridge is love, the only survival, the only meaning.

Blessed Are the Powerful

By James Luther Adams

Delivered at the inaugural convocation of the Boston Theological
Institute in 1968.[1]

*The Institute is a consortium of nine seminaries and theological schools:
Andover Newton Theological School, Boston College, Boston University
School of Theology, Episcopal Divinity School, Weston Jesuit School of
Theology, Gordon-Conwell Theological Seminary, Harvard Divinity School,
Holy Cross Greek Orthodox School of Theology, and Saint John's Seminary.*

***

We live in a time when almost everyone is acutely conscious of the
struggle for power that is going on, in the international theater and also
on the home front. Indeed, over wide stretches of the earth revolutionary
forces are at work in various ways. Some places, to be sure, remain in
a happy state of innocence, but this happiness may soon pass. Our
situation today is fraught with danger, readily evident in the appearance
of the "confrontation politics" that rejects normal political methods. One
of our sages, a seasoned commentator on the political scene, noting the
importunate demands for reform, questions whether popular democracy
as we know and cherish it is capable of bringing about the changes required
in a technological age. There are many paradoxes in the situation.

Ordinarily, the churches and theological seminaries are not
expected to concern themselves with struggles for power. What is the
world coming to, the pious will ask, if churches and seminaries turn
aside from their true vocation to join in the struggles of power politics?
It is therefore significant, it is even a sign of audacity, that the opening
convocation of the Boston Theological Institute focuses attention on
the problem of power.

---

1 The address was subsequently published in *The Christian Century*, vol. 86,
no. 25 (June 18, 1969), copyright 1969, Christian Century Foundation.

The word is highly ambiguous, for power can take a great variety of forms. In some circles, power has a very bad reputation. Everyone is familiar with Lord Acton's maxim, "Power *tends* to corrupt, and absolute power corrupts absolutely." Acton apparently aims to be somewhat ambiguous: Power tends to corrupt. Henry Adams is more blunt when he says, "Power is poison." A contemporary American political analyst who aims to reflect a theological perspective says that "man is born a slave, but everywhere he wants to be a master." Somewhat similar was the view of Jacob Burckhardt, the eminent Swiss historian who formulated a basic axiom of his philosophy of history in these words: "Power is not a stability but a lust, and *ipso facto* insatiable; therefore, unhappy in itself and doomed to make others unhappy." Looking back at the period of the Reformation and the Protestant-Catholic struggle, Burckhardt concludes that the confession that became dominant in any region of Europe was the one that possessed the strongest battalions. This view reminds me of a definition I heard recently at a church conference on black power: "Power is not something to be shared. It is something you have to take away from others."

Yet "power" has not always been defined as simply synonymous with coercion or corruption. In the history of religion and thus also of Christianity, it is a venerable concept. God is addressed as the Lord Almighty. In its extended version, the Lord's Prayer concludes with the words, "Thine is the kingdom, and the power and the glory." And the Gospel is said to be the power of God for salvation.

I

Obviously, if one is to speak of power, everything depends on how one defines it. Generically, power is ability, capacity, to get things done, and as such is essential to any person or society and also to God. On the human scene it may be the ability to dominate, to communicate, to manipulate, to play the piano; or it may be the capacity simply to go on existing. Plato said the first quality of anything is that it has power. Reality is power. One of the most familiar definitions asserts that power is the ability to exercise influence. Max Weber spoke of power as the ability to issue a command that must be obeyed, and he added that it might take the indirect form of manipulation. He overlooked Plato's definition of the passive dimension of power: the capacity to be influenced. Plato hints that an essential difference among people is that between their susceptibility to good or evil influence.

But if power as such is evil, then impotence could appear to be divine. Yet God, we are told, is perfect in power. Kierkegaard would say that this perfection of God's power is to be seen in his giving the human being the power to turn against him; for communion with God is not possible if no alternative exists. Here we approach the paradox contained in the dialectic between divine and human power. Human freedom is a gift from God. From a religious perspective, both God and the human being would be impotent but for this grace of freedom.

Much more than this must be said, however, if we are to consider the nature of God's power and the human response. A familiar way of stating the fundamental insight of biblical faith is to say that it is the faith that informs a historical religion which views the human being as a historical, social creature, and that it aims to be confident in the ultimately reliable power. Thus it is a faith that defines and fulfills the destiny of the person as an individual and in community. In a rudimentary fashion, this faith is expressed in Exodus: God is a dynamic power that liberates from slavery—has brought a people out of Egypt and guided it across the Red Sea and the wilderness. "With thy hand thou hast redeemed; thou hast guided them in thy power." This power makes a covenant of faithfulness with a people (and eventually also with individuals); it requires of them that they pursue righteousness and mercy. Because this power is based on affection as much as on law, unfaithfulness is more than violation of law; it is betrayal of affection and trust.

The Old Testament prophets see unfaithfulness not only in idolatry but also in the separation that breeds injustice and destroys community. Sin begins in the human heart and finds social expression in class separation, in neglect of the poor, in the pursuit of vengeance instead of mercy. The sins specified by the prophets turn out to be the sort of thing that appears in today's newspaper, especially in the black press. Indeed, one historian has said that the Old Testament prophets anticipate the modern free press.

The Old Testament conception of the most reliable power, the divine community-forming power, is remarkable. It contains the element of command and at the same time the idea that we are free to respond or not to respond; and it envisions a power that becomes manifest in a community that struggles for righteousness, for justice and mercy. Much of this concept is summed up in Micah's words: "I am full of power in the Holy Spirit, full of judgment and might to declare unto Jacob his transgression, and to Israel its sin."

This conception of the power attributed to God served not only as a standard for and a criterion of all other powers; it also became the basis of hope for the future—so much so that it was projected into the future in the form of an expected Messiah. To be sure, there were nationalist as well as universal ingredients in the idea of the Messiah.

II

It is, of course, not easy to characterize precisely the changes that come with the advent of Jesus and of Christianity. In principle, the nationalist element is eliminated and the messianic kingdom is viewed as already breaking in and also as to come later with power. A new eon is already here in actuality, yet the historical process is brought under radical eschatological judgment and tension. The intermediary powers in the world which make for separation and strife and idolatry among people are viewed as demonic. To himself and to his followers, Jesus is the spearhead of the divine power, breaking into history and pointing beyond history, bringing healing to men and women, calling them into a new covenant of righteousness—a covenant that in the outcome formed a new universal community.

We can agree that this new kingdom movement was not a social reform movement. But a look at the character of the new community they thought was demanded shows us what the early Christians believed to be the truly authentic, the truly ultimate reliable power. In this community economic status, social rank, racial origin, were all subordinated to a broader, transcending, and transforming power. At the same time, the individual was brought into more intimate relationship both with God and with the other members of the fellowship. The direct response to the Holy Spirit gave rise to new problems of organization, for this responsiveness brought into existence a charismatic community under charismatic leadership. Yet it is not possible to interpret the ethic of the new community under any single rubric—for example, under the rubric of spirit to the exclusion of law, or of otherworldliness to the exclusion of this-worldly concerns, or of consistent eschatology to the exclusion

234

of concern and responsibility for the present. Nor can that community be interpreted as being either politically conservative or apolitical. Time was required for it to explore the implications of its confrontation with the dynamics, the power of the kingdom. Actually, the fact that the data regarding this community can be laid hold of in a variety of ways lends it perennial freshness. The many pertinent perspectives reflect the richness of motifs that become available here, and explain why early Christianity is seen as one of the great innovative moments in history, bringing forth treasures new and old.

Especially striking is the fact that here is a community independent of the state, a community freeing itself from idolatrous intermediary powers, promoting and exemplifying a heightened sense of responsibility, not only to and for itself but also to and for the individual—witness its concern to care for the weak and the elderly, slaves and widows. Some early Christian parishes even undertook to provide vocational education for orphans; others formed credit unions. What we see here, then, is a dispersion of power in the sense of dispersion of opportunity to assume responsibility.

Not the least of the latent functions of these new communities was to give and undergo training in the skills of organization and reconciliation. In short, it is not enough to say that a new spirit, a new ethos, here came to birth. That spirit, that ethos found practical and indeed institutional expression precisely among people who previously had been denied opportunities to participate. The new sense of hope cannot be understood merely in terms of eschatological expectation; it was engendered and sustained by the common experience of freedom in Christ, which took shape in new expressions of community. In other words, the hope stimulated and was supported by social participation.

In that day, however, the possibility of political participation was practically nil for the Christian or for anyone—a fact that probably explains in part the largely apolitical character of the early Christian ethos and the Pauline admonition to be subject to the governing authorities. How different it is with us. In a democratic society Christians participate in government—at least in the sense that, as citizens, they have the opportunity and the responsibility to share in shaping the nation's policy.

It is therefore understandable that the ecumenical discussion, and specifically the Zagorsk Consultation held in preparation for the recent World Council Assembly in Uppsala, has turned attention to a redefinition of power and of Christian responsibility with respect to power. Quite properly, Zagorsk recognized a variety of methods of dealing with Scripture and of "doing" social ethics; at the same time, it was able to agree on a definition of power—one more or less familiar to us from other, sociological sources—as "conscious and active participation in the decision-making processes of society" which make for justice and "for more meaning for human life in society." The Zagorsk statement applies this criterion not only to the domestic situation in the Western countries, but also to those regions of the world that, in relation to the West, "have not." It even articulates a theory of revolution to justify the effort to change the locus of power in certain countries, to the end of enabling "participation of the masses in the making of decisions." Thus it asserts that Christians "can be free both to accept and to criticize the revolutionary trends in the world."

In the main, however, the Zagorsk statement is a summons to the Christian to shoulder responsibility for promoting justice. It calls for "participation of the masses in the making of decisions." Who are the masses? They are not only the anonymous, readily replaceable man and woman of the labor market. They are also those who do not participate in the decision-making processes that affect the community. They are especially the blacks upon whom impotence has been imposed; the alienated people who have not been permitted to have their say in public and institutional undertakings that affect their own way of life.

III

In face of the alienated, of the marginal men and women and children, power must be newly defined: as a creative, innovative relationship between those who have the freedom to participate in making social decisions and those who do not have that freedom. Obviously, the Christian cannot be content with philanthropy, for philanthropy may be a means of keeping others powerless; nor can one be content with simple majority rule. Conventional philanthropy and majority rule can be a means of still further alienating the marginal people, and thus increasing their self-hatred and resentment. There is a good deal of evidence to show that the deeper the sense of alienation the greater the sense of hopelessness, and the more likely the resort to violence. In this context, the people with power engender the violence. One theological tradition has called this process the wrath of God, the strange work of God's love. The Old Testament calls it hardening of the heart.

The Boston Theological Institute comes into being at a time in our nation's history when resentment is growing not only among the powerless but also among the powerful. On the part of the latter, the resentment is a reaction to the demands and the chaotic apocalyptic of the powerless—a reaction that cannot or will not distinguish between the melodrama and the genuine drama of protest. Thus resentment on both sides is every day splitting the nation further apart and is showing itself to be a distinctly dangerous and destructive force. We must recognize that the polarization, the opening to the right, which is appearing among us is supported by large numbers of church people. And the consequence is less and less rationality and mutual understanding, more and more appeal to spurious notions of "law and order." It is precisely these "law and order" people who are demonstrating the weakness of their strength, the sterility of their power.

Commenting on the student revolt in Europe today, the Tübingen New Testament scholar Ernst Käseman recently asserted that the rebels are revealing "what is rotten among us." "When they kicked up a row," Käseman said, "people thought only of the police club. These people did not shriek when they became aware of the millions who are perishing, but they have suddenly found their voice again, and they sing the old song of 'authority and order,' and one now faces new citizen terrors."

The question now before us is whether our churches and theological schools can summon the power to bring about conversations between the powerful and the powerless, to moderate polarization and to encourage self-determination on the part of the alienated. Perhaps the best contribution to society theological schools could make would be for them to demonstrate to the community, and especially to the churches, their capacity to respond to student demand. The challenge facing these schools is typical of what is going on all around us, and creative response to it requires something more than change of procedures: it requires profound changes in theological education. For theological education is not on a pedestal outside, it is part and parcel of our society.

IV

At this juncture, it is highly important that we recall that progress in the authentic use of power has been marked by the inclusion of the marginal people in the systems of power. In the early modern period, the middle class and then the working class were the marginal men and women, and successively they were allowed to acquire power. Unfortunately, the labor movement, like the previous middle-class movement, gradually took on the spirit of exclusion. But just as language is constantly enriched and enlivened from below, so society can be constantly enriched and enlivened by the marginal people with their highly creative potential. Let us hearken to the Exodus theme as expressed in the black spiritual, "Way down in Egypt land... Let my people go."

The authenticity of power, however, is determined not alone by the freedom of all individuals and all groups to participate in the making of social decisions, but also by the quality and purpose of their participation. The authenticity of power is determined by the ends it serves and the means it uses. The truly powerful are those who serve large purposes and can accomplish them. This kind of fulfillment requires "power with," not "power over"; it requires love.

The tensions that surround us today can be a source of strength; they provide the occasion for the renewing, community-forming power of God to work. Among women and men this power becomes manifest as they grope for new solutions. Authentic power is a gift to human being, issuing from response to the divine power. To them who have the power to hear, the saving Word of reconciliation will be given. From them who have not this power, even what they have will be taken away. Authentic power is neither poison nor insatiable lust, neither coercion nor corruption born of pride. It is the power that can exhibit the imagination of bold invention, that can respond to the ultimate power that shapes new communion with God and new community among men and women.

It is in this sense that we venture to make a beatitude: Blessed are the powerful. Blessed are the powerful who acknowledge that their power is a gift that imposes ever new responsibilities and offers ever new, though costing joys. Blessed are the powerful who acknowledge that authentic power is the capacity to respond to the covenant, the capacity to secure the performance of binding obligations.

A James Luther Adams Chronology

1901	Born November 12 at Ritzville, Washington; son of James Carey and Lella May (Barnett) Adams
1916	Left high school to help support family; learned stenography and worked for a prosecuting attorney
1917-1920	Private secretary to the Superintendent, then Chief Clerk of the Operating Division, Northern Pacific Railroad
1920	Entered the University of Minnesota as an undergraduate
1923-1924	Co-editor of undergraduate sheet, *Angels' Revolt*
1924	A.B., University of Minnesota
1924-1927	Harvard Divinity School student, receiving the S.T.B. degree in 1927
1924-1925	Student assistant to the minister of All Souls Church, Lowell, Massachusetts—the minister being Arthur C. McGiffert, Jr.
1925-1927	Student minister of the Second Church in Salem, Massachusetts
1927	Summer study in Germany
1927-1934	Ordained to the Ministry by the Second Church in Salem on May 15, 1927, and served there as Minister
1927	Marriage to Margaret Ann Young on September 21. They have three children: Eloise, Elaine (Miller), Barbara (Adams Thompson)
1928	One of the organizers of the Greenfield Group, an Eastern liberal ministers' study group meeting semi-annually
1929-1932	Instructor in English, Boston University
1930	M.A. in English, Harvard University
1930-1935	One of "The Religious Associates" of the Congress of Industrial Organizations (CIO)
1933-1934	Editor, *The Christian Register,* American Unitarian Association periodical
1934-1935	Minister of the Unitarian Society, Wellesley Hills, Massachusetts
1934-1936	Co-initiator and then member of the Commission of Appraisal, AUA, which brought about a denominational reorganization as outlined in the Commission's book, *Unitarians Face a New Age*

1935-1936	Study with Rudolf Otto in Germany, research on Bishop Hurd at Hartlebury Castle, seat of the Bishop of Worcester; weekly visits with Albert Schweitzer; St.-Sulpice Seminary, Paris, under spiritual director, Levassor-Beruz; associated with anti-Nazi "underground"
1936-1957	Professor at the Meadville Theological School, then also the Federated Theological Faculty, University of Chicago (beginning 1943)
1938-1948	Editorial Board, then Associate Editor, *The Protestant*
1938	Studied in England; lectured at international (I.A.R.F.) youth conference in the Netherlands; lived in Germany in '36 and '38 in Benedictine monastery, Maria Laach, to study Liturgical Movement
1939	"How My Mind Has Changed in the Past Decade," *The Christian Century*
1939-1944	Editor of *The Journal of Liberal Religion*
1940	"On Being Human—the Liberal Way," AUA Pamphlet 359
1941	Co-author of "Memoir" in *Irving Babbit: Man and Teacher*
1941	Delivered the Berry Street Lecture, "The Changing Reputation of Human Nature," published in expanded form in 1942-1943
1942-1945	Member of Ecumenical Theological Seminar, Middle West. See JLA articles in *The Journal of Religion:* "The Law of Nature in Graeco-Roman Thought," "The Law of Nature: Some General Considerations." Later JLA taught, every third year at Chicago and Harvard, seminar on natural law
1942-1957	Helped to found the anti-isolationist Independent Voters of Illinois and held continuing leadership role during the Chicago years, including 3 terms as Chairman
1943-1954	Consultant, Chicago Council Against Racial and Religious Discrimination
1943-1957	Professor of Religious Ethics, University of Chicago; Chairman, Department of Ethics and Society
1944	"The Religious Problem," in *New Perspectives on Peace*, University of Chicago Press
1945-1954	Advisory Board, Chicago Chapter, American Civil Liberties Union
1945	Ph.D., University of Chicago
1945-1962	National Theological Discussion Group, College of

Preachers, Washington Cathedral

1945-1955	Advisory Board, American Christian Palestine Committee
1945	With Leo Szilard and some 60 professors, JLA released the first public protest against the atomic bombing of Hiroshima and Nagasaki
1946	"A Faith for Free Men," *Together We Advance*, Beacon Press
1947	Co-author of "Unitarians Unite!"—the report of the AUA Commission on Planning and Review, 1945-1947
1948	*The Protestant Era* by Paul Tillich. Translated, edited and with concluding essay by JLA, University of Chicago Press
1950	Officer of the Chicago Chapter, Christian Action
1950-1956	Associate Editor of the English Unitarian periodical, *Faith and Freedom*
1950	Dudleian Lecturer, Harvard Divinity School: "Natural Religion and the 'Myth' of the Eighteenth Century"
1951-1956	Co-editor, *The Journal of Religion*, University of Chicago
1952	On tour of Israel and the Middle East; lectured on Martin Buber at Cyprus, auspices of American Christian Palestine Committee
1952	"Paul Tillich's Interpretation of History" in *The Theology of Paul Tillich*
1952	Lecturer at Albert Schweitzer College, Switzerland; lecturer on sociology of religion, Anglo-Catholic Theological College, Ely Cathedral; lecturer on "Our Responsibility in Society," International Association for Liberal Christianity and Religious Freedom (I.A.R.F.), Oxford, England
1952	Chairman of the Advisory Board, Beacon Press
1953	William Belden Noble Lectures, Harvard University Visiting Professor, Harvard Divinity School
1954	Member of the International Council of La Societe Europeenne de Culture; annual columnist, *Comprende*
1954	Chairman of the Board of Trustees, The First Unitarian Church of Chicago, Illinois
1956-1962	Co-conductor, Seminar on Religion and Business Decisions, Harvard Graduate School of Business Administration
1957	*Taking Time Seriously*, published by The Free Press
1957-1968	Edward Mallinckrodt, Jr. Professor of Divinity; Chairman, Department of Religion and Society, Harvard Divinity

School; now Professor *Emeritus*

1957-1959	Massachusetts State Board, Americans for Democratic Action
1957-1959	President of the Society for the Scientific Study of Religion (of which he was one of the founders in 1953)
1957-1963	Massachusetts State Board, American Civil Liberties Union; Chairman of its Church and State Committee, 1966-1968
1957	JLA the first theologian to be a member of the Society for Political and Legal Philosophy, for whom he wrote his essay on "Civil Disobedience," *Nomos XII, 1960*
1958	Honorary Doctor of Divinity, Meadville Theological School
1958	Major articles published on "Ethics" and "The Social Import of the Professions"
1958	Fellow, American Academy of Arts and Sciences; as Chairman of the Committee on International Organizations, visited major learned academies of Europe, 1966-1968
1958	Lectured in Japan and India: International Association of the History of Religion, Tokyo and Kyoto; World Center for Buddhist Studies, Rangoon; Theological College, Bangalore
1960-1967	Co-conductor, extracurricular seminar on Religion and Law, Harvard Law School
1960	Honorary Doctor of Theology, University of Marburg, Germany
1960	Lectured in Holland at the Arminius Symposium. See "Arminius and the Structure of Society" in *Man's Faith and Freedom*, edited by G. O. McCulloch
1960-1965	Massachusetts State Board, American Association for the United Nations
1961-1964	Coordinating Council, American Unitarian Association Commission on the Free Church in a Changing World
1962-1963	Delivered the Hibbert Lectures, "By Their Groups," at Oxford, Manchester and Liverpool Universities; plus lecturing at Marburg, Bern, Berlin, as well as Padua, Italy
1962	Vatican Council II, First Session, Protestant Observer on behalf of the International Association for Religious Freedom
1963	"Ernst Troeltsch" and "Christian Socialism" articles published in *Encyclopedia Britannica*

1963	Translator of *The Dogma of Christ*, by Erich Fromm
1963	Fulbright Research Scholar, University of Marburg
1964-1968	Advisory Committee, Council for Population Studies, Harvard University; initiated Department for Population Studies at Harvard Divinity School
1965	*Paul Tillich's Philosophy of Culture, Science and Religion*, published by Harper and Row
1965-1969	Chairman of the Advisory Committee, Department of Social Responsibility, Unitarian Universalist Association
1965	"James Luther Adams and His Demand for an Effective Religious Liberalism," Ph.D. dissertation by James Dennis Hunt, Syracuse University, 700 pages
1966	International Congress on "Marx and the Western World," Notre Dame University
1966	*Voluntary Associations:* A Study of Groups in Free Societies, Essays in Honor of James Luther Adams, edited by D. B. Robertson. Foreword by Paul Tillich; biographical intellectual sketch by Max L. Stackhouse; bibliography of JLA writings by Ralph B. Potter, Jr., Jean Potter, and James Hunt
1967	"Is Marx's Thought Relevant to the Christian? A Protestant View," in *Marx and the Western World*, edited by Nicholas Lobkowicz
1967	Lectured at the University of Mainz, Germany: "Theokratie, Kapitalismus und Demokratie: A Critique of Max Weber's *Protestant Ethic*
1967-1968	President, American Society for Christian Ethics
1968	At the General Assembly of the Unitarian Universalist Association in Cleveland, Ohio, the UUA Holmes-Weatherly Award was presented: "To James Luther Adams as universal man, Christian socialist, apostle of voluntary associations, and prophet to the prophets"
1968-1972	Distinguished Professor of Social Ethics, Andover Newton Theological School
1968	Contributor to Wilhelm Pauck Festschrift, *Interpreters of Luther*
1968	Lecturer, Christian-Marxist Seminar, Charles University, Prague, Czechoslovakia
1969	Edited and translated *What Is Religion?*, by Paul Tillich

1969	Former HDS students of JLA formed FREE: the Fellowship for Racial and Economic Equality, to combat white racism. JLA has been chairman of the board. This developed into the Southeast Institute
1970	Co-author and co-editor with Seward Hiltner, *Pastoral Care in the Liberal Churches*
1970	Participant, Ciba Foundation Symposium. See *The Family and Its Future,* published in London
1970	Vice President, Unitarian Universalist Christian Fellowship (also 1977-)
1971	Editor and translator of *Political Expectations* by Tillich
1971	Contributor to Festschrift for Erich Fromm
1971	Vice President, Association for Voluntary Action Scholars
1971	Minister of Adult Education, Arlington Street Church, Boston
1971-1973	Chairman of the Board, Society of the Arts, Religion and Contemporary Culture
1972-1973	President of the American Theological Society
1972-1976	Professor of Theology and Religious Ethics, University of Chicago; Distinguished Scholar in Residence, Meadville/ Lombard Theological School
1973	The Award for Distinguished Service to the Cause of Liberal Religion presented by the Unitarian Universalist Association
1973	Editorial Board, *Journal of Religious Ethics;* Editorial Adviser, *The Unitarian Universalist Christian*
1974	Executive Committee, North American Society for Tillich Studies
1974	Board of Associate Editors, *Journal of Voluntary Action Research*
1975	Honorary Fellow, Manchester College, Oxford University
1976	James Luther Adams Festival, Boston
1976	*On Being Human—Religiously: Selected Essays on Religion and Society,* by JLA, edited by Max L. Stackhouse, Beacon Press
1976	"God and Economics" in *Belief and Ethics: Essays in Ethics, the Human Sciences, and Ministry in Honor of W. Alvin Pitcher,* edited by W. Widick Schroeder and Gibson Winter
1977	*James Luther Adams at 75,* Special Issue of *The Unitarian Universalist Christian,* with an autobiographical essay and articles by JLA from six decades, edited by Herbert F. Vetter

1978	*The Reconstruction of Morality*, by Karl Holl, edited by JLA and Walter F. Bense
1979	D.H.L. (Hon.), Middlebury College
1980	"Being Human—the Liberal Way," Cambridge Forum national public television series, *I Call That Mind Free* (videotape and audio tape)
1982"	Foreword" in *Crisis and Consciousness: The Thought of Ernst Troeltsch*, by Robert J. Rubanowice
1984	"Dialogue on Nazism," JLA and George H. Williams
1984-1985	President of the Society for Art, Religion and Contemporary Culture
1985	*The Thought of Paul Tillich*, co-authored with Wilhelm Pauck and Roger L. Shinn
1985	"Legitimation," with Thomas Mikelson, *The Encyclopedia of Religion*
1986	*The Prophethood of All Believers*, edited by George K. Beach
1986	*Voluntary Associations: Socio-Cultural Analyses and Theological Interpretation*, edited by J. Ronald Engel
1988	"The Weightier Matters of the Law," in Festschrift for Harold Berman
1990	"Reminiscences of Paul Tillich," *Harvard Divinity Bulletin*
1991	*An Examined Faith: Social Context and Religious Commitment*, edited by George K. Beach
1991	Translator with Walter F. Bense of *Religion in History*, by Ernst Troeltsch, with introduction by JLA
1991	"Voluntary Associations and Struggles for Human Rights," chapter for a memorial volume honoring R. W. Taylor, for the Christian Institute for the Study of Religion and Society, Bangalore, India
1992	"Preface," *The Social Teaching of the Christian Churches*, by Ernst Troeltsch, Harper Torchbooks
1993	*James Luther Adams Papers*, edited and with an introduction by Herbert F. Vetter, *The Unitarian Universalist Christian*, Fall 1993-Winter 1994
1994	Death of James Luther Adams, July 26, 1994
1995	*Not Without Dust and Heat: A Memoir*, by James Luther Adams, Exploration Press of the Chicago Theological Seminary

CPSIA information can be obtained at www.ICGtesting.com
Printed in the USA
BVOW041107070413

317507BV00001B/47/P